BOA
EDITIONS LTD

Black Buffalo Woman

T0243985

■

Black Buffalo Woman

An Introduction to the Poetry
and Poetics of Lucille Clifton

Kazim Ali

■

American Reader Series No. 42

BOA Editions, Ltd. ■ Rochester, NY ■ 2024

First Edition
23 24 25 26 7 6 5 4 3 2 1

For information about permission to reuse any material from this book, please contact The Permissions Company at www.permissionscompany.com or e-mail permdude@gmail.com.

Publications by BOA Editions, Ltd.—a not-for-profit corporation under section 501 (c) (3) of the United States Internal Revenue Code—are made possible with funds from a variety of sources, including public funds from the Literature Program of the National Endowment for the Arts; the New York State Council on the Arts, a state agency; and the County of Monroe, NY. Private funding sources include the Max and Marian Farash Charitable Foundation; the Mary S. Mulligan Charitable Trust; the Rochester Area Community Foundation; the Ames-Amzalak Memorial Trust in memory of Henry Ames, Semon Amzalak, and Dan Amzalak; the LGBT Fund of Greater Rochester; and contributions from many individuals nationwide. See Colophon on page 294 for special individual acknowledgments.

Cover Design: Sandy Knight
Cover Art: Courtesy of the Clifton Family Archives
Interior Design and Composition: Isabella Madeira
BOA Logo: Mirko

BOA Editions books are available electronically through BookShare, an online distributor offering Large-Print, Braille, Multimedia Audio Book, and Dyslexic formats, as well as through e-readers that feature text to speech capabilities.

Cataloging-in-Publication Data is available from the Library of Congress.

State of the Arts

NYSCA

BOA Editions, Ltd.
250 North Goodman Street, Suite 306
Rochester, NY 14607
www.boaeditions.org
A. Poulin, Jr., Founder (1938-1996)

NATIONAL
ENDOWMENT
for the ARTS
arts.gov

Contents

to Rukia Ali

"the only mercy is memory" — Lucille Clifton

Introduction: Mentor and Muse

1.

I have been reading and thinking and talking about Lucille Clifton's work for a long time. One of the first poems I read by her was "the thirty-eighth year." Its closing lines haunted me all that cold and lonely year:

> i had expected more than this.
> i had not expected to be
> an ordinary woman.[1]

Though I was barely turning twenty myself, the regret that the older poet felt at unfulfilled possibilities in her own life felt fresh and real to me: I was young, gay, and Muslim, unsure whether I would ever be able to live openly, let alone have love in my own life. This older Black woman, a mother of six, to the outside world appearing to have every success, was able to write a poem very specific to her own circumstances that nonetheless spoke to me with the greatest of clarities. Clifton's emotions are so deeply felt and her mode of expression so clear and musical, that this poem and countless others of hers have become touchstones for me throughout my life. So many other readers feel the same.

I met Lucille Clifton for the first time the day before my twenty-fourth birthday, and I saw her for the last time fifteen years later to the day—as it happens, the last day of my own thirty-eighth year. Lucille was magic like that, equally connected to the physical and material world and to the mystical and spiritual one. She was a "two-headed woman," as she referred to herself in a poem, and anyone who knew her well can tell you about their own experiences with Lucille, coincidences and occurrences that are far stranger than fiction, including, for example, that Clifton passed away on the anniversary of her own mother's passing.

One way I thought about this book as I was writing it was as a conversation with Lucille herself. Understudied then as now, Clifton's work engenders such *personal* responses from her readers that the intentions of critical or analytical attention might feel like obfuscation. Poets who did write about Clifton often did so with effusive praise for the *feeling* in her work, without much care or attention for her artistic achievement, or contextualizing her within critical or literary frameworks. As Toni Morrison pointed out in her introduction to Clifton's *Collected Poems:*

> "Accolades from fellow poets and critics refer to
> her universal human heart; they describe her
> as a fierce caring female. They complement
> her courage, vision, joy—unadorned (meaning
> "simple"), mystical, poignant, humorous, intuitive,
> harsh and loving. I do not disagree with these
> judgments. Yet I am startled by the silence in
> these interpretations of her work. There are no
> references to her intellect, imagination, scholarship
> or her risk-taking manipulation of language. To
> me she is not the big mama/big sister of racial
> reassurance and self-empowerment. I read her
> skill as that emanating from an astute, profound
> intellect—characteristics mostly absent from her
> reviews."[2]

While there have been numerous articles and book chapters on her work—including some that I engage with in this book—there are only two monographs, both published during her lifetime, between fifteen and twenty years ago, and one of those appeared before her final two (groundbreaking) books were published. *Black*

Buffalo Woman aims to look at Clifton as a poet, a thinker, even as philosopher and theologian. I want to examine her poetic craft as well as her intellectual interests.

For my own part I do remember one particular time right before I was supposed to deliver a lecture on Clifton's use of traditional prosody to a room full of students and teachers and writers. I panicked, imagining that I was making it all up, that none of the dactyls and trochees I was planning to talk about were intentional, that someone would tell me I was projecting my own interest in formal poetry onto a poet who wrote in free verse. I ducked into a side room and called Lucille up on the phone to tell her what I was about to do. She laughed and said, "Oh thank god you're doing that! I'm tired of people thinking I'm like Grandma Moses or something!"

Toni Morrison went on in her introduction to confess, "I crave a book of criticism on Lucille Clifton's work that scours it for the meanings therein and the stone-eyed intellect on display."[3] With respect to the esteemed Ms. Morrison, I'm not sure I "scour" here, but I do try to sift, turn over, listen to, tune in, sound out.

At any rate, in the last ten years or so a number of brilliant scholars and critics have been working on Lucille Clifton's oeuvre in new and compelling ways, including Marina Magloire, William Fogarty, Omar Miranda, Sumita Chakraborty, Bettina Judd, Sylvia Hennenberg, and Scarlett Cunningham. My interest in this book here is not as a scholar per se, but rather as a passionate and devoted reader. Or maybe these are two aspects of the same condition, after all.

The title of this book, *Black Buffalo Woman,* has multiple meanings: Clifton herself identified strongly with her own Black womanhood, even using the word "woman" as part of the title for three different books of hers, and had planned on using the words again as part of the title for a fourth book that she ended up deciding not to publish. Buffalo, NY, was her hometown, and it was a hometown that was extremely important to her on a personal level; it also resonated throughout her poetry. Finally, there is the historical figure of Black Buffalo Woman, a Lakota woman who was associated with Tasunka Witko, the indigenous leader better known as Crazy Horse, who had captivated Clifton's imagination. Clifton—who was interested in mystical and spiritual practices including past life regression—felt a kinship and affinity with the historical figure of Black Buffalo Woman, and regarded her name as a sign of relationality of some kind.

2.

Championed by such giants as Robert Hayden, Toni Morrison, Carolyn Kizer, and Langston Hughes, Lucille Clifton was one of the major American poets of the late 20th and early 21st centuries. Readers flock to the poetry of Clifton for spiritual relief, for sharp social and political critique, for plangent music, for wit and humor, and certainly for a mastery of the economy of language and prosody. She condensed powerful emotional impact into often brief, even epigrammatic forms. She has become somewhat a legend for a whole generation of poets, and even inspired a character on the animated program *Family Guy* (on the writing staff of which her son-in-law served), the high school English teacher Ms. Clifton.[4]

Clifton was born in 1937 in Depew, NY, a town outside Buffalo, NY where her family later moved. Raised by a father, who—as Clifton has written about, painfully—abused her as a child, and by a mother who was herself a poet, Clifton grew up in a mixed family that included a brother and two half-sisters, one older and one younger. She attended Howard University (where she was acquainted with fellow students Morrison, Ishmael Reed, Roberta Flack, and Amiri Baraka), and later Fredonia State College, but never received a degree.

After returning to Buffalo, she met and married Fred Clifton, a philosophy student at the University of Buffalo who was also a practitioner and scholar of the ancient science of Yoga. The couple were involved in activism that resulted in the founding of Africana Studies programs at Buffalo State College, and later at Harvard University, where Fred Clifton worked briefly. They settled in Baltimore, and lived there for many years, raising their six children until Fred Clifton's death at age 49 from cancer, a shocking event that resounded through Lucille's life and is reflected throughout her poetry.

All this time, while she was feeding and caring for children at home, she was finding time late at night to sit at the big dining room table and write poetry. When she writes about this time in a short poem from her book *quilting*, she writes about it in the present tense, about a woman who is not her, writing that "somewhere/some woman/just like me" is laying out the childrens' clothes and setting the table for breakfast.[5] Remarkably, the pen this woman uses to write is one she finds between the cushions of the couch, that is to say, one that is incidental, one that probably belongs to someone else, or was forgotten, that slipped out of a pocket. Nonetheless, the woman has found time to be a poet: and the words she writes on the top of the blank page in front of her are "Good Times," the name of Clifton's own first book. With that gesture of course, Clifton establishes herself twice in time—Lucille Clifton, the successful and acclaimed poet in the present moment, and Lucille Clifton, the woman from the past, exhausted at the end of the day, finding any time she can in order to write. That the imagined woman in the present day of the poem "somewhere" writes the same words Clifton did decades earlier reinforces the kinship she feels with other writers who may share the same familial, material, or social conditions that once governed her life.

In another poem from *quilting*, "when i stand around among poets," she writes that when she is with other poets, "I am embarrassed mostly,/their long white heads,/the great bulge in their pants,/their certainties." When she mentions both the whiteness and the maleness of the poets she is standing around, she is making a commentary on the state of poetry rather than the actuality of Clifton's own community—in addition to Morrison, Reed, Baraka, and Kizer, she was friendly with and was championed by Maxine Kumin, Sonia Sanchez, and others. But I appreciate that the poets' "certainties" was one thing that troubled her; for her own part she claims "I don't know how to do/what I do in the way/that I do it. It happens/despite me and I pretend//to deserve it."[6]

This too is somewhat of a pose. Clifton was indeed a master of prosody and poetic form and the use of language. It may have been instinctual and learned by ear rather than studied and learned by formal education, but it was mastery nonetheless. She talked in interviews about influences that included Blake, Milton, Yeats, Aiken, and Sanchez (herself influenced by Spenser). She expressed her own opinion that her readers might be surprised she was influenced by such writers. I don't mention these writers in order to legitimize Clifton (or Sanchez) by showing that she was indeed a part of an Anglo—European-American lineage of poetry, but merely to point out that her use of metrics and skillful manipulation of the poetic line was neither incidental nor instinctual or happenstance. Despite the poem that perhaps cheekily claims otherwise, she did know how to do what she was doing, and she knew why she did it in the way that she did it.

I believe that "when i stand around among poets" rather speaks to the keen sense of exclusion she felt, both from the power structures at work in the literary world, but also to the extremely personal and inborn sources of poetry, more trustworthy than knowledge or formal education or access to an audience or "certainties."

I myself encountered Lucille Clifton's poetry for the very first time not even as a poem but as a lyric in a song by Ani DiFranco, also a Buffalo artist. DiFranco writes about an experience going to have an abortion in her "Lost Woman Song," the title of which is a riff of Clifton's "lost baby poem." In Clifton's poem she describes an early home abortion. Unlike Gwendolyn Brooks, who was famously silent about what the politics of her own poem about an abortion, "The Mother," were, Clifton was clear with people who misread the poem as potentially being about a miscarriage; she would confirm that the poem was about an abortion, and aver her pro-choice politics. Despite this difference in approach by the two writers, Clifton has said that it was reading Brooks' "The Mother" that gave her the courage and permission to write the "lost baby poem." DiFranco honors Clifton in the same way, singing:

> Lucille, your voice still sounds in me
> though mine was a relatively easy tragedy.
> The profile of our country looks a little less hard-nosed

but you know, that picket line persisted
and that clinic's since been closed."[7]

It wasn't until the following year, the cold spring of 1991, my sophomore year at the University at Albany, while the first Gulf War roared to life, that I read Clifton's poetry, including "lost baby poem" as well as "the thirty-eighth year," in a class called Black Woman Poets, taught by Dr. Barbara McCaskill. It meant something that I was reading Clifton's work in the context of other Black women, among them Sanchez and Brooks, along with Mari Evans, Angela Jackson, Colleen McElroy, Leslie Reese, and others. McCaskill wanted us to see the aesthetic and linguistic context these women were working in. It was a formative class for me because the various Englishes these writers were using made me aware of the possibilities, not only in a different cultural perception than the mainstream of the Anglo-American literary tradition, but of the possibilities in the language of English itself. I also realized that writers marginalized by the mainstream literary establishment often published with tiny presses. Many of the books we studied were chapbooks and pamphlets published in small ephemeral editions.

Dr. McCaskill put *two* books by Clifton on the syllabus that year, both *good woman* and the then-recently published, *Next*. The very first poem we looked at was "cutting greens," included in Clifton's 1974 volume—along with "the thirty-eighth year"—*an ordinary woman*. This poem is still, in my mind, a model Clifton poem. Concise at fifteen brief lines, it tells the story of an ordinary domestic chore, yet makes of that chore an extended metaphor with wide political and spiritual implications:

cutting greens

curling them around
i hold their bodies in obscene embrace
thinking of everything but kinship.
collards and kale
strain against each strange other
away from my kissmaking hand and

the iron bedpot.
the pot is black,
the cutting board is black,
my hand,
and just for a minute
the greens roll back under the knife,
and the kitchen twists dark on its spine
and i taste in my natural appetite
the bond of live things everywhere.[8]

The greens in the poem are immediately more than mere vegetable, they have bodies held in "obscene embrace." The collards and kale, both part of traditional Southern cooking, and specifically Black cooking, do not feel "kinship," but rather "strain against each strange other." This hostility and alienation is contrasted with the moment of unity between both knife, board, greens, and woman. When this unity is achieved, reality itself unhinges. In a surreal moment, "the kitchen twists dark on its spine." One travels from the intimate to the infinite so quickly in this poem, and to me the turning point is that small moment where Clifton truncates the otherwise repeated adjective "black": "my hand." She herself, the woman cutting greens, has a personal revelation of the most universal sort.

My final paper for McCaskill discussed Clifton's series of poems about the Virgin Mary which she writes in a Caribbean English vernacular. I focused on the poem "island mary." Written in longhand with a ballpoint pen in three little bluebooks, the essay represented my first attempt to write about Clifton, which I would continue to do off and on for the next several decades. Having published four earlier essays on Clifton, in the spring of 2022, I delivered a series of lectures for an on-line course organized by the Community of Writers, for whose Poetry Week in the mountains near Tahoe Clifton was a longtime staff member. This book grew from those lectures.

As I mentioned, I met Clifton in person the day before my 24th birthday, in 1995. I was living in Albany, working for a social justice organization. I had not been a particularly distinguished student (I was too busy protesting or handing out leaflets or making phone calls!), nor was I yet particularly skilled as a poet, but what I lacked in ability, I made up for in heart. A sentence that is probably still true. In addition to the reading she was to give that evening in the grand auditorium of the downtown campus (with its very grand and ornate podium—which she would decline to stand at, of course) she was meeting graduate students for a smaller discussion.

At the end of the session, I lined up with everyone else to say goodbye. When it was my turn—I cannot now defend my impudence—I asked her if I could give her a hug. She laughed out loud and threw her arms open and said, "Oh, sure honey, come here."

The reading the next day was transcendent. What a birthday gift! Lucille did something I had never seen a poet do before, which was that she came out from behind the podium to stand before the audience on the proscenium, and she read her poems to us without looking down at the book she held in one hand. After completing each poem, she would lift the book and turn to the next dog-eared page.

After the reading, my professor, the poet Judith Johnson, was driving Lucille back to her hotel and I managed to tag along. We all went into the restaurant of the hotel and sat down for a late dinner. I've scarcely had a better birthday dinner than that one: sitting at a little table with Judy and Lucille Clifton and another graduate student, Sally, discussing *Jeopardy!*, eastern philosophy, comic books, Ouija boards, who our favorite characters from *Star Trek: The Next Generation* were, and maybe even, every once in a while, about poetry. For the curious, as to our favorite Star Trek characters, though I was partial to the ethereal beauty, lustrous hair, and psychic abilities of Deanna Troi, Clifton was firmly on the side of the Klingons, including imposing security officer Lieutenant Worf and the villainous and campy Duras sisters, Lursa and B'Etor.

3.

Clifton's work appears on the surface plainspoken and its address is direct, but as Morrison pointed out, "unadorned" does *not* mean "simple." The accessibility of the texts has made the poems dear to many readers from varied backgrounds and with varying relationships to contemporary poetry, but these same qualities may be one reason the work has not yet (in my view) garnered the level of critical and scholarly attention it deserves. The closer one looks at these poems, the more one finds within them rich and complex dimensions of meaning.

In Chapters 1 and 2, I look at Lucille Clifton's poems dealing with American social and political history. I jump right into the middle of things in Chapter 1 by engaging in a close reading of the "buffalo war" sequence that appears in her first book *good times.* Chapter 2 looks at a range of her poems on historical figures, particularly in her second book *good news about the earth.*

In Chapters 3 and 4 I look at Lucille Clifton's most personal (and probably most famous?) poems, those dealing with her body. These poems deal with gendered experiences of womanhood and motherhood, with Blackness, and also with the eros, sexuality, and precarity of the body, culminating with an examination of a few of the many poems Clifton wrote about illness and mortality, including her own cancer.

In Chapter 5 I look at Clifton's prose memoir, *generations,* as well as assorted poems she wrote in later years that simultaneously illuminate further and problematize and trouble the times described therein.

Chapter 6 treats Clifton's rich array of texts drawn from biblical sources, focusing on five sequences, "some jesus," from *good news about the earth,* the mary poems from *the two-headed woman,* "tree of life," from *Quilting,* "brothers," from *The Book of Light,* and "from the Book of David," which appears in *The Terrible Stories.*

Chapter 7 examines Clifton's use of popular culture and advertising, including discussion of her extensive writing for children, and of Fred Clifton's single book, a young adult novel written in epistolary form called *Darl.*

Chapter 8 makes a case for Clifton's careful and skillful use of prosody and metrics and poetic form in her poetry. In addition to analyses of several poems' formal strategies, I include an extended comprehensive close reading of the metrics and mechanics of the poem "sarah's promise."

Chapter 9 looks at a previously underexplored facet of Lucille's work. Often thought of as a poet of affirmation and positivity, Clifton's work took a definitive turn in her last two published books, *Mercy* and *Voices*. These poems engage mortality and racism and her own personal history with much more trenchant emotions and a growing pessimism, even despair. This chapter looks at and considers this period of her life under the metaphorical sign of the term "dark," which typically denotes in English negative emotions like anger and fear, but which, of course, in Lucille's work takes on greater and finer nuance.

Finally, in Chapter 10, I examine work Clifton did not publish during her lifetime. I focus mainly on the masterful sequence "The Book of Days" included among Lucille's last papers and drafts, but I also discuss briefly two major bodies of unpublished work, Lucille Clifton's spirit writing, and poems she left uncollected during her lifetime.

This book is my own response and engagement with these poems, and is offered in the hope that others will follow, in reading, reciting, teaching, and writing about these poems. In general, what I try to do is not exhaust or explain, but invite. I hope to introduce an interested reader to some of the main aspects and concerns of Clifton's work, examine some of the poems, tell you what I see and hear, and by doing so give you the tools that will enable you too, on your own, to hear some of the many-tongued voices spoken within.

Please consider this a content warning of every kind: Clifton's poems treat violence, racism, historical and generational and personal trauma, childhood sexual abuse, and other difficult subject matter. In Clifton's work you'll see the N-word, the F-word, the G-word, the B-word, all the words.

As a non-Black BIPOC scholar, I recognize and contend with my own class and race and gender privilege in relationship to the experiences described in these poems, even at the same time my own various and intersectional identities place me in positions of both allyship and affinity.

In between the writing of the first draft of this book and the last, my mother Rukia Ali passed away—suddenly, unexpectedly. Though I mentioned that one way I thought of this book was as a conversation with Lucille Clifton, the other way was as a conversation with my own mother, who knew of my love for Clifton. Of course, Lucille lost her own mother at a far younger age, and her poems about Thelma Sayles are helping me through my own time of grief.

To both of them, I offer this book.

Chapter 1: Buffalo War

Lucille Clifton had won the Discovery Award, made her first national appearance (as a fiction writer in the children's magazine *Highlights for Children*) and begun publishing her poems in journals and magazines when the young Random House editor Toni Morrison, whom Lucille was acquainted with from their time together as students at Howard, published her first book *good times*. Embedded in the book, not set apart in a section nor otherwise marked as an official 'sequence,' are a series of poems I have termed the "buffalo war" poems.

The "buffalo war" poems are a series of poems which begin with an untitled poem whose first line "love rejected" is its designation, and continues with persona poems in the voices of two boys, Tyrone and Willie B., who are participating in civil unrest in the city of Buffalo, NY, Clifton's hometown. Each boy speaks in four poems, titled with his name and the number, and the sequence—as I've identified it—ends with a concluding poem called "buffalo war."

The poems take place during riots that happened in Buffalo, NY during the summer of 1967. That summer, called "the long, hot summer," was a period in time when a series of riots erupted in urban centers across the United States in response to social and economic inequity and injustice. It was a period of heightened tension around race issues, framed by the assassinations of Malcolm X in 1965 and Martin Luther King, Jr and Bobby Hutton in 1968 and Fred Hampton the year after. In the summer of 1967, more than one hundred and fifty riots erupted in cities like Denver, Newark, Buffalo, Atlanta, Chicago, New York, and other places. Tremendous property damage resulted and upwards of eighty people were killed in the violence. In today's heightened atmosphere of activism highlighting structural racism and police violence against Black communities, the "buffalo war" poems feel as relevant and resonant as they must have seemed to audiences in 1969 when they were initially published.

The sequence opens with a poem in the form of an epigrammatic dialogue of sorts between the poet and someone commenting on the riots, it seems. Again, neither the "opening" of a sequence, nor the positionality of who is speaking in either the opening or closing poems, is clearly stated. The poems occupy a seamless place in the contents of the book as a whole:

> love rejected
> hurts so much more
> than love rejecting;
> they act like they don't love their country
> no
> what it is
> is they found out
> their country don't love them.[9]

One will see throughout this series of poems Lucille Clifton's ability to create specificity and emotional weight and resonance with very few words. I think that's one of the major powers of her poetic talent. On the page one might be tempted to call it minimalist, and yet the emotions expressed are neither cool nor removed or restrained in any way. In very concise and precise lines, Clifton opens up an imagined dialog between an outside detractor of the riots, which resulted in extensive property damage ("they act like they don't love their country") and the critical justification from the observing poet. It's an exchange I heard again and again in the summer of 2020 during the protests which followed the killing of George Floyd.

This short poem also demonstrates a masterful switch between diction or register. It opens with a magisterial and formal "love rejected/hurts so much more/than love rejecting," but transitions to "what it is/is." This may at first appear to be a simply casual and colloquial register, but the specific doubling of the verb "to be" as both temporal and emotional intensifier is particularly common in African American Vernacular English. In the past tense one might say "what it was was" or, for emphasis in past perfect tense, "what had happened was." This use of a doubling of the verb "to be" as intensifier in AAVE does not exist in the future tense, but more on how AAVE uses the future tense in the next chapter.

This kind of change between registers becomes characteristic throughout the "buffalo war" poems, identifying that the series is intentionally epic in its scope and ambition; it is written—as were ancient epics like *the Iliad*, and *the Divine Comedy*—in the colloquial spoken vernaculars of their moments precisely because epics are meant to be accessible not solely to kings or educated classes, but to wide audiences, most especially for the community about which it is written. In fact, it has been the ancient epic of a culture—with its vast corpus of texts collected across many generations with many collaborative contributors, and normally in oral form that has often become our primary source of understanding of the shifting development of language and forms of historiography.

We get very little specific typical descriptive detail about either Tyrone or Willie B. in the eight short poems in which the two boys speak—for example, what they look like, what they are wearing, how they sound—and yet, with Clifton's characteristic economy, we do get a very clear picture of who these boys are—how they felt, what happened to them during the riot, what they did and why they did it. There is also a geographical specificity to the description. One could get out a map of Buffalo, NY and track the movements of the two boys throughout the day, the way the maps at the openings of translations of *The Odyssey* do, or as readers of Joyce's *Ulysses* have done in Dublin in tracking the steps of Leopold Bloom through the city. This geographic precision is one more way Lucille Clifton grounds her embedded sequence in an epic tradition.

Here is "tyrone (1)":

on this day
the buffalo soldiers
have taken up position

corner of jefferson and sycamore
we will sack the city
will sink the city
seek the city[10]

Clifton continues her mythological positioning of Tyrone as a classical hero with the opening, "on this day." The phrase puts the listeners on notice that we are bearing witness to historical events, meant to be registered as meaningful. Tyrone is making sure that his audience knows this is a momentous occasion as he himself is also well aware. As Martin Luther King, Jr said that same summer in a speech at Stanford University, "A riot is the language of the unheard." A riot is an upending of social norms and of "civil" order. In a riot the unexpected can occur. When Tyrone says "on this day," we know that Tyrone doesn't just see the moment as ordinary and doesn't just see himself as a kid who's going to act violently or destroy property as an act of mischief or vandalism or petty theft. Rather he sees himself as having a role that is larger in events that are much larger.

"On this day" announces a *beginning*, a proclamation of a sort. He follows up this mythical positioning by assigning to himself and his colleagues a historical appellation: "buffalo soldiers." It's a witty move because they are in Buffalo, New York, so naturally they are "Buffalo" soldiers, but of course here he is invoking the historical (and historic) Buffalo Soldiers—black enlisted regiments who fought in the Indian Wars and the Civil War, and about whom Bob Marley sang—finding in their army service proof of Black resilience and a will to survive the institutions of racism. It is also telling that he chooses to think of himself as a soldier, which is a noble fighter in service of a cause, whether nation or community, rather than the way rioters are commonly seen by people in privilege—as either instigators, criminals, mercenaries, or thugs. To say one is a "soldier" is to claim one is part of a larger vision or institution, not a mere instrument of individual or selfish violence.

Thus Tyrone historicizes himself in a position of actual nobility, and, once again, reinscribes the social and political significance of what these young people are doing. The following two lines of the poem continue this epic framing, both in the description of the boys' actions in military terms—they have "taken up position"—and in the specifics of the geographic location: the corner of Jefferson Avenue and Sycamore Street, in Buffalo, NY just south of the predominantly Black neighborhood on Buffalo's east side known as the Fruit Belt, so named for the orchards once planted there by early immigrants to the area. This corner that Tyrone stands on in Clifton's poem is not very far away from the Tops grocery store that was the site of a racist mass shooting in May of 2022. In fact, Aaron Salter, Jr., the retired police officer-turned-alternate-energy-entrepreneur who was working as a security guard at Tops that day and was killed in the attack, was a cousin of Lucille Clifton's on her father's side.

Once a prosperous part of the city, the neighborhood's fortunes declined when it was bisected by the construction of the Kensington Expressway in the mid-1960s under Robert Moses' controversial urban planning modality which resulted in many historic Black neighborhoods across New York State being diminished, dissected, or demolished by public works projects, including highway construction, usually without any consultation or collaboration with the residents of the affected communities themselves.

One might imagine a historical marker, such as the kind you see in front of important houses or historical sites, placed at the corner of Jefferson and Sycamore, where these poems begin. What follows is a triad of lines describing the boys' intentions: in diminishing construction and repetition of three verbs. Graphically on the page the two verbs "will" are lined up right on top of each other, reinforcing the intention visually, and the three actions—sack, sink, seek—are similarly aligned visually to give them further emphasis. By calling attention to the actions (further focused by the sonic repetition of first and last letters and by their monosyllable), Clifton drives forward the momentum and anticipation inherent in impending violence. William Fogarty, in a study of Clifton's use of language, highlights these lines as both a gesture toward Tyrone's shifting feelings about the riots and an example of the various tonal registers within the poem.[11] The word "sack"—an archaic word that might recall the sack of Troy—might not often be found in the vocabulary of a sixteen-year-old boy.

Of course, after this "sacking" and destruction of the city, Tyrone transitions in something altogether different: an effort to *find* the city within. The historic Buffalo Soldiers were participating in a war of liberation, and while the first two of these actions ("sack" and "sink") might be expected in any war, Tryone ends by wanting to preserve the city, or at very least reveal something which had been to that point concealed. He means to seek it by means of its own destruction, i.e. at the point of seeking, the city will already have been both sacked and sunk. Fogarty also points out that the final act of "seeking" returns sonically to the sound of the place Tyrone stands, Sycamore Street, giving physical and material primacy to the neighborhood itself, regardless of its diminished state after the construction of the Expressway.

The boys on the corner are on a quest for something, after all—something they hope to find. And if they have to tear up the existent (or burn it down) in order to find it (the city itself in some way more elemental and essential that can be expressed), then they will do that. It's a startling, and startlingly self-aware, opening to the unfolding story of the "buffalo war." We will see Tyrone again, we will come to know more about him, in the rest of the poems. And as we have come to understand Clifton herself as an intentional and careful poet, the reader will come to see Tyrone as a self-aware and critical thinker who knows what's happening around him, and who knows the import of what he is planning to do.

But for the moment, and for the rest of the epic, Clifton will pivot from the one boy to the other.

Willie B. is a very different boy than Tyrone and his innocence and even more destructive tendency serve as counterpoint to the older boy. Immediately we sense that Willie B. is younger. Rather than Tyrone's determined "on this day," Willie B.'s poem opens "mama say." Unlike Tyrone, he tells us how old he is a few lines later—12, and it sounds like a young 12—but he too, like Tyrone, is indeed aware of the greater significance of the riot:

willie b (1)

mama say
i got no business out here
in the army
cause i ain't but twelve
and my daddy was
a white man

the mother fucker[12]

The positioning of the opening of this poem is interesting because he is responding to and invoking his mother—as "mama"—but refers later to his biological father, a white man, as a "mother fucker," a double entendre rude to both the man and the mother. The mother seeks to protect the son from the riot for two reasons: his age is mentioned first—implying, perhaps, that Tyrone is older—but the second reason is both more important and more complicated: in the mother's eyes Willie B. does not belong in the streets with the Black protesters because he is half white. On the other hand, the fact that he is white does not register with Willie B. as important or relevant, and may even be a cause of tension with his mother and scorn for her, as evidenced by the final line. He, like Tyrone, knows these riots are about more than mere destruction: while Tyrone refers to himself as a "soldier," Willie B. also recognizes the organization and intentionality behind the movement when he refers to the protestors as an "army."

The war continues in the second poem in Tyrone's voice, and he describes the spirit of the people around him as "beautiful" and they are all "laughing and shouting." "We happy together," he says, and "we turning each other on/in this damn war."[13]

"Tyrone (2)" describes moments of violence and destruction, but in gleeful terms. As in an army, Tyrone and his friends are finding a sense of community and purpose in what they're doing, "turning each other on" in an energetic way, in an energizing way. Although Tyrone and his friends are almost seeming to have fun, these riots continued through the east side of the city for nearly six days, and the streets were flooded with police amid incidents of arson, property damage, and looting.

Despite his mother's objections, Willie B. does eventually join the "army" outside, but with less noble intentions than Tyrone and his friends:

willie b (2)

why i would bring a wagon into battle
is
a wagon is a help to a soldier
with his bricks
and when he want to rest
also
today is mama's birthday
and i'm gone get her that tv
out of old steinhart's store[14]

While Tyrone and friends intend to sack, sink, and *seek* the city, the child-like Willie B. is at once more practical, and more devious too. Willie B. has taken his toy wagon, his little radio flyer perhaps, out into the street with bricks and is going out into the riots to steal a television for his mother's birthday. It's a moment of humor in the poem, and also tenderness, but it also delineates the difference between these two speaking boys, the representative cast of the epic: Tyrone has a very strong sense of what he's doing, what his intentions are in this riot, the importance of it, and the social and historical significance of it, while Willie B.'s desire is simpler: he wants to get the TV for his mom's birthday.

As the riots continue, the awareness of the two boys finally converge in each boy's third poem. By the third or fourth day of the riots, over forty people had been wounded, including by gunshot, many of those from police fire. Governor Nelson Rockefeller called in baseball legend Jackie Robinson, famed for integrating Major League Baseball, who was at the time serving as Rockefeller's Special Assistant for Urban Affairs, to Buffalo, NY, to meet with the mayor of the city, and try to talk to the rioters. "Ex-Dodger Star to

Counsel Angry Negro Youths" read the headline of one newspaper article describing Robinson's visit.

Here's Tyrone commenting on Robinson's visit:

tyrone (3)

the governor has sent out
jackie robinson
and he has sprinted from center
and crouched low
and caught the ball
(what a shortstop)
and if we buffalo soldiers was sports fans
we sure would cheer[15]

Robinson was nationally famous, having originally played in the Black baseball leagues (called at the time the "Negro leagues"), and then was selected to be the first black player in the major leagues, playing for the Brooklyn Dodgers. Ironically, Robinson breaking that color barrier in 1947 put a lot of Black professional baseball players out of work as the flourishing Black leagues could not compete as more and more Black players joined the integrated major leagues. By 1958, the last of the Black leagues had disbanded. After Robinson's sports career he had gone into politics as a Republican, having mostly conservative views on issues like the Vietnam war, but drifted toward the more liberal wing of the Republican party after Goldwater's victory at the 1964 nominating convention.

It was in this context that Robinson, an integrationist, part of a liberal Republican administration, appeared in Buffalo. The young men, as evidenced by Tyrone, were not impressed; mocking Robinson's political work by describing it with sports analogies, he concludes: "if we buffalo soldiers was sports fans/we sure would cheer." Tyrone also refers to Robinson's role as a shortstop, a position he played only in the Black leagues, having become most renowned in Major League Baseball as a second baseman. By returning to Robinson's previous position in his reference, Tyrone is perhaps dismissing Robinson's achievement of integrating the formerly all-white Major Leagues.

Willie B.'s take is, if anything, even more dismissive, as he claims to not even know who Robinson is:

willie b (3)

mama say
he was a black hero
a champion like
muhammad ali
but i never heard of it
being not born till 1955.[16]

The humor of Willie B.'s voice—he must depend on his mother to provide him with information and context—leavens the seriousness of what we otherwise understand to be happening. Of course, the appearance of Muhammad Ali here is telling, because in all the ways that mattered in 1967, Muhammad Ali was very *unlike* Jackie Robinson. Willie B.'s mother, who believed his mixed-race background meant he should not risk himself by being in solidarity with the protestors, also tries to present a sanitized version of Muhammad Ali to Willie B. Ali was no mere sports hero: the year prior to the riots in Buffalo, Ali, already a champion boxer, had been drafted for military service in Vietnam and announced his intention to refuse to serve, famously saying, "Why should they ask me to put on a uniform and go ten thousand miles from home and drop bombs and bullets on brown people in Vietnam while so-called Negro people in Louisville are treated like dogs and denied simple human rights?"[17]

Ali's boxing license was suspended and he was stripped of his title. He was eventually indicted and the week before the riots broke out in Buffalo, he was convicted of refusing the draft, a crime punishable by up to five years in prison.

When Willie B.'s mother tries to explain who Jackie Robinson is to Willie B. by saying Robinson is "like" Muhammad Ali, she too, like Tyrone, is only invoking the sports accomplishments of both men, ignoring Robinson's conservative politics (though they did evolve from conservativism to an abandonment of those ideals and eventually the abandonment of the Republican Party), and similarly ignoring Ali's much more radical politics, shaped by his spiritual teacher, Malcolm X, who had been killed two years earlier, in 1965.

Ali would not be able to box again until three years later when his conviction was overturned on appeal.

The appearance of Jackie Robinson here in both boys' poems performs a kind of parallax where the boys—so far separate in the actions of the poems—have a perception of the same event. Narratively speaking, Robinson's appearance signals the entrance of the external—the governor has sent him to try to cool temperatures—and heralds the end of the riots. It's worth saying that Clifton herself had more esteem for Robinson than either of the boys in the poem do. In a later poem from an ordinary woman called simply "jackie robinson,"she praises him, calling him "brave as a hit/over whitestone fences."[18]

This epic ends as most epics do, without a satisfying conclusion. The purpose of an epic in classical antiquity is to create the larger-than-life framework, normally on behalf of a political elite or a national idea. Yet all of these ancient epics, every single one of them, attempt to build characters who struggle in the circumstances of the founding of the nation, or in promotion of the social ideals of heroism. The Iliad ends with Achilles surrendering his role as the main character to Hector, whose funeral is the subject of the final book; the Odyssey ends with a kind of failure on Odysseus' part: thirsty for vengeance, he is dissuaded from further massacre by Athena in the form of Mentor; the Aeneid has the most infamously problematic ending of them all: everything Aeneas has learned to that point, including the lessons of Achilles and Odysseus implied from the earlier epics of which his is a conceptual and translingual sequel, would lead him to spare Turnus' life—his killing of Turnus precludes any further development of his character: the epic ends.

While it can be argued that these truncated endings are the result of the degradations of time or the failure of the poets to complete their tasks, Aeneid translator Shadi Bartsch points out that the problematic endings of epics may be intentional: the adjective and verb used to describe Turnus, in line 952 of Book 12 of Bartsch's translation, as he collapses onto the earth in death is the same phrase used to describe Aeneas at the beginning of the tale, in line 92 of Book 1, collapsing in despair on the deck of his ship. There is a synchronicity connecting the two men as the phrase is used nowhere else in the epic, Bartsch points out.[19] Perhaps this is one way of understanding that no epic can truly "end" because the ending itself betrays the flaw in the founding myth: that it is possible to halt growth, to freeze political and social development in place in the form of the authority of an emperor, who is himself mortal, or in the form of a nation or country, which itself may have already passed.

Here is the end of the epic in Tyrone's voice:

tyrone (4)

we made it through the swamps
and we'll make it through the dogs
leaving our white man's names
and white man's traditions
and making some history
and they see the tear gas
burn my buffalo soldiers eyes
they got to say
Look yonder
Tyrone
Is[20]

Tyrone continues to place the riots in Buffalo in a historical continuum, linking it to the struggles for African liberation that characterized the period of enslavement in the United States. Not only does he invoke the escapes of enslaved people (the "swamps" and the "dogs"), but also the cultural and spiritual erasure that attended enslavement, when the languages, social traditions, and family names of African people were suppressed and erased by the enslavers. Clifton invokes this erasure many times in her work, including the later poems such as "at the cemetery, walnut grove plantation, south carolina, 1989," where she writes of the cemetery, "nobody mentioned slaves/and yet the curious tools/shine with your fingerprints."[21] Later in the same poem she begs, "tell me your dishonored names." It is, of course, an entreaty that cannot be answered. The African names of the enslaved people are lost to history. She hopes, in the poem, "slave cabin, sotterly plantation, maryland, 1989," that such a name could be remembered; she imagines the old woman, known as "aunt nanny," sitting and "humming for herself   humming/her own sweet human name."[22]

Clifton recounts also, at the beginning of the prose memoir *generations*, the argument between her father and his grandmother, Caroline, known to all as "Mammy Ca'line," who was born in Africa and enslaved, about her African name. She refuses to tell him the name. "But it'll be forgot!" he hollers. "Don't you worry, mister," she replies, implying that knowing the name is not important.

Tyrone might agree. After declaring that he and his comrades are "leaving our white man's names/and white man's traditions," he invokes his own name: eyes stinging with tear gas fired to disperse the rioters, he says about the police and any observers, "they got to say/Look, yonder/Tyrone/Is."

These three brief lines show Tyrone claiming for himself a significance that he was never given in his life before, doubly significant because of what's happening at the end of the poem: the boys are being tear gassed.

One understands the significance of the declaration very subtly because of Clifton's atypical use of capitalization in her work. Most often she lowercases everything, including initial capitalization at the start of a sentence or line, including proper names of people and places (as in "buffalo"), including the personal pronoun, rendered by Clifton as "i", and including the word "god." Here, in quick succession, she capitalizes three words in each of the last three lines of the poem, and they are three different kinds of capitalization. In the first case, she capitalizes the declarative "Look," following it with the very formal "yonder," giving especial significance to the observers seeing Tyrone, sinking under the assault of the might of the state, represented by the tear gassing. Secondly, he gives himself emphasis by capitalizing his own name—the name he now claims for himself. The moment of claiming "Tyrone" as his own, as not a "white man's name," is reminiscent of the moment in her poem "light" where she reflects on her own name Lucille as an African name. She makes this claim because she was named after an ancestress Lucy, who as described in generations as having killed a white man who wronged her; she sees this action as one of transgression and bravery and, because of it, she claims "mine already is/an afrikan name."[23] In so saying this, Lucille Clifton declares her name, though European, is not a "white man's name," meaning a slave name.

Finally in the last line of the poem, Clifton goes back to the powerful and flexible and various alternative uses of forms of the verb "to be" in African American Vernacular English: she gives emphasis to Tyrone's declaration of selfhood with the singular utterance "Is."

Tyrone reifies himself as historically significant in the eyes of any observer.

Willie B. has, throughout the series of poems, provided a necessary counterpoint to Tyrone's earnestness and self-awareness. He almost seems like he's out in the riot for fun, and if not for fun, then for potential personal gain. We're not told whether or not he retrieves the desired television, but there's no reason not to believe that he hasn't. In Willie B.'s final poem, the riot has already ended and he is making a confession to the reader, in his child-like way wanting credit for the destruction he has wrought:

willie b (4)

i'm the one
what burned down the dew drop inn.
yes
the jew do exploit us in his bar
but also
my mama
one time in the dew drop inn

tried for a white man
and if he is on a newspaper
or something
look I am the one what burned down the dew drop inn
everybody say i'm a big boy for my age
me
willie b
son[24]

Willie B. targets the inn for two reasons: first because of a general feeling that the members of the community may be exploited by the owner of the inn, who are presented by Willie B. in prejudicial terms as outsiders ("the jew do exploit us"), but secondly, and more importantly, because his mother "tried for a white man" there. We already know that Willie B.'s father is white, and ostensibly not present in his life based on what he recounts in the first poem, but we don't know anything else about him. Willie B. implies that the site of their meeting may have been the Dew Drop Inn. The fact that the mother "tried" for the white man is a shameful incident in Willie B.'s eyes, and the fact that he refers to his father as a "mother fucker" confirms that for Willie B. the relationship is not meaningless: his feelings of animosity toward the absent white father justify his action of arson.

Further, it appears that the white man in question might be famous, a business leader or a politician of some kind since he is in the paper, though this information is tossed off by Willie B. as incidental and does not connect causally or grammatically in the poem, i.e. he interrupts himself to return to the more important matter, even capitalizing his first person pronoun: "look I am the one what burned down the dew drop in".

Like Tyrone, Willie B. asserts himself at the end of the poem, but rather than assert himself in a grand and historical and rhetorically elevated way, as Tyrone did, Willie B.'s assertion is local and immediate, reconnecting him in his relationship to his mother: "everybody say i'm a big boy for my age/me/willie b/son."

Throughout his poems, Tyrone's relationship is to the city and the larger social and political issues surrounding the riot, while

Willie B. has been focused on the personal, and in particular, on his mother. He often introduces information with "mama say." Later, as he heads out to the riots, he vows, "i'm gone get her that tv," and here in the final poem he sees in some way the father's act of sleeping with the mother to produce Willie B. as an act of violence, or violation, whether or not the relationship was consensual or not, information we as readers are not given. In his own way, he is engaging in an act as metaphorical as Tyrone's when he sets fire to the inn where his mother either met his father or tried to pick up another white man. The injustices Willie B. sees and reacts against are not grand and historical and social. They're extremely personal.

The sequence ends without demarcation in the book itself, but with a poem bearing the title "buffalo war." It is, as all ending epics are, anti-climactic:

buffalo war

war over
everybody gone home
nobody dead
everybody dying[25]

As in life, there's no real conclusion to the boys' "war"; the riots did not result in any political or social gains for the community. Clifton's "nobody dead," while technically true—unlike in the other riots during the Long, Hot Summer, no one in Buffalo lost their life— still sounds a down note. Indeed, many were injured in the unrest, and some grievously. The final line continues this note of giving in to despair, naming a present tense condition from which there does not seem to be any escape. Everybody alive is still suspended there, in the process of death, the process of dying.

Clifton, who by June 1967 had relocated from Buffalo with her family to Baltimore, curiously follows the downbeat ending of the "buffalo war" poems with a quite light-hearted poem called "Flowers," which ends with an optimistic line, "and the name of the place/is Love."[26] Note the rare capitalization of the final word.

This juxtaposition almost seems to give the sequence's pessimistic ending a little bit of breath, a thin ray of hope.

Chapter 2 : All Clay is Kin and Kin

When Lucille Clifton writes about historical events, she is looking in both directions at once: she seeks to illuminate or find hidden meaning in the past, but is also interested in how her own view of the past acts upon, and creates, new visions of the present and the future. She is clear-eyed and realistic and yet even in the moments of greatest hardship, she seems to want to make sure her vision toward the future includes hope and survival. In an uncollected poem written just prior to the events of the summer of 1967, she tunes this vision to the subtlest word, once more invoking the specific particularities of African American Vernacular English.

Here is "5/23/67: R.I.P.," an elegy for the poet Langston Hughes, who was one of the first people to publish Clifton's poetry, including it in an anthology he was editing. Clifton wrote this poem on the occasion of Hughes' passing, though it remained uncollected in book form until her *Collected Poems*:

5/23/67: R.I.P.

The house that is on fire
pieces all across the sky
make the moon look like
a yellow man in a veil
watching the troubled people
running and crying
   Oh who gone remember now like it was,
   Langston gone.[27]

(9)

Aracelis Girmay notes, in her introduction to Clifton's selected poems, *How to Carry Water*, that this poem mourns the recent death of Langston Hughes and "is an attempt to remember a community's loss while simultaneously marking the impossibility of that record ever being precise enough."[28] Girmay is correct, but the supposed mourning of the people in the closing couplet is also belied by the double meaning of the final word.

As we have seen in both the penultimate line of this poem and in Willie B.'s second poem in the "buffalo war" sequence, the term "gone" has two meanings: it is an adjective in Standard English meaning 'absent,' but in African American Vernacular/ Black English, it is also a form of the transitive future tense, i.e. an oral elision of the construction "going to." In other words, "who gone remember" here means "who is *going to* remember," (though Black English/AAVE typically eliminates/elides "to be" as a helping verb in present participial form) so the mourning line "Langston gone" *does* mean 'Langston is gone,' i.e. dead, but it *also* means "Langston is *going to.*" Clifton not only mourns Hughes' passing, but affirms the continued presence of his spirit and the continued and continuing relevance of his work.

Regardless of Clifton's dual emotions of grief at Hughes' passing and determined understanding that his legacy would live on, she was nonetheless committed to addressing the political in her work. As in the "buffalo war" poems, her manner of doing so continued to be intimately personal and emotional, and always with a deeply felt awareness of the relationality between her own individual life (and the lives of her children and community) and the larger social and political events that were unfolding in the world outside.

There was no opportunity for remove, in other words. Clifton is no Keats, writing the ode "To Autumn" mere weeks after the Peterloo Massacre in which fifteen demonstrators were killed (to whom Keats compares his poetic labor in a letter to his brother the day before he wrote his ode, as scholar Anahid Nersessian points out in her excellent book *Keats's Odes: A Lover's Discourse*).

Rather Clifton always saw her own fate as inextricably bound with actors in historical events, and not solely the Black actors.

Because her sympathies and her empathies were universal, she often mythologized and essentialized experiences in these early poems, writing in a more communal voice rather than telling the stories of specific lives that she came to do in later books. Even though she was writing in a public voice, the poems were anything but expected; she often used the language and form to undo old associations and assumptions of meaning. Let us look at a short representative poem called "after kent state," a poem, like Keats' "To Autumn," composed in the immediate wake of an act of civil unrest and violence. The event the title refers to is the May 4, 1970 murder of 4 unarmed student activists, and the wounding of 9 others by the Ohio National Guard, who fired upon a demonstration by unarmed student protestors against the invasion of Cambodia on the campus of Kent State University in Ohio. The four students who were killed were all white. Two of them were activists involved in the protests; the other two were students who had stopped to watch the protest between classes. I include that detail only to point out that Clifton seemed to recognize and acknowledge the precarity of life here and the dangers posed by state violence, regardless of the nature of the individual as active or passive participant:

after kent state

only to keep
his little fear
he kills his cities
and his trees
even his children   oh
people
white ways are
the way of death
come into the
black
and live[29]

On the surface of it, at the beginning of this poem, we are not sure who is being addressed, nor do we know who is being spoken of: the possessive pronoun "his" appears first, followed by "he," but there is no antecedent given. We can only assume: Nixon? The "Man" or the "establishment"? Both the essentialized and the actual person who gave the order to the Ohio National Guard? One can assume all of these meanings.

After connecting the killing of both cities and trees—a rare moment of solidarity and understanding between activism around conservation and preservation and political activism in urban communities, activisms that then, as now, were often exclusive and at odds with each other for resources and national attention—she names the tragedy of the moment. To keep his "fear," i.e. continue to prosecute his war, the "white man" is willing to kill his own children. (In fact, the father figure's willingness to kill his son will recur in the later poem "sarah's promise," a poem about the biblical Sarah, Abraham, and Isaac, that we will look at in Chapter 8).

It is not until the fifth line of the eleven-line long poem "after kent state" that Clifton makes her address, "oh," and increases the impact by enjambing the audience of this entreaty onto the next line, the "people." And who are the "people" that are being so addressed? She may be addressing white people or she is addressing black people who still follow or subscribe to what she essentializes as "white ways"—i.e. holding on to one's fear, killing trees and cities, prosecuting wars, and so on. Probably she is addressing both groups. Interesting to note here that while she pluralizes "white ways," her warning is that they—all of them—are the singular "way" of death. In other words, there is no possibility of redemption or rescue down the path of the various "white ways."

She positions "white" as dangerous, as selfish, as lacking a future, while "black" is inclusive, welcoming, life-affirming, and holds the possibility of rebirth for all, a possibility enacted by her strategic line breaks: "come into the/black/and live."

Naturally, it's important to point out that Clifton here is working within a linguistic context of the term "white" and its variants normally having positive connotations and associations, i.e. "white glove," "white lie," "white wedding," etc. and "black" or "dark" having negative or even morally corrupt or evil connotations and associations, i.e. "blackmail," "blackball," "blacklist," "blackguard," to "blacken" a reputation, etc. Clifton plumbs this inversion of racist connotation in other poems, such as "bodies broken on," where she writes of "red dust and black clay/pulling white men down" and action she calls "good news about the earth;" in another poem, "her hiding place" she includes a curse on those who would forget the plight of Angela Davis, then in police custody, that their hair (and she includes herself) would "fall straight on our backs/like death." In the poem "ordinary woman" she uses the word "europe" as a synonym for a decline into death and in a poem called "apology (to the panthers)," she confesses "i grieve my whiteful ways."[30]

It's in this framework that Clifton chooses to invert to normative associations and declare "white ways are/the way of death" and that one could "come into the/black/and live." At the time Clifton wrote these lines, not only were poets and writers attempting to undo the colonizing destruction wrought by language, but theorists and thinkers were trying to posit new ways of understanding the world, including a repositioning of African history, philosophy, and political thought as essential and central to a development of modern society. Anthropologist and philosopher Molefi Asante described this school of thought as "Afrocentricity," a term he chose to highlight that "Africans were not simply removed from Africa to the Americas, but Africans were separated from philosophies, languages, religions, myths, and cultures."[31]

In both Asante's configuration and Clifton's, Afrocentricity is not meant to be exclusive, solely returning African thought and experience to a central role, but rather is by its own nature inclusive of various orientations, undoing a sense of centrality and marginalization in human cultural experience. It is important to note, however, that though Clifton is inclusive and generous in her view of history, her opinions are trenchant, clearly stated, and she does not dither when asked to choose a "side." In the poem "whose side are you on?" the opening line answers the question, and she continues through repetition to reinforce her solidarity with working people and the dispossessed:

whose side are you on

the side of the busstop woman
trying to drag her bag
up the front steps before the doors
clang shut   i am on her side
i give her exact change
and him the old man hanging by
one strap his work hand folded shut
as the bus doors i am on his side
when he needs to leave
i ring the bell   i am on their side[32]

Note how the formal choices of line break and the eschewing of punctuation along with the occasional midline caesura creates
both the forward movement and slight sense of claustrophobic
closed space of a bus. The opening two lines have a more normative
line break that happens on the clause, but with that enjambment on
"doors," the poem—and the bus—is off and running. Similarly, the
lack of punctuation in the phrase "and him the old man" keeps the
poem moving forward. Both the man and the woman mentioned
are struggling physically: in her case, she may have a grocery bag
or a bag of possessions that she must carry, in his case his hand is
either tired or sore from manual labor or else it is injured. In any
case, she anticipates their need and helps them.

She continues in this expression of solidarity and makes
clear her allegiances:

i ring the bell   i am on their side
riding the late bus into the same
someplace   i am on the dark side always
the side of my daughters
the side of my tired sons

The end of this poem once more demonstrates the relationality between the general and personal I mentioned before. While

she is abstracting by characterizing all of the passengers' destinations as the common "same/someplace" and clarifying that her devotion is universal and unflagging ("always"), she personalizes the people she is helping: they become metaphorically her family, as actual as her own four daughters and two sons, that she will always support.

Two adjectives here in this closing section hold a lot of weight. Firstly, of course, there's "dark": though Clifton has not specifically identified whether these people on the bus are Black people or not—in fact the sole marker besides economic class which might necessitate the use of late night public transit is physical need, i.e. to get home from work on a late shift—yet this adjective implies that to be the case. And then at the close of the poem, it works rhythmically, but also adds an extra dimension of tenderness when she gives the men in the poem the additional descriptor "tired."

In other poems, Clifton engages with slavery and the legacy of the enslavement of African people, and she delves very particularly into the problem of determining meaning when written history and personal memory diverge. What does the legacy of history mean to her and her own family in particular? She contends, in many of these poems, with these difficulties of history as a Black woman poet struggling with what is knowable and speakable.

In the poem "atlantic is a sea of bones," Clifton opens with a traditional Black spiritual song from the African American South based on the episode from the biblical Book of Ezekiel where the prophet commands the dry and dead bones in the Valley to come to life. "Now hear the word of the Lord," commands Ezekiel in the Bible. The story from the Book of Ezekiel was adapted into song by poet and activist James Weldon Johnson with music composed by his brother, J. Rosamond Johnson; if the brothers sound familiar, it may be because they teamed up as lyricist and composer often, most famously to create the song "Lift Ev'ry Voice and Sing," promoted by the NAACP at the beginning of the 20th century as the "Negro National Anthem." The traditional spiritual song "them bones" describes the bones of the body knitting back together to rise up, but is more commonly heard in a version sung by school-children to learn skeletal anatomy, devoid of either Biblical context or context of African liberation. Clifton uses the older version of the song, with the refrain from Ezekiel:

> them bones
> them bones will
> rise again
> them bones
> them bones will
> walk again
> them bones
> them bones will
> talk again
> now hear
> the word of The Lord
>
> – Traditional[33]

By appending her own response to these traditional and haunting lyrics, Clifton participates in an ancient tradition of call-and-response, which has characterized Black social rhetoric, as well as the religious services of Black Christianity, and which may have its roots in not only the cultures and musical structures of West Africa, but in the patterns of Muslim prayer which includes call-and-response between the officiant or imam or the prayer and the congregants/participants.

Importantly, she switches tone. The Johnsons' jaunty tune beloved in churches and schools alike is met by Clifton's ominous first line which immediately opens up a darker and more historical interpretation of the seabed between Africa and the Americas as the Valley of Dry Bones of Ezekiel's text. If the bones knitting to-gether to rise up again in the presence of God is meant, in Johnson's lyrics, to be celebratory, Clifton's oracular vision is darker, and potentially terrifying:

> atlantic is a sea of bones,
> my bones,
> my elegant afrikans

connecting whydah and new york,
a bridge of ivory.

seabed they call it.
in its arms my early mothers sleep.
some women leapt with babies in their arms.
some women wept and threw the babies in.

maternal armies pace the atlantic floor.
i call my name into the roar of surf
and something awful answers.

As in other poems, Clifton immediately claims historical truth as her own personal experience, i.e. "my bones,/my elegant afrikans." One notices here that Clifton adopts a different spelling for Africa and Africans, using a "k" instead of the normative "c." This spelling, among Afrocentrist thinkers, such as poet Haki Madhubhuti and others, came about as way of critiquing the more common orthographic rendering of the word in English as "Africa," and also as a rejection of the Latin origins of the word as an imperial term for the southeastern coast of the Mediterranean used by early Romans during the time of the empire. Of note, there is also an alternative spelling of the name of America as "Amerika" (which Clifton also uses) to highlight the racist and fascist aspects of American life. This spelling of "Amerika" is thought to be a spelling drawn from the German spelling of the name.

Whydah is a city on the coast of modern day Benin, which was once a part of the old kingdom of Dahomey, from which Clifton traces her ancestry, according to the oral testimony of her great-grandmother Caroline Donald which Clifton recounts in her memoir *generations* and in various poems of hers. When Clifton talks about the women leaping or throwing their babies in, one is reminded not only of the biblical story of Miriam the Prophetess casting the basket with her baby brother Moses inside onto the surface of the Nile, but also the historical accounts of African women doing precisely this, to spare their infants from the horrors of enslavement. More ominously, as recounted in NourBese Philip's powerful work *Zong!*, sometimes enslaved persons were murdered intentionally, thrown into the water by the ships' crews, a fate reserved for the most rebellious on board, or those who were sick or infirm and thus likely to infect others and/or die before arrival in the Americas.

The closing lines of the poem re-enact the practice of call-and-response as Clifton shouts her own name to the ocean in response to the roar of the surf. We know now that names are a powerful totem and mantra: in *generations*, Caroline holds her own African name secret, while in the "buffalo war" poems Tyrone declares his own as powerful and significant; the woman in the poem "slave cabin, sotterly plantation" hums hers to herself so she will not forget it. Here as Clifton shouts her name into the surf, she both expects and imagines the answer, though she does not tell us what the answer is, only that "something awful" answers. Here "awful" may be used in its traditional sense—to denote the absolute unspeakable horror of the Middle Passage, but it is also being used in its older and original usage: as "awesome," or "awe-filled." In other words, perhaps horrible but somehow by that horror sanctified. Clifton takes us to the lip of the unspeakable and leaves us there. It is a strategy she repeats in other poems, such as "it was a dream." In this poem, when Clifton is confronted by her "greater self" that self is "whirling in a gyre of rage/at what my days had come to." When Clifton begs the wrathful other self "what could i have done?" the spirit tears her hair and:

> screamed as long as
> i could hear her
> This.   This.   This.[34]

By staying in the general and the abstract, the figure becomes even more frightening.

It is most often the dead or the divine or otherwise spiritual that is vague in Clifton, their message seeming to be that there are certain experiences so vast as to be incomprehensible to the human mind. There may also be practical reasons why the spirits do not speak to humans about the essential truth of matters: when in a later poem Clifton is (once more) visited by the spirit of her departed husband Fred, she begs him to tell her "why/cancer and terrible loneliness/and the wars against our people," Fred's spectral hand becomes flesh and spells out to her a kind of cold comfort: "it does not help to know."[35]

There is something particularly painful, of course, when one's own personal history is bound up in the social trauma of slavery, which itself actively erased and displaced family history and continuity. As Tracy K. Smith writes, in her introduction to the new edition of generations, "What if the largeness of those lives—what they endured, yes, but also what they carried, remembered, witnessed, and made—has been hushed up, negated, overwritten, or outright erased?"[36]

In "atlantic is a sea of bones" Clifton tries to confront this erasure of the history of African lives, their griefs and joys. She creates a new geography for the ocean, or more precisely, a new topography. Rather than invoke the anonymity of the ocean and the impossibility of those who were lost within it to ever speak legibly—as NourBese Philip does brilliantly in her work Zong!—Clifton gives the ocean itself agency as a speaking being, something that could "answer," and she positions it as place with physical features on its floor, notably the bones of the dead Africans. The knitting together and rising up of these "maternal armies" becomes something unspeakable, something "awful," meaning perhaps ominous or even dangerous.

I think of Clifton's complicated positioning of herself in a vexed history in the terms Christina Sharpe describes in her book In the Wake: that Black existence "is to occupy and be occupied by the continuous and changing present of slavery's as yet unresolved unfolding."[37] Sharpe, in asking what has survived Black exclusion from history (and how Black literature and art mediates that "un/survival"), argues that Philip and other Black writers "do not seek to explain or resolve the question of this exclusion in terms of assimilation, inclusion, or civil or human rights, but rather depict aesthetically the impossibility of such resolutions by representing the paradoxes of blackness within and after the legacies of slavery's denial of Black humanity."[38]

Sharpe's thorny questions help us to realize how and why Clifton comes up to the edge of what is speakable, how she wrestles with the problem of the personal in the historical—and it's very personal indeed, in that her great-great-grandmother—not *that* many generations removed—was "born free in Afrika in 1822/died free in America in 1910."[39] Sharpe uses the term "wake" in its many contexts: to be "awake" or, more accurately perhaps, "woke," to actively wake another, the wake as a witnessing after a death, and to be metaphorically "in the wake" of historical events, or literally in the wake of a ship, in this case a slave ship. For Sharpe, the ship is not only the ship; its implications continue to unfold "from the forced movements of the enslaved to the forced movements of the migrant and the refugee, to the regulation of Black people in North American streets and neighborhoods...to the reappearances of the slave ship in everyday life in the form of the prison, the camp, and the school."[40]

In this way, Clifton herself finds the legacy of racism and enslavement to be present in a broad political and social sense but also immediately present in her own life. In a series of poems from her book *Next*, she even places herself at various points in history—the first letter of the poems are either a lowercase "l" or an unusual capital "I," and it's equally possible Clifton meant both to be seen: in the title index of her *Collected Poems* these poems are filed neither with the "I" nor the "L" but under "A" for "at". The poems put the upper case "I"/lowercase "l" (as whichever case may be) at creation itself, as well as at significant other locales of both human and Black historical importance: Nagasaki, Gettysburg, and Jonestown. The first of these poems puts Clifton and her body (literally separate entities in the poem: "i and my body rise/with the dusky beasts") at the moment of "creation," which identifies not as Adam and Eve in the moments of their creation (whom she interestingly calls "eve and her brother"), but rather in their "long/slide out of paradise."[41] Creation is not the traditional moment of the making of either Adam or Eve but rather in the *expulsion*. Their state of separation from Paradise and the presence of God is the actual beginning of their existences.

It is in "I. at creation" that Clifton most clearly articulates her underpinning and oft-quoted spiritual belief, namely that "all life is life. /all clay is kin and kin."

Of course, this belief is complicated multiple times over by history and the way it has unfolded. The choices of Gettysburg, Nagasaki, and Jonestown as the other venues are not incidental. Gettysburg, as the site of a major battle in the Civil War, was also the place Abraham Lincoln delivered his famous Address, an important moment on the rocky, twisting road of the liberation of Black people from American enslavement. Nagasaki was the second of two cities destroyed by the American atomic bombs in the second World War. Clifton's choice of Nagasaki is significant because the first—and more deadly—bomb was dropped on the city of Hiroshima. While the use of atomic weapons at all has been hotly debated by historians—many of whom believe the Japanese empire was already preparing to surrender and the deployment of the weapons had broader strategic purposes, such as cementing American soft power (in the hardest of ways)—certainly the bombing of Hiroshima sixteen hours earlier had already had its desired effect; in other words, the bombing of Nagasaki—an unplanned target, substituting for another city then covered in clouds—was unnecessary, even within the framework of forcing the surrender of the Japanese. 40,000 people lost their lives in an instant. The final poem is set at another location of death: Jonestown, the outpost in the Guyanese jungle where some 900 people who were followers of Jim Jones and his People's Temple, most of them African American, perished in a mass suicide, drinking cyanide-laced juice.

In the poem called "I. at jonestown," the speaker glumly surveys her own history saying "i believed this white man...was possibly who he insisted he was." This faith is not rewarded, as she says, "if i have been wrong, again,/father may even this cup in my hand turn against me."[42] History does not have a logic, Clifton seems to suggest in the poem "I. at nagasaki." "i/have done nothing/to deserve this," Clifton says there. In a later as-yet-unpublished poem called "no one deserves anything," she says even more broadly, "no one deserves anything/but it happens."[43]

It is in "l. at gettysburg" that Clifton asks the hardest question. There on the field of Gettysburg she challenges the notions of causality and purpose in violent histories, putting racist language into the ghost-soldiers' mouths:

l. at gettysburg

if, as they say, this is somehow about myself,
this clash of kin across good farmland, then
why are the ghosts of the brothers and cousins
rising and wailing toward me in their bloody voices,
who are you, nigger woman, who are you?[44]

Despite the obvious relevance of the place to her as a Black woman, Clifton acknowledges the ugliness and the contradictions of history. Rather than merely accepting the well-meaning platitudes about the liberation of slaves as an essential part of the North's motivating in the war, she engages with the complicated politics of the time by positioning the souls of the dead soldiers—she does not say whether they are Northern or Southern— as rejecting her, still confrontational, still as racist in death as many of them must have been in life. The exclusion of which Sharpe spoke does not elude well-meaning historians. It is for this reason, I believe, that Clifton always writes from the position of present tense relevance of events perhaps considered "removed" by history.

In a poem called "slaveships," Clifton lets the language of history speak for itself. As in Robert Hayden's poem "Middle Passage," the "bright ironical names" of the slave ships turn in on themselves without any editorializing or explaining in a narrative voice from the poet.[45]

slaveships

loaded like spoons
into the belly of Jesus

where we lay for weeks for months
in the sweat and stink
of our own breathing
Jesus
why do you not protect us
chained to the heart of the Angel
where the prayers we never tell
and hot and red
as our bloody ankles
Jesus
Angel
can these be men
who vomit us out from ships
called Jesus   Angel   Grace Of God
onto a heathen country
Jesus
Angel
ever again
can this tongue speak
can these bones walk
Grace Of God
can this sin live[46]

By allowing the names of the ships themselves, as in
Hayden's poem, to provide ironic and violent counterpoint to the
events around their existence, Clifton juxtaposes registers as she
did in the "buffalo war" poems, allowing a scriptural elevated tone
to give deeper lie to the brutal legacy of slavery. The Christian country becomes "heathen," the actions in the ships named for holy
beings becomes sinful.

She continues the ironic comparison between Christianity
and the slave trade by riffing off of several biblical texts. The ships
"vomit" the people onto the far shore, as the Leviathan did to Jonah.
The question "can these bones walk" recall Ezekiel's encounter
with God in the Valley of the Dry Bones, in which God promises the Israelites eternal life. Finally, the closing line, "can this sin

live," echoes the passage in Ezekiel in which God tests the prophet, asking him, "Son of Man, can these bones live?"

Unlike in Ezekiel, scholar Jeannine Thyreen-Mizingou points out, in "slaveships" the voice speaking is not God, but seems to be the collective and communal voice of the enslaved. The voice is "asking why Jesus did not protect them from the hardships of slavery, and how this sin can live when there is such a thing as the 'Grace of God.'"[47] As Christian Wiman points out, the subject of the poem is "the limits of grace." The poem does not really accuse God, says Thyreen-Mizingou, but critiques "the hypocrisy and misuse of Christianity."[48]

Clifton's calling America "heathen" summons to mind Phillis Wheatley Peters who, in her poem "On Being Brought from Africa to America" refers to Africa as "Pagan." Clifton's contrasting view denies Wheatley's exhortation to her fellow (White) Christians around treating Black people with greater dignity. On the other hand, as Honorée Jeffers has pointed out in her book *The Age of Phillis*, there is no reason not to believe that Wheatley was merely being strategic in how she was addressing a particular audience; in a later poem of Wheatley Peters, "To the Right Honorable William, Earl of Dartmouth," she writes "I, young in life, by seeming cruel fate/was snatch'd from Afric's fancy'd happy seat."[49]

Clifton's view of her own role as a historian within the rubric of poetry is perhaps best summarized by the short poem "why some people be mad at me sometimes":

why some people be mad at me sometimes

they ask me to remember
but they want me to remember
their memories
and i keep on remembering
mine.[50]

Obviously, the line breaks are doing a lot of work here, dividing the perception of history into the dominant version, whether approved by family, nation, or god, and the personal one. And the most powerful and affirming thing a person can have is their own memories, their own version of the past, the one they and only they know to be the "true" one.

Memory is different than history because memory is personal and history is a narrative created, revised, and meant to be agreed upon. When Clifton is asked that horrible question at the end of "I. at gettysburg," we witness the clash between what history purports to be and what Clifton, as a Black woman near the end of the 20th century, knows it to be. So here in this poem, we see how one person creates the past for the other, and the power of a person is in refusing the history of the other.

Let's look at a poem where this concept of contested memory actually comes to the forefront. The relationship and separate outlooks of Lucille and her mother Thelma are at the heart of this poem, called, aptly, "memory":

memory

> ask me to tell how it feels
> remembering your mother's face
> turned to water under the white words
> of the man at the shoe store. ask me,
> though she tells it better than i do,
> not because of her charm
> but because it never happened
> she says,
> no bully salesman swaggering,
> no rage, no shame, none of it
> ever happened.
> i only remember buying you
> your first grown up shoes
> she smiles. ask me
> how it feels.[51]

At the very opening of the poem, Clifton positions the reader/listener in a collaborative role—it may appear confrontational, but it is also an invitation to understand: "ask me to tell how it feels." And true to that privileging of emotions over facts, she doesn't give a visual description but rather a metaphorical one: the child remembering how she felt when she saw her mother's face "turned to water." We might imagine tears here, or a face that goes slack in surprise or shock. What do we know about the words of the man at the shoe store? Clifton does not quote the encounter but rather refers to his speech as "white words," which we the readers must imagine to be some kind of racist treatment. In fact, it may even be better not to know the precise language.

In classroom settings, we often talk about offensive language as it appears in texts we may read, and we wonder if we reproduce offensive language, if we write a poem, including offensive language, do we reproduce that offensive language by reciting it out loud in the classroom? We may have seen many different instances of language that would not be considered to be used in mixed company—she certainly does not shy away from those type of words (including, for example, the closing question of "I. at gettysburg"—but in this case, greater power is given to the experience of the Black women, Lucille and her mother, by not quoting the man at the shoe store directly.

So this is how memory works: something horrible has been said to the mother, and she lets you know exactly how horrible, without ever saying what it is. We understand that with the image of the mother's face turning "to water." Once more, Clifton uses a strategic line break on the second "ask me,"; this time it feels more confrontational.

We don't really know whether Thelma Sayles remembers something different than what the child Lucille is remembering; it is more likely that with her denial she is trying to either protect her daughter or merely preserve the memory. But in so doing, she is indeed denying the experience of the daughter's shame and rage. The child may be embarrassed by her mother, just trying to get by, get along, trying to smile through it, trying to make the horrible experience go away, but the adult Lucille knows much better. The mother is trying to make something ugly that happened in the past not be true anymore. The conflict here is that the daughter and the mother grew up in different worlds with different survival strategies and different ways of making it through the lived world.

So Lucille Clifton wants her audience in on this conundrum: "Ask me/how it feels," she says one more time, and this time we know that this memory from decades earlier is still very fresh and immediate in the memory of the adult woman.

The mother's action of reclamation is not necessarily condemned outright by Clifton, but still held up as having impact on the daughter. The shame the daughter feels after this many years is still tempered by some kind of admiration, I think, for the steely resolve of the mother in trying to preserve for the child a loving memory of buying shoes.

In place of a conclusion, let's look at a last poem that encompasses the breadth of Clifton's treatment of history—another poem set in the very specific geography of Buffalo, NY. The poem, "lot's wife, 1988" recounts a trip Clifton took back to the sites of her childhood homes after the Cliftons moved from Buffalo to Baltimore, Maryland. Clifton invokes the Biblical figure of Lot's (nameless) wife, who famously turned back to look at the burning cities of Sodom and Gomorrah and in that act was turned into a pillar of salt. While there have been revisionist interpretations of the act of Lot's wife and the aftermath/consequence of her transformation (notably by poets Alicia Ostriker and Scott Cairns; I too have written a poem after this moment, called "The Plaint of Marah, Woman of Sodom"), her transformation is generally considered to be a punishment for doubting. It is not the only ancient story which punishes a wayward glance: Orpheus is also so punished for looking away from where he has been told to look, i.e. back at what lies behind, rather than ahead; Icarus, too, is punished for this: for looking up toward the sun as he flies.

Clifton has, in various poems, consecrated the ordinary and daily. For example, in her poem "auction street," she recounts visiting a street with that name in the city of Memphis and discovering that it is so named because of the sale of African people that once took place there. Clifton admonishes the reader at the end of that poem, as God did to Moses on Sinai: "take off your shoes/the ground you walk is holy."[52] So too in "lot's wife 1988" she mythologizes her own family's origins, assigning it spiritual significance by taking on the role of Lot's wife looking back at destruction. Of course, looking back means looking at history, and as Clifton has already pointed out in the poem, "why some people be mad at me sometimes," one is punished doubly so for looking at history critically, at odds with received narratives, i.e. myths of the past.

lot's wife 1988

each of these weeds is a day
i climbed the stair
at 254 purdy street
and looked into a mirror
to see if i was really there.
i was there.   i am there
in the thousand days.
the weeds.   and these weeds

were 11 harwood place
that daddy bought expecting it
to hold our name forever
against the spin of the world.

our name is spinning away in the wind
blowing across the vacant lots
of buffalo, new york,
that were my girlhood homes.

sayles, i hear them calling, sayles,
we thought we would live forever;
and i look back like lot's wife
wedded to her weeds and turn to something
surer than salt and write this, yes
i promise, yes we will.[53]

One hears in that moment of self-affirmation "i was there" echoes of Tyrone's "look yonder." And so Clifton asserts her own *thereness* amidst the empty lots which were once her childhood homes. As it happens, the lot that still bears the number 254 has been assigned to the property deed of the lot numbered 248 Purdy Street. It is an asphalt paved lot, the driveway from the street still there. The woman who lives in 248 leases it to a church based in the house on the other side, at 264 Purdy Street, called the Refuge Temple of God in Christ. I am unsure whether the Refuge Temple or its congregants are aware of the history of their parking lot.

The house at 11 Harwood Place is also gone: it's now the side yard of the house at 13 Harwood Place. Ironically, if you were to search on Google Maps to find 13 Harwood Place, the photograph offered of the site is the green lawn where 11 Harwood Place once stood. Both homes are but a five-minute drive from the corner of Jefferson and Sycamore where Tyrone once started a momentous day.

Samuel Sayles, Clifton's father, bought the houses, one after the other, hoping they would "hold our name forever/against the spin of the world," and Clifton feels the disappearance of the houses keenly. She hears ghosts now too, "them"—who? Ancestors? Her father and mother and uncles and aunts? She does not say, but unlike in "atlantic is a sea of bones," she *does* tell us what she hears: the name of the family repeated over and over again: "sayles." While there is tragedy in being the last of the family that lived in those places, Clifton feels a determination. "We thought we would live forever," Lucille-as-Lot's-Wife thinks glumly, in a brief moment of despair, before she herself transforms to "something surer than salt." But the critical moment comes next: after she transforms, she *writes* the particular poem, and it is in that act of writing that she finds her affirmation, "yes/i promise, yes we will."

Clifton is, by sharing the poem, by looking back, making a history—indeed a place in the canon of American literature— for a family that would otherwise have been forgotten.

Chapter 3: The Blacker She Do Be

Nobody writes a funnier, sexier, sassier poem about the body than Lucille Clifton, and yet her poems about the body also address the specific precarity and conditions that Black people in America contend with. She has commonly been misread as a Christian poet, an identification she contested.[54] Her spiritual foundations—we will explore them more fully in chapters 6 and 9—owe much to Eastern philosophies such as Yoga and Buddhism, and draw from indigenous practices from both the Americas and Africa, including what might be termed "pagan" or "shamanistic." "One set of my godchildren is Jewish-Catholic and the other set is Hindu," she told Susan Somers-Willett. "I've been to all those places of worship. In my house I have a Bible, a Bhagavad-Gita, a Torah, and the Bahai book. My husband was a Yogi. I do believe in spirit and the world of spirits but I don't think of myself as Christian because that word is so laden with baggage."[55]

For Clifton, the "body" and the "spirit" were intertwined. Often, even when she is being witty or funny, she hallows the experience of the body and rejects a more typically Christian view of the duality of the physical and the spiritual, and the attendant idea of the "mortification of the flesh"—that the flesh must be transcended or denied or even destroyed in order for spiritual enlightenment or liberation to take place.

For the dualist, what is human and what is divine are separate. In this theological paradigm, one imagines that mortification—life (and death)—of the flesh is necessary to achieve immortality, i.e. we are born in these lesser forms, we live, we suffer, we die, and our lives are then accounted for against a balance sheet of good and evil or sin and sanctity. For the Christian dualist, one may have the chance to live and die in Jesus' name, since he was believed to be divine but subjected himself to the humiliation and destruction of his flesh. Christians believe that by so doing he removed original sin and reset the scales for humans. In Clifton's view of the body, we see something different. She does not often see the body as a lesser to the spirit nor a thing that is impure, but, as in the yogic view, something that is itself holy and offers potential for experiencing the divine.

Let us look at a representative poem, untitled but referred to by its first line:

> if i stand in my window
> naked in my own house
> and press my breasts
> against my windowpane
> like black birds pushing against glass
> because i am somebody
> in a New Thing
>
> and if the man come to stop me
> in my own house
> naked in my own window
> saying i have offended him
> i have offended his
>
> Gods
>
> let him watch my black body
> push against my own glass
> let him discover self
> let him run naked through the streets
> crying
> praying in tongues[56]

The rhetorical structure of the poem enacts the form of a spell or charm, or curse if you prefer. She sets up the situation with the drama of the naked woman and the archetypal man coming to police her (it must be said: Black) body, and then follows it with the elevated construction of "let him," reminiscent not only of magic, but of scripture. What's noteworthy is that she has created a moment in which the Black body exists in the privileged position, not the denigrated one. It's she who is in the house, who is displaying herself to be viewed, and this position of privilege and power is asserted in the poem through the concept of ownership; repeatedly the speaker emphasizes this positionality as she asserts "my own house" and later "my windowpane," "my own window," and "my own glass."

It is compelling that this poem from more than fifty years ago places a Black woman in the place of certitude and strength, indeed in the possession of prosperity and power. In the current moment, as explored by Sharpe and Philip and Rankine and many others, Black peoples' physical embodiments are precarious, still considered threats, and are disposable. One witnesses time and time again—Ahmaud Arbery, Breonna Taylor, Sandra Bland, Johnny Mims—Black people denied the personal and bodily rights that would be due any other person. They are denigrated, acted against violently, beaten, shot, or tased, and most often these actions have no consequence for the perpetrators, often times themselves police.

This conceptual position of the speaker of "if i should stand in my window" is only made more interesting by what the woman in the position of power is doing: exhibiting herself, and not *just* exhibiting herself, but pressing her body up against the glass. It's a curious collision, but nonetheless celebratory, transgressive, and body positive. She describes the breasts quite beautifully, as "black birds," following it with the powerful statement "i am somebody" in a "New Thing." The "New Thing" she is speaking of (in those rare capital letters) is her own book: "New Thing" was the working title of the manuscript that eventually became *good times*. Clifton compellingly leaves that remnant of the prior iteration of the book, the phrase "New Thing," to represent here a new life: the Black woman poet now has both authorship and authority.

When the generic "man" complains that she has offended his "Gods," the divinity is not only capital but plural, and also alone occupying its own one-word stanza. The capitalized "God" is the received God, not the personal and lowercase "god" Clifton most often (though not exclusively) uses. In this case we might be reminded of a Christian God who would be offended by a Black woman's nakedness. The uppercase God is narrowly conceived by individual communities for their own individual social purposes, yet is still made here *plural*, the one thing that the uppercase God cannot abide. Its position alone in the stanza does not feel like a position of privilege but rather one of being singled out—even ashamed. One is also reminded—Jesus, Angel, Grace Of God—that the Christian God is far from holy: His scriptures and traditions both sanctioned and justified slavery.

Of course, here the woman in the window has her own power: by watching her body push against the glass she knows he will find his own liberation. He will "discover self" and the curious thing is what happens after that discovery: the man loses the previous sense he may have had and behaves in ways that might be similarly considered against notions of social order: running "naked through the streets/crying/praying in tongues." This final moment might immediately recall the practice of speaking in tongues in churches, but glossolalia has ancient roots in pre-Christian prophetic traditions. Perhaps for the modern reader the first association is the Christian revival tent, but it ought to also summon up an extra-lingual, extra-sensual, ecstatic (literally: to be outside oneself) relationship with the divine. This new spiritual condition of the condemning man has no words attached to it and was occasioned by his vision of a Black woman's breasts pressed against a window.

Clifton here disorders the ordinary tropes of Black womanhood—stereotypically either an oversexualization or a dehumanizing erasure—with a declaration of the transformative power of a Black woman's body. What might ordinarily be described as a sexualized or pornographic situation becomes here a body in a state of majesty, a state that could induce others into spiritual fervor. As Sylvia Hennenberg writes in her essay "Fat Liberation in the First World: Lucille Clifton and the New Body," "Lucille Clifton has been a steady, if often unacknowledged, champion of the New Body, proudly showcasing in her poetry the fat black body as a force of resistance against the oppressive effects of racism, sexism, ageism, ableism, and classism that join ranks to beleaguer black women."[57]

Let us turn from this poem to another, that on the surface appears tonally different, yet uses the same kind of rhetorical structure of an inducement or prayer or curse, though more subtly. The poem "lost baby poem" is a well-known one of Clifton's. It describes an abortion she had in pre-Roe v. Wade days, and, as mentioned earlier, inspired Ani DiFranco, a fellow Buffalo artist, to write a song about her own abortion called "lost woman song."

The poem may follow in the tradition of Gwendolyn Brooks' poem "The Mother," but from the outset its tone is different. Brooks' poem is in uneven rhyming couplets, a structure which Ogden Nash used to skillfully comic effect. The lilting, even jaunty, line contrasts with the serious treatment of the subject, a woman remembering abortions she has had, speaking to the unborn children. Brooks' "The Mother" opens, "Abortions will not let you forget./You remember the children you got but you did not get."[58] The first line has four heavy stresses in it and alternates between iambs and anapests, with a trochaic substitution in the third foot; the second line, purely anapestic, has five heavy stresses. Throughout the rest of Brooks' poem, the poet keeps the reader off balance with generally metrical lines and plenty of end-rhymes and internal rhymes continuously switching meters, line lengths, and even enjambing at unexpected moments. The general feeling is light-heartedness but it is made uneasy by the constant changes in scheme.

Clifton's poem, on the other hand, starts dark and stark and gets darker and starker, settling into a somber, even dread-filled, cadence:

the lost baby poem

the time i dropped your almost body down
down to meet the waters under the city
and run one with the sewage to the sea
what did i know about waters rushing back

what did i know about drowning
or being drowned

you would have been born in winter
in the year of the disconnected gas
and no car   we would have made the thin
walk over genesee hill into the canada wind
to watch you slip like ice into strangers' hands
you would have fallen naked as snow into winter
if you were here i could tell you these
and some other things

if i am ever less than a mountain
for your definite brothers and sisters
let the rivers pour over my head
let the sea take me for a spiller
of seas   let black men call me stranger
always   for your never named sake[59]

The poem opens with a direct address to the "lost baby," who is nonetheless described as having an "almost body" in the opening line. For her part, Brooks never wanted to reveal what her feelings about abortion were, nor did she ever give permission for the poem to be used in a political context. As Annie Finch explains, "'the mother' firmly undermines two of the most common false generalizations about people who choose abortions: that they are uninterested in motherhood and that they feel no emotion about the experience." Brooks did not mean to be clear to a reader of "The Mother" what the actual feelings of the speaker of the poem were about abortion, in general nor whether or not she regretted the abortion.

In contrast to Brooks, Clifton was forthright about the circumstances in the poem and about her own feelings. Often questioned by audiences at her readings who wanted to know whether the poem was about an abortion or a miscarriage, Clifton was clear: it was an abortion she was describing, and though she was trying to address the complexity of feelings surrounding such a moment, she did not have regrets. Clifton also spoke and wrote about trying to terminate another pregnancy unsuccessfully and somewhat ironically: her youngest daughter Alexia, who was born despite Lucille Clifton's efforts, ended up being the sole match among all her children to become her mother's kidney donor. The poem "donor," about this moment (it is dedicated "for lex"), she describes "the hangers i shoved inside/hard trying not to have you," and calls Alexia her "stubborn baby child,/hunched there in the dark/refusing my refusal."[60] It says something about Lucille Clifton that she describes the failed attempt at a home abortion with a mixture of regret, humility, self-deprecation, and even humor.

Besides all of those things, Clifton was also brave in the face of social and personal danger: "donor" was published in 2000, but "lost baby poem" was originally published in her second book, *good news about the earth.* That book came out in 1972, the year before the Supreme Court's *Roe v. Wade* decision. At the time, Clifton lived in Baltimore, where abortion, except in cases of rape or "fetal deformity," was still illegal.

It's important to say here that for years after, right wing political forces continued to assault women's reproductive health care, and by the time DiFranco wrote her "lost woman song," multiple states had made it more and more difficult for poor women to access abortions. Clinic protests were in full swing, and violence against providers was rising, culminating in the sniper-like killing of OB/GYN doctor Barnett Slepian. Slepian was murdered by a militant who shot him through the window of his house as he stood in his kitchen preparing soup after having returned from the memorial service for his recently deceased father at the local synagogue. Slepian's wife and son were in the kitchen with him.

"Lucille, your voice still sounds in me," sang Ani DiFranco six short years earlier about having to walk through a picket line for her own abortion, "though mine was a relatively easy tragedy/ the profile of our country's grown a little less hard-nosed/but you know, that picket line persisted/and that clinic's since been closed."

It's unknown whether James Kopp, the man who murdered Dr. Slepian, was also responsible for the attempted murder of another doctor in Rochester, NY, who was also shot through his kitchen window the previous year but survived the incident. Since the 1973 Roe decision nearly a dozen healthcare workers, including physicians, nurses, security guards, and clinic staff such as receptionists and orderlies, have been killed in clinic violence; many more suffered injuries, some of them grievous. In the wake of the Slepian murder, Operation Rescue held multiple demonstrations in Buffalo and Rochester, with one of their leaders, Flip Benham, saying calls for nonviolence were "pitiful." Of course, one is now aware that in 2022 the Supreme Court would strike down Roe v. Wade in Dobbs v. Jackson Women's Health Organization, once again curtailing access to reproductive medicine. Clinic violence has not abated. Shelley Lynn Thornton—the daughter Norma McCorvey (aka Jane Roe) was pregnant with at the time she sued for the right to her own reproductive decisions—said, at that time of the Dobbs decision, "I believe that the decision to have an abortion is a private medical choice that should be between a woman, her family, and her doctor."[61]

I describe these social conditions so that a reader can better understand the larger tensions around the writing and later reading and performance by Clifton of this very personal poem, which neither mentions nor addresses them. This exclusion is powerful in its own way, because the concern of the woman in the poem is not for her own safety nor around the moral implications of what she has done, nor even for the "lost baby," but rather for the "definite brothers and sisters." For Clifton, in this poem, the decisions a woman makes about her own body are hers to make, and the implications and repercussions of those decisions are hers to bear. What Brooks said bears true for Clifton: "abortions will not let you forget."

The poem opens in water, in this case not a life-giving element, but rather dirty, profane: sewage water, the water of waste being carried out to the sea. Of course, when Clifton invokes "drowning/or being drowned," one is reminded of the Atlantic, the "sea of bones," which heightens the sense of the ocean as a place of death, of Black erasure and obliteration, a place where "maternal armies pace." Clifton is a mother at odds with these mothers of lost babies who acted to save their infants from the horrors of slavery, babies lost under much direr and different circumstances. The sea, too, is an ancient feminine symbol and Clifton invokes it as such in later poems, such as "poem in praise of menstruation."

She moves into the conditional tense in the following stanza, though keeps the address focused on the lost child of the title, saying, "you would have been born." The event is mythologized, Clifton describing it as taking place in a year the family recognizes as "the year of disconnected gas/and no car," hazardous in a Buffalo winter, a moment that perhaps also speaks to the poverty and precarity of the family's situation. When Clifton uses metaphors of wintry cold to describe the "thin walk" and the child slipping "like ice" into the hands of an adoptive family "naked as snow" we are given to understand the gravity of the decision being made by the mother, and its difficult emotional toll. There is also the geographic specificity of the references: the hill on Genesee Street is very near the Niagara River; Canada is less than a mile to the northeast, across the narrow river. Clifton's references are anything but abstract here; they are specific to a time and a place.

The regret the mother feels takes on an even more melancholic tone when we realize that even should she have been able to carry and give birth to the child, the child was to be given away. The loss is absolute in either condition. Here, at the end of the second stanza of the poem, Clifton moves into the more direct conditional structure present in "if i stand in my window." "If you were here" she says to the lost child, "I could tell you these/and some other things." It's that "some other things" that gets me, for the same reason the vague phrasing from "it was a dream" lands: in this case though, it's the *ordinary* rather than the elevated spiritual—things any mother might say to her child—that becomes unspeakable.

While the curse of "if i should stand in my window" was directed at the man in the street—a condemning, narrow-visioned, puritanical man—in "lost baby poem," the dire curse is reserved by Clifton for herself, summoning up a condemnation should she fail the "definite brothers and sisters" in any way. Here again, the water is not warm and nurturing—it is the dangerous water, the water that drowned mothers and babies, the water between Afrika and Amerika, what could drown this mother should she fail. And finally, the last curse, the closing curse, is that her own community ought to disown her, call her a "stranger" for the sake of the "never-named" imaginary child. It is important to note here that Clifton is not subscribing to any particular politicized view of a fetus or zygote as a fully formed being; the baby being addressed in the poem is being spoken to as a figure, an imagining of the poet.

In contrast to Brooks' poem, an apology and a farewell ("I loved you all" it closes), Clifton's poem is a dark warning to her own self. It is a pose Clifton takes in several poems, including a poem I quoted a piece from earlier, the poem "for her hiding place," about the philosopher and academic Angela Davis.

Davis, a political philosopher and activist, had been charged by the state of California with kidnapping and conspiracy to commit murder. Before the trial of the "Soledad Brothers" in 1970, a brother of one of the defendants stormed a separate trial, taking the judge hostage and arming the three defendants to demand the freedom of the Soledad Brothers. The three men were standing trial for killing a prison guard at the jail where they had been incarcerated. The guard in question had killed three inmates by shooting them from a guard tower during recreation in the prison yard. Prisoners had begun a hunger strike in protest during the inquiry but a grand jury immediately exonerated the guard, calling the shooting justifiable as the guard was breaking up a fight in the yard by firing the live rounds. The prisoners rioted and the guard in question was killed in the ensuing violence.

Davis' involvement was peripheral: she was charged in connection with the case because the younger man who charged the courtroom used a gun (one among many he armed himself with) purchased by Davis some time earlier. Davis proclaimed her innocence in the matter of how the young man came into possession of her firearm. The defendants, along with the trial judge and the young brother, were all killed in the escape attempt. Authorities issued a warrant for Davis' arrest. Amid a highly charged and tense political environment, Davis fled. Her escape as a fugitive became somewhat of a cause célèbre among both those on the left and the right, one group cheering her escape and the other calling for her swift apprehension. The FBI added her to its Most Wanted List, and she was arrested three months later in New York. Black writers and academics immediately organized defense committees calling for her release. Davis, politically committed to remaining in the United States and fighting the charges against her, fled neither south nor north to the closest international borders, but east across the country.

What's interesting about Clifton's poem is that she conflates place and time in terms of said "hiding place." The immediate association is, of course, the many hiding places Davis utilized as she traveled from Los Angeles, staying with friends and supporters as she went. But Clifton writes of "the scholarships to hide in," implying it was also Davis' life as a student in the academy, and later career as a professor, that were part of "her hiding place/in whiteness."

She was already a well-known academic by this time, having studied first at Brandeis, then at University of California, San Diego, receiving a Master of Arts degree in philosophy under Herbert Marcuse, before leaving and following Marcuse back to Germany to complete her PhD. She had been hired on the faculty of UCLA but the university dismissed her from the position because of her Communist sympathies. When this firing was deemed illegal, they terminated her again for unprofessional behavior due to inflammatory language and uncivil expression. If you think such a pretext wouldn't stick, it did, and if you think we're much past those repressive days, keep in mind that Indigenous literature scholar Steven Salaita had the offer of a tenured position at the University of Illinois rescinded ostensibly because of the tone of tweets he had sent from his personal Twitter account during the Israeli aerial bombardment of Gaza City in 2014. For many years after, Salaita was unable to secure full time academic employment; he currently teaches at the American University of Cairo. Angela Davis went on to teach at the Claremont Colleges briefly, later being hired as a professor of philosophy and gender studies at the University of California, Santa Cruz, where Clifton also taught.

Clifton is interested, in her poem, in Davis' dual existence, nearly disguised, as a radical Black woman in American society, in particular in higher education:

for her hiding place
in whiteness
for angela
straightening her hair
to cloud white eyes
for the yellow skin
of angela
and the scholarships
to hide in
for angela
for angela
if we forget our sister
while they have her
let our hair fall
straight on to our backs
like death[62]

What Clifton declares here is that Davis was hiding *before*— in the scholarships, with light ("yellow") skin. When she says Davis was "straightening her hair" she means it metaphorically: in the popular imagination Davis is nearly more famous for her iconic tight voluminous Afro style than her activism, though she wore dreadlocks in the 90s and wears looser coiled tresses now. Often policed in both professional settings, educational institutions, and in public spaces, Black hair traditions—particularly those of Black women—are powerfully invoked by Clifton to show how far Davis was willing to go in order to "hide."

In her installation "The Hair Craft Project," artist Sonya Clark presents drawings of various hairstyles created for Black women, crediting the stylists and hairdressers, all Black women, who created them. Clark writes of the project, "The poetry and politics of Black hairdressers are central to my work...rooted in a rich legacy their hands embody an ability to map a head with a comb and manipulate the fiber we grow into a complex form."[63] In exhibiting the work of the stylists in both photographs of the stylists' work and her own drawings of Black hair designs, Clark posits both hair salons and art galleries as sites of "aesthetics, craft, skill, improvisation, and commerce." Hair, in other words, becomes an essential part of the expression of Black identity, as much as clothes, or jewlery.

Clifton, once more, in this poem, says in the rhetoric of entreaty or bargain or curse, "if we forget our sister/while they have her." When she says "they," she means not only the criminal justice system—the police who arrested her and the courts who tried her—but *also* the academy of higher education that employs her. A successful person may often be warned by their community, "don't forget where you came from," but here Clifton asks the community not to forget Davis, not to abandon her while "they have her."

It may have come from a deeply personal fear: Clifton, who was left on her own to raise six children by the premature death of Fred Clifton at 49, worked in the academy as well, first at Coppin State College, then at UC Santa Cruz with Davis, at Duke University, and finally at St. Mary's College of Maryland. I myself had many a conversation with Lucille where she confessed to still feeling some level of Imposter syndrome, even decades later, teaching at institutions of higher education, prestigious ones, including in graduate programs, when she had no college degree herself.

If Davis and others had to straighten their hair—surrendering their identities in some unspeakable way—to "cloud white eyes," then Clifton begs members of her community to honor the sacrifices made by those who assimilated into the institutions of power. The price to community for forgetting them would be dire: their own hair "straightening" metaphorically and falling onto their backs, "like death."

There is a powerful image of tamed hair at the heart of Clifton's well-known poem "fury." This poem published in 1993's *The Book of Light* tells the story of Clifton's mother, Thelma, also a poet, according to Clifton, who wrote formal verse in iambic pentameter. At some point Thelma Sayles received an invitation to publish her poetry, which her husband Samuel, Lucille's father, forbade. In response, Thelma burned her poems in the furnace of the house. In a heartbreaking scene, Clifton describes that moment, saying "her hand is crying" as she feeds the poems to the fire, and, "her eyes are animals." When describing her mother, she says also, "each hank of her hair/is a serpent's obedient/wife."[64]

Since ancient times, the serpent has been seen as a powerful symbol for feminine wisdom. Witness both the sacred serpents of the Oracle of Delphi as well as the serpent in the Garden of Eden encouraging Eve to eat the fruit of knowledge. There is also, of course, the snake-haired Medusa, described by Barbara Walker in *The Woman's Encyclopedia of Myths and Secrets* as a dread-locked Libyan wise-woman rather than the monstrous villainess of later misogynistic Greek legends.[65] Her name, Walker explained, came from the Sanskrit "medha," meaning wisdom or knowledge, which became the Greek "metis." Medusa, in other words, was the destroyer/crone aspect of Athena; her conquest by Perseus— with Athena's assistance—was a politically motivated narrative inscription of northern Mediterranean supremacy. The vanquished Medusa's snake-haired head was displayed as evidence of her defeat. Similarly, in "fury," the hanks of the wise woman's hair are each an "obedient/wife," which makes Samuel, Clifton's father, the serpent in question, a rather more sinister and controlling figure rather than the initial evocation of the snake as an ancient feminine symbol and partner of Eve in transgressing against the patriarchal God.

This inversion of power heightens the tragedy of the burning of the poems: though she feeds the poems to the flames, the truth is that the woman's creativity and power are destroyed by the conditions of her life. Thelma dies young at forty-four and the daughter who witnessed the destruction grows up to become a poet, saying to her mother in an early poem, "Dear Mama," "here are the poems/you never wrote."[66] In saying so, she connects her own life as a poet to her mother's, though the poems Thelma wrote are no longer extant. The poem concludes "all that i do/i do for you." As much as "fury" is a poem of rage at how Thelma Sayles was treated, and an acknowledgement of what she had to give up, it is also the daughter Lucille's commitment to live a bold and open life. Over and over again in Clifton's work, the emotion of "fury" appears as determination as much as anger: "i am furious," she declares in both of the later poems "leukemia as white rabbit" and "dialysis," which we will look at more closely in the next chapter.

Clifton wrote about her body in a celebratory way, critiquing the mainstream beauty standards that might minimize or denigrate Black bodies, large or fat bodies, and aging bodies. Scarlett Cunningham wrote about an evolution in Clifton's writing about the body, as well, saying, "The late poetry forges strong connections in relation to aging, decline, and impending death at the same time that it celebrates the possibility of an afterlife and the continuity of the universe."[67] Three well known poems from this moment, "homage to my hair," "homage to my hips," and "what the mirror said," appear back to back early in Clifton's collection *the two-headed woman.*

These three poems are, in the vein of Neruda, odes to ordinary parts of the body, but parts that in Black women have been policed, exoticized, and sexualized by mainstream American culture. Black women's hair and their hips and bodies as well have been denigrated and diminished according to typical commercial beauty standards, which favor European features and body types. Sylvia Hennenberg comments, "Unless it is strategically and exceptionally displayed as the cash cow of a specialized niche market (e.g., 'Big Black Booty Pornstar Cherokee') or as the token figure that saves the face of a capitalist enterprise (e.g., Tyra Banks and her handful of successors at Victoria's Secret), the black body is obliterated by the paradigm of the white female body that knows no fat, age, color, poverty, or disability."[68]

homage to my hair:

when i feel her jump up and dance
i hear the music! my God
i'm talking about my nappy hair!
she is a challenge to your hand
black man,
she is as tasty on your tongue as good greens
black man,

she can touch your mind
with her electric fingers and
the grayer she do get, good God,
the blacker she do be![69]

The first thing to notice is the punctuation. When Lucille Clifton reprinted her first four poetry books (along with the memoir *generations*) with BOA Editions in 1987, she radically altered her mechanics by eliminating capitalizations, and reducing or eliminating much punctuation, particularly included exclamation points and question marks. She still sparingly used commas and periods. But here we see not only three early exclamation points (and there will be another before the end of the poem) but also an upper case capitalized "God" twice. Of course, this God seems like a loving and affirming one, so maybe the upper case is appropriate. Her use of the adjective "nappy" is important here because a "nappy" quality of Black hair is often denigrated, both within and from outside the Black community, being considered ungroomed and undesirable. Here Clifton celebrates what might be seen as imperfect.

Unlike most of her poems, here she is clear about the audience of the poem: twice she uses the address "black man." Lest we skip over how overtly sexual this poem is, let us recognize the moment when she says the hair is "tasty on your tongue," suggesting the man will eat as well as he does when "good greens" are on the plate. After all, there is really only one normal circumstance in which a woman's hair would be on a man's tongue, i.e. she is talking about all her hair, not just the hair on her head.

In addition to embracing Black hair in all its uniqueness and beauty, she also embraces the sexuality of an older woman when she talks about the hair getting "grayer" the older the woman gets. This aging actually makes her "blacker," referring to Blackness as a state of being rather than to the (fading) color pigment of her hair. There is also that musical quality of scat singing due to the use of Black English grammar—"she do be"—sounding a little riff at the end of the poem. Scarlett Cunningham notes, "Clifton challenges the dominant script on female aging through an uncharacteristic insistence that the aging process intensifies rather than negates her desirability by deepening these qualities of blackness that made her desirable in youth."[70]

The other two poems are equally musical and equally committed to a vision of the large body as beautiful and sexually desirable. Clifton performed all of these poems frequently in her public readings. In "homage to my hips" the large woman's hips are described as "mighty" and "magic" and have the ability to "put a spell on a man and/spin him like a top!"[71] At the end of "what the mirror said" Clifton talks about the large body having a "geography" that would require a map and directions to navigate and says, "mister with his hands on you/he got his hands on/some/damn/body!"[72] This final line simultaneously exalts the physical body and affirms the beauty of the large and aging woman's body, but also, "if i should stand in my window" does, refusing the normal power dynamic inherent in sexual objectification by affirming the personhood of the woman being desired, i.e. that she is "somebody."

In addition to "homage to my hair," "homage to my hips," and "what the mirror said," Clifton continued to write witty and funny poems about the body, most notably a series of praise poems in *Quilting*, "poem in praise of menstruation," "to my last period," the oft-quoted "wishes for sons," and "poem to my uterus," in which, after a hysterectomy, she bids farewell to her "old girl," calling it "my bloody print/my estrogen kitchen/my black bag of desire."[73] In other poems, she writes flirtatiously and erotically, most particularly in "there is a girl inside," about the desire an older woman feels. Clifton published this poem when she was fifty-four, saying about the girl that "she is randy as a wolf."[74] The poem continues:

> she will not walk away
> and leave these bones
> to an old woman.
>
> she is a green tree
> in a forest of kindling.
> she is a green girl
> in a used poet.

she has waited
patient as a nun
for the second coming,
when she can break through gray hairs
into blossom

and her lovers will harvest
honey and thyme
and the woods will be wild
with the damn wonder of it.

There is certainly something saucy and daring about the older woman thinking about her own sexual awakening as a "second coming," and the ending of the poem is lush and luscious oration, involving all creation in the sexual flowering of the woman in her maturity. Cunningham points out that Clifton is occasionally ambiguous about aging, particularly in this poem where it is still youth (the "girl inside") that allows the older poet to experience the richness of sexuality, that she can "break through" age in order to the experience the "blossom" of younger days. Cunningham explains that sometimes "the celebratory impulse, especially in relation to the aging body, declines as her poetry progresses."[75]

The sequence "a dream of foxes," published sixteen years later, in the book The Terrible Stories, when Clifton was seventy, is a more complex examination of these same feelings. It is at once sadder and more chillingly honest (and pessimistic) about loneliness and sexual desire and frustration, but ultimately more revealing and fulfilling at its conclusion.

In six characteristically short poems, a form consciously echoing, though not precisely, Galway Kinnell's seven-part poem "The Bear," Clifton is visited by a fox who stands at her doorway, waiting, refusing to leave, "the only blaze in the dark/the brush of her hopeful tail/the only starlight/her little bared teeth."[76] In Kinnell's poem, he is stalking the bear. He devises the meaning for both wounding it and tracking it, and finally he assimilates both the bear's body and spirit. Clifton, on the other hand, goes through a journey of reconciliation with the animal, but she is stationary—in her house—and the relationship with the animal is not violent; if there is a violence in the poem it is one of transformation and it is the animal who acts upon and transforms the woman.

In the first poem, Clifton only imagines the fox, but by the second poem she is real, "haunched by my door," coming "next night again/then next then next."[77] Clifton is curious and finally speaks to the fox in the next poem, but not to ask any question, only to express some kind of kinship with the fox: "it is not my habit/ to squat in the hungry desert...it is not your habit/to watch."[78] It is not until the fourth poem of the six that the fox's nature—or what it might stand for as an allegorical symbol—is revealed:

> leaving fox
>
> so many fuckless days and nights.
> only the solitary fox
> watching my window light
> barks her compassion.
> i move away from her eyes,
> from the pitying brush
> of her tail
> to a new place and check
> for signs. so far
> i am the only animal.
> i will keep the door unlocked
> until something human comes.[79]

The lonely woman desires human contact, and this time the brush of the tail is not "hopeful," but "pitying," yet the unsubtle pun between "fuck" and "fox" seems playful, even challenging in a way. As Clifton asks in an earlier poem "song at midnight," "brothers,/this big woman/carries much sweetness/in the folds of her flesh./[...]/who will find her beautiful/if you do not?"[80] This poem calls attention, too, to the woman's age, saying "her hair/is white with wonderful."

In the fifth poem of "a dream of foxes," "one year later," Clifton arrives at the same point at which Kinnell arrived in his last, and seventh, poem. The close of Clifton's "one year later" echoes the closing of Kinnell's "The Bear." Time has passed since she has abandoned the fox, her sexual desire. "What if,/then," she wonders, the fox "had called me out?"[81] Kinnell, at the close of his poem, is confused too, and wonders what has happened: "I awaken/I think... wandering: wondering/what, anyway,/was that sticky infusion, that rank flavor of blood, that poetry, by which I lived?"[82]

Clifton goes on in her own poem, echoing Kinnell's question:

> what if,
> then,
> i had reared up baying,
> and followed her off
> into vixen country?
> what then of the moon,
> the room, the bed, the poetry
> of regret?

Her poem, while inspired by his, and tracking the same kind of transformative relationship between bestial and human, is different than his in important ways. Firstly, as I mentioned earlier, the power relationship between the human and the animal is fully different: Clifton's speaker is reticent, perhaps even afraid, while Kinnell's speaker, as early as the second poem in "The Bear" sequence, is already devising the death of the animal he is following.[83]

As the woman in the fox poems encounters the animal spirit she comes to a greater and greater understanding of her own regrets, her own desires, until she is finally able to express them: "so many fuckless days and nights." On the other hand, Kinnell's speaker slowly loses his own humanity and human consciousness as he merges with the bear. By the end of his poem, he barely remembers he is human at all. In his own mind he confuses the blood he drank earlier in the poem with the poetry by which he himself as a man once lived.

Clifton's poem does not end with the expression of regret at the conclusion of "The Bear." While the question near the end of Clifton's sequence evokes the closing of "The Bear," Clifton continues on in one final poem, once more entering the dream.

a dream of foxes

in the dream of foxes
there is a field
and a procession of women
clean as good children
no hollow in the world
surrounded by dogs
no fur clumped bloody
on the ground
only a lovely line
of honest women stepping
without fear or guilt or shame
safe through the generous fields[84]

The women here, who once bemoaned their "fuckless days and nights" are described as being "clean as good children" and "honest," now living "without fear or guilt or shame." They are free from the violence and pain of their previous lives. Though they may still have their regrets, may still dream about "vixen country," they have found themselves both "lovely" and "safe" and find the fields "generous."

It's that final description of the field as "generous" that leads me to believe that this is not a poem of acceptance or resignation, no matter how benevolent, on behalf of the women. Rather one questions the title and first line: is this the dream of the woman about foxes? Or is this the dream of the foxes? In the second case, the foxes themselves, whom the woman abandoned, now dream of women who have learned to live without shame or guilt or fear and can accept the generosity of the fields, all the riches that sexuality has to offer.

Chapter 4: Trouble is Coming Round

While Scarlett Cunningham is correct when she points out that Clifton's "celebratory impulse" is dramatically tempered in the poetry she published in the last ten years of her life, there had always been, in Clifton's work, an abiding elegiac quality. Even before the paradigm-shifting events of the loss of two of her children, in 2002 and 2004, there were other losses: her mother at a young age, then her husband, her sister, her brother, her father. Amid all of Clifton's poems contending with grief and death, there was a kind of recognition of grace in acceptance or loss. She says in an early poem "the lesson of the falling leaves," "the leaves believe/ such letting go is love/.../I agree with the leaves."[85] Later in the poem "the thirty-eighth year," which I mentioned at the start of our journey, Clifton bemoans her lack of accomplishment by the time of her thirty-eighth year: "i had not expected to be/an ordinary woman."[86] She's on a short timeline: Thelma Sayles died at forty-four. She catalogs the ways she has not met her own expectations: "i had expected to be/smaller than this,/more beautiful,/wiser in afrikan ways," ultimately "i had expected/more than this."

Though she begins in a broader address, Clifton shifts in the poem to speaking directly to Thelma Sayles, invoking her, summoning her into the poem and telling her about the family she has surrounded herself with. Interestingly, Clifton does not refer to her two sons when she tells her mother, "i have taken the bones you hardened/and built daughters."

The end of the poem is complicated because Clifton swings between expressing her sorrow and regret and stating something that feels like acceptance, a realization that she has become "an ordinary woman." Though haunted by the early death of her mother, she seems determined here to rise from that tragedy and make her own destiny, saying "let me come to it whole/and holy/not afraid/not lonely/out of my mother's life/into my own."

In earlier books, Clifton strains to find herself in a position of comfort, ultimately, after contending with the shadows of doubt and danger. Witness Tyrone's own declaration at the end of the "buffalo war" poems even as the narrative voice declares at the end of the following and concluding poem, "nobody dead/everybody dying." In another poem from this period, the worried Anna says about her daughter Mary, destined for greatness as the mother of Jesus, "work is the medicine for dreams." This grounding in the material world is complicated, of course, by Clifton's deep commitment to simultaneously explore realms of spiritual mysticism and connections between the present world and what might be considered the supernatural or the "otherworldly." Clifton never felt that these were opposing impulses, nor that she could be both kinds of poet. "I am one who can feel the sacred, sometimes," she told Charles Rowell, "and the one who's profane at other times."[87]

Indeed, despite being a profoundly spiritual poet, Clifton was a witness to the lived material conditions and the communal grief around her, including that of her parents. "I'm the only poet I know who's been evicted twice in her life," she confessed to Rowell, speaking of her own economic struggles, but speaking inadvertently, perhaps, to the exclusivity of the world of poetry at the time. "In my family," she went on to say, "we have everything, even a lot of relatives in jail."[88] In one early poem, "miss rosie," she gives dignity to the abject Miss Rosie, who huddles, "wrapped up like garbarge":

> you wet brown bag of a woman
> who used to be the best looking gal in georgia
> used to be called the Georgia Rose
> i stand up
> through your destruction
> i stand up[89]

The body of the woman here is tenuous, Rosie is not fully conscious ("sitting, waiting for your mind") and in poor physical condition ("sitting, surrounded by the smell/of too old potato peels") and yet still worthy of the younger woman's respect.

This mythographic treatment of denigration and degradation, the mortification of the body, presents the speaker as heroic for being able to live through these types of traumas. In "poem on my fortieth birthday to my mother who died young," Clifton describes herself running a race, coming to the forty-fourth lap, the age at which Thelma Sayles died, calling that significant lap, "the place where you fell." She declares, "i might not even watch out for the thin thing/grabbing towards my ankles but/i'm trying for the long one mama,/running like hell and if i fall/i fall."[90] Holladay sees it as a refusal to share Thelma's fate, but to me it feels more like resigned solidarity with the older woman.[91]

The full impact of the resignation present in both "the thirty-eighth year" and in "poem on my fortieth birthday" can be seen by comparing them to a later poem called "climbing." In this poem, Clifton is approaching her sixtieth birthday, having long outlived that deadline of the shorter lifespan of Thelma Sayles. She climbs up a rope after another woman with "dangling braids the color of rain." She does wonder about the lost potential of the past—"maybe i should have had braids./maybe i should have kept the body i started,/.../maybe i should have wanted less," but ultimately she has come to a different kind of relationship with her own age by this point. As the woman ahead of her passes a notch in the rope marked "Sixty," Clifton says, "i rise toward it, struggling,/hand over hungry hand."[92] Here Clifton is neither satisfied to accept her role as "ordinary" nor to not look at the "thin thing" that threatens her. She is immediately present in the struggle to rise, she is defiant and "hungry" to reach that notch in the rope.

But she will not arrive at this point before a significant rupture, both in tone and chronology, which followed the publication of *the two-headed woman* in 1980, the year Clifton turned forty-four. Clifton, who published regularly, releasing a new book every two or three years—five books in the eleven years between 1969 and 1980—did not release another book for seven more years.

It perhaps does not seem like a long time between books, but it is the longest gap in publication between books of poetry that she would ever have. Much happened in the interim, including the loss of the Cliftons' Baltimore home to foreclosure and the subsequent death of Fred Clifton in 1984 from cancer, events that would haunt Clifton the rest of her life. She relocated her family to California, to teach at the University of California, Santa Cruz.

Clifton had always been generous in her work, writing poems that were autobiographically specific, but also wide-ranging, dealing with both history and the politics of the day. Of the "speakers" in her lyric poems, she told Charles Rowell, "My 'I' tends to be both me Lucille and the me that stands for people who look like me, and the one that is also human."[93] Clifton did want her poems to be appreciated and read by Black audiences, but she also felt they had a universal readership. "Either/or is not an African tradition," she explained to Rowell. "Both/and is the tradition."

Even considering this, the tragedies she contends with in *Next* and in the books which follow—*Quilting, The Book of Light*, and *The Terrible Stories*— are less socio-political and communal and more intimate and personal. She becomes less forgiving of the failures of her father. As she herself ages, she contends with illness, loss, and mortality, though always with, as Hilary Holladay says, an "imaginative juxtaposition of hope and grief."[94] The poems in her earlier books dealt primarily with ancestral loss, both with the African community at large, but also in Clifton's own family. In these later books, illness and death came directly into Clifton's immediate present. Besides losing her husband, she writes compellingly of the death of a friend's young daughter from cancer in *Next*, and recounts her own journeys with cancer and kidney failure in *The Terrible Stories*.

As the "buffalo war" series existed as a sequence embedded within *good times* without formal reference, so does a series of poems hide at the end of the second section of *Next*. The first section of this book is called "we are all next" and the second section is called "or next." The term "next" itself is inspired here by the Galway Kinnell poem "December Day in Honolulu," a quote from which serves as epigraph for the collection. The actual phrasing of "we are all next" and "or next" is drawn from a poem in the collection, "the one in the next bed is dying." From these references, we already know that the collection as a whole will be concerned with mortality, but also with a forward-looking hope and belief in continuity: the Kinnell epigraph reads, "This one or that one dies but never the singer...one singer falls but the next steps into the empty place and sings..."[95]

Because they are framed by three poems on the death of Thelma Sayles and four poems on the death of Fred Clifton, the series of nine poems regarding the death of "joanne c." in 1982 are necessarily amplified in position in the canon of Lucille's grief. They are, as poems about a woman's battle with cancer, also made even more resonant knowing that Lucille herself will battle a virulent and recurrent cancer less than ten years later. There is no hope of survival in Joanne's poems: the very first of the series of nine poems is called "the death of joanne c." and includes a date. One particularly haunting image comes from a poem written in Joanne's own voice: she describes her chemotherapy treatment by saying "i host the furious battling of/a suicidal body and/a murderous cure."[96] Because of this line, one comes to understand the "death" to be metaphorical—i.e. the death engendered by the extreme duress of chemotherapy—but it nonetheless presages and privileges the actual death soon to follow. In another poem Joanne's mother enters, her presence made more poignant by the recent reminder of an absence of the mother figure of Thelma in Lucille's own life. Joanne's mother takes on mythic powers as she sweeps in, "the witch of the ward,/.../incanting Live Live Live!"[97]

In the following poem, "leukemia as white rabbit," Clifton fuses the playful with the deadly serious, also fusing the mother roles: the voice of Joanne's mother, the witch of the ward of the previous poem, and Clifton's own lyric voice merge at the close of the poem:

leukemia as white rabbit

running always running murmuring
she will be furious   she will be
furious, following a great
cabbage of a watch that tells only
terminal time, down deep into a
rabbit hole of diagnosticians shouting
off with her hair   off with her skin and
i am   i am   i am   furious.[98]

Leukemia, the disease itself, is personified as the terrified white rabbit from *Alice in Wonderland*, worrying about the mercurial queen. Followed down the rabbit hole, one only witnesses the diagnosticians pronouncing the dire sentences, while the mother—and Lucille Clifton herself—now share the fury, powerless to act before the onslaught of cure.

Toward the end of the section in which the "joanne c." poems appear, we find the poem which gives the book its title, a two line poem which demonstrates the absolute power and mastery that Lucille Clifton had in the epigrammatic form:

the one in the next bed is dying.
mother we are all next. or next.[99]

In this short couplet, Clifton continues the conflation of the women: Joanne speaks to her mother, trying to comfort her, but with Thelma's voice echoing in our ears from her poems, one can also read this poem as Lucille speaking to her own mother. There is a resignation in the continuation of the word "dying" that we saw in the poem "buffalo war," and will see in a moment in an earlier poem called "richard penniman," a recognition that "dying" is not a terrifying or unusually dire exceptional condition but merely (*merely. as if.*) an ever-present component of what it means to be alive.

Each of the three sets of poems in this portion of the book—the poems about Thelma, the poems about Joanne, and the poems about Fred—end with a poem called "the message of," (i.e. "the message of thelma sayles," "the message of fred clifton," and "the message of joanne c.") and what Joanne says to her mother after this epigrammatic summation is tinged with the kind of regretful acceptance that characterizes Lucille Clifton's poems about illness and mortality: "death is life."[100]

Thelma, as a poet herself who gave up her own poems, as Lucille described in the poem "fury," has a very different message for her daughter. Speaking of her own epileptic fits and the swollen bitten tongue that sometimes followed, Thelma advises her daughter, "when you lie awake in the evenings/counting your birthdays/ turn the blood that clots your tongue/into poems. poems."[101] Thelma, in Lucille's lyric voice, is aware of the poems Lucille writes, such as "the thirty-eighth year" and "poem on my fortieth birthday to my mother who died young," and admonishes her to convert the tragedy—both of Thelma's death but also of her suppressed ambition as a poet—into her own triumph. It is a powerful affirmation of the creative urge: though Thelma was not able to live fully, governed by the gender politics and material realities of her time, she wants to ensure that her daughter will.

Following Joanne's poems, there is a brief interlude, called "chorus: lucille," that functions as a prelude to the series of Fred's poems, positioning Clifton in the classical role of the observer as in the ancient Greek dramas. But it is a mistake to think of the chorus in the dramas as mere witnesses describing the action; they are also meant to comment and react to the unfolding events, and in doing so they *define* the events for the audience. It's the audience in the seats that are passive witnesses; the members of the chorus on stage are far more than that, and in many plays (for example *The Eumenides*, the closing play of Aeschylus' *Oresteia* trilogy) their thoughts and words can actually influence the outcome of the play. In the case of this "chorus," she reflects after the death of Joanne on Fred's illness and impending death.

chorus: lucille

something is growing in the strong man.
it is blooming, they say, but not a flower.

he has planted so much in me. so much.
i am not willing, gardener, to give you up to this.[102]

The "strong man" of the poem is Fred Clifton himself, and what is growing in him may be the cancer. When Lucille says "not a flower," she does call the actual flower to mind, and follows it up with "he has planted so much in me," acknowledging the powerful synergy of the relationship, which resulted in six children after all. As Mary Jane Lupton has described in her book, Fred Clifton was an academic, sculptor, philosopher, and writer, publishing a young adult novel and numerous poems, which he would read at various community events when the Cliftons were in Baltimore.[103]

When Lucille Clifton speaks to the "gardener" in the last line, there is a conflation in it—she is both admonishing the gardener who planted the bloom—God?—that she will not give up Fred Clifton, but she is also telling the second gardener, Fred himself, who has planted "so much" in her, that she is not willing to give him up to the cancer. Though moving, it is nonetheless futile, the poem immediately following being called "the death of fred clifton." In Fred's case, unlike Joanne's, the death is actual and the poems that follow are all narrated from beyond the grave, so to speak.

In the "death of fred clifton," Lucille posits death as an achievement of knowledge—in this way the theological implications of death are less Christian and more in line with the Vedantic philosophy Fred Clifton believed in and studied in his life. In Fred's voice, Clifton realizes that after death, "i had not eyes but/sight" and that "there was all around not the/shapes of things/but oh, at last, the things/themselves."[104] It's not only the goal of reincarnation to realize more and more the connectedness of human and divine, but there is an achievement of the Platonic ideal in realizing the true nature of objects and beings rather than the signs and names by which we only partially apprehend them. "There is no deathless name," Fred says in the subsequent poem, "a body can pronounce."[105]

As if to accentuate the difference between the person who has died (who has now realized the boundlessness of the spirit released from human form) and the person who remains behind,

Clifton includes now a poem called "my wife," which tells of Lucille after Fred's death, but still in Fred's voice. The bereft wife wakes up from sleep, "having forgotten," momentarily, the death of the husband, as survivors sometimes do, and is shocked into remembering by the closet, previously emptied of the deceased's clothing, his shirts and his ties. It's a small moment, an ordinary one, compared to the grand and metaphysical pronouncements of the ghostly Fred.[106]

The concluding poem of the sequence is one of Clifton's best known and oft-quoted:

the message of fred clifton

i rise up from the dead before you
a nimbus of dark light
to say that the only mercy
is memory,
to say that the only hell
is regret.[107]

Fred Clifton's death will continue to haunt Lucille throughout her life, and she will write about this death and its impact on her and her family in each of her following books. If there is a sense of closure here, it is only closure that mercy is a memory: to serve that memory. Clifton will continue to engage this grief; she will never let it go.

Later, when Clifton herself is diagnosed with cancer, undergoes a lumpectomy, and then later, when the cancer returns, a mastectomy, the engagement with mortality becomes intimate and personal. Unlike in these earlier poems, each starting with the description of the death and concluding with a "message," the poems on Clifton's cancer from The Terrible Stories are more desperate, more fearful, and somehow, more tender.

In the opening lines of "amazons" Clifton seeks to create a sisterhood for herself, linking the mythical warriors of ancient Greek mythology with the Dahomey warrior women from whom she is descended. Considering her love of the Klingon warrior women Lursa and B'Etor, one can only imagine how much she would have loved the Dora Milajie, the warrior women from the comics and film *Black Panther*. As the Amazon women have sacrificed one breast—so the legend goes—for greater skill in combat, the poet is asked what she is willing to sacrifice. Audre Lorde appears in the closing motions of the poem, which is a celebration of the early detection of Clifton's cancer. In the following poem, however, Clifton tells the story of the night before the lumpectomy, a surgery meant to halt the cancer and save her life. The title of the poem, referring to time of day, nonetheless evokes the primordial mother figure as well as her somewhat diminished scriptural counterpart:

> lumpectomy eve
>
> all night i dream of lips
> that nursed and nursed
> and the lonely nipple
>
> lost in loss and the need
> to feed that turns at last
> on itself   that will kill
>
> its body for its hunger's sake
> all night i hear the whispering
> the soft
>
> > love calls you to this knife
> > for love   for love
>
> all night it is the one breast
> comforting the other[108]

The opening of the poem evokes multiple contexts: lips of a lover, lips of a child, and the nipple as something itself with agency, with a "need/to feed." The poem makes of cancer somewhat of a metaphor by implying it may have in its sources some kind of personal loneliness or emotional hunger. It is still love—or at very least, self-preservation—that leads a person to choose the surgery that can save them and there is something tender in the closing image of the two breasts in their own private communion.

This dialog continues in the next poem "consulting the book of changes: radiation." As we have watched Joanne C. suffer through chemotherapy ("a suicidal body/hosting a murderous cure"), and Lucille undergo surgery, now we will see the poet undergo radiation treatment. The poem is in a call and response format with alternating sections.

The main left justified sections are in second person, an omniscient narrator speaking to the person undergoing radiation, opening: "each morning you will cup/your breast in your hand/then cover it and ride/into the federal city."[109] These discursive narrative sections are punctuated by indented sections that are always questions, meant to be understood as being asked by Clifton herself. One section reads, "if there are no cherry blossoms/can there be a cherry tree?" Near the end of the poem, she dispenses with metaphor, asking, "what is the splendor of one breast/on one woman?"

In describing her own life, Clifton highlights the loneliness of the experience: "after," she says, "you will stop to feed yourself. you have always had to feed yourself." It's a poignant moment realizing that she is going through this experience alone, that whatever support system she imagined herself in the earlier poem "amazons" are not present here, either in flesh or spirit. There is no comfort to be had either from the omniscient, oracular, god-like voice in the poem either. As this same oracular voice once, in an earlier poem, admonished Clifton when she was looking for answers to questions too big to ask ("why cancer why loneliness?") by saying "it does not help to know," here it answers her sad question "will i begin to cry?" by warning, "if you do, you will cry forever."[110]

There is another turn toward a darker outlook in the next poem "1994." While the narrative voice in the other poems has been firm and determined, here she falters a little, saying "you know that the saddest lies/are the ones we tell ourselves/you know how dangerous it is//to be born with breasts/.../to wear dark skin." This invocation of her race and gender is far less empowering than the similar summoning present in her famous earlier poem, "won't you celebrate with me," where she declares the strength in being "born in babylon/both nonwhite and woman."[111] Published several years after that affirmative poem, in "1994" Clifton despairingly asks, "have we not been good children/did we not inherit the earth," but before she can allow herself to sink fully into pity, she rouses herself in a moment of empathy with the listener and reader for the commonality of various tragedies that humans must bear by conceding, "but you must know all about this/from your own shivering life."[112]

Let us leave these later poems aside for a moment (we will return to them in Chapter 9) and look at two earlier poems, from long before these shadows began gathering in Lucille's life. These two earlier poems show how Lucille Clifton mythologizes or gives outsized emphasis to small individual moments, even when she is writing about historical or mythological characters or public figures. As Clifton conceded to Rowell, "Someone once said to me that what she does is find the human in the mythic, and the mythic in the human."[113] The first poem is "richard penniman." A reader might be more familiar with Richard Penniman by his stage name Little Richard. A gender-bending performer who was one of the pioneers of rock music, Little Richard was a forerunner to showman-musicians like Prince, Michael Jackson, and James Brown. Richard was more or less open about sexuality decades earlier than it was safe— or even legal—to be so, though he maintained a complicated and changing relationship to gender and sexuality throughout his life, even disavowing homosexuality at certain points. Interestingly, this conflicted swing between hedonism and religiosity was evinced also by Jackson and Prince during their own careers.

Lucille Clifton wrote about Little Richard in her second book, *good news about the earth*, in the section of the book called "heroes" in which she writes about other Black figures like Angela Davis, Malcolm X, and Bobby Seale. The poem is interesting because it positions Little Richard, calling him by his pre-fame birth name, in a relationship with these other figures, all political. It's further compelling because it, as early as 1972, defends Little Richard's effeminacy and sexuality in a time and place when it might have been considered rare—even brave— for a Black woman poet, mother of six, publishing with Random House, to do so. Even then, and throughout her life, Clifton was an ally to the LGBT community, arguing against the exclusion of lesbians from some early feminist movements, and arguing against homophobia in general.[114]

The poem about Little Richard has no title and opens with his name, grammatically unconnected, as a kind of invocation:

> richard penniman
> when his mama and daddy died
> put on an apron and long pants
> and raised up twelve brothers and sisters
> when a whitey asked one of his brothers one time
> is little richard a man (or what?)
> he replied in perfect understanding
> you bet your faggot ass
> he is
> you bet your dying ass. [115]

Here, Little Richard's act of raising his siblings qualifies him as a "man" more than any gender-based behavior or sexuality would. The brother has a "perfect understanding" of both what the interviewer is implying and of Little Richard's nature as a "man." When he replies to the interviewer, calling him a "faggot ass," he turns the interviewer's assumptions and behavior back around on him, i.e. it is the interviewer who has acted "unmanly" in posing the question at all. The term, which must have been used against Richard at some point, turns into a badge of honor. The use of the adjective "dying" here is reminiscent of other times Clifton has used the term as a condemnation of a life being lived without hope or spiritual connection, as in the closing poem of "buffalo war."

In "richard penniman," as in "leukemia as white rabbit," the light-hearted, or even humorous, opening belies the seriousness within the poem itself and the reader is jolted into a different relationship with what one thought might be a witty or funny poem.

This same strategy of a jolt from playful to serious is used to great, even heartbreaking, effect in the short poem "photograph."

"Photograph" has a brief descriptive text at the beginning that sets up the scenario of the poem. It reads "my grandsons/spinning in their joy," presumably the subject of said photograph.[116] The poem begins:

> universe
> keep them turning   turning
> black blurs against the window
> of the world

In this entreaty or prayer, we are reminded of the woman of Clifton's earliest book, pressing her breasts against the window. In that case it was the window of a house, but metaphorically functioning as a window of the world, the same window through which the young gleeful boys are seen and in much the same way, "black blurs," instead of the earlier "black birds."

But it's the close of the poem that includes the gut-wrenching turn:

> for they are beautiful
> and there is trouble coming
> round and round and round

An innocuous poem about two little black boys whirling around takes on new awful meaning in our contemporary age of Trayvon, Tamir, Elijah, Sandra, George, Breonna, Eric, Ahmaud, and all of the countless Black youth and Black grown folk who have been the victims of violence, structural racism, and policing. The final line turns the child-like play of the movement of the spinning into something ominous and terrifying. Claudia Rankine's book *Citizen* includes a page upon which are named Black people killed by police; in subsequent printings of the book, the page is added to and expanded; Clifton's final lines have the same kind of recognition of the ongoingness of racist violence against Black people. They carry with them a terrible and resigned warning.

Chapter 5: Things Don't Fall Apart

Lucille Clifton's prose memoir *generations* was released in 1976, the same year as Alex Haley's more famous *Roots*. It was a time when a new generation of writers of African descent, including Toni Morrison, Toni Cade Bambara, Alice Walker, and Gloria Naylor, among others, were publishing dynamic and widely read books about Black life in America. Many of these books won major prizes and were also being adapted to film, like Walker's *The Color Purple* and Morrison's *Beloved,* or being serialized on television, as *Roots* famously was in two miniseries, or Naylor's *The Women of Brewster Place*, which began as a miniseries, but later became a short lived regular series, starring Oprah Winfrey who also had roles in both of the films *The Color Purple* and *Beloved.*

While Clifton draws from her personal life, family history, and even generational history, throughout her body of work, *generations* was the most extended view of her family in her published corpus, and the only prose. This text offers sustained and significant clarity on the various figures who appear only briefly in poems, often in single episodes. Critic Hilary Holladay points out about Clifton's *generations*, "In contrast to the bold, novelistic storytelling of the 688-page *Roots*, Clifton's 54-page narrative of her paternal family lineage is meditative, elliptical, and elegiac."[117]

In her own review of *Roots*, Clifton does begin by commenting on its length, saying, "It is a big book. It costs more than some of the family can afford to spend for a book. It seems at first to have too many pages, too many words," but eventually she concedes, "The accomplishment of finding and assigning true names is one beyond words...it is what the poet spends her/his life trying for. The naming of things; I spend my life. Alex Haley took only 12 years and did it truly. Not so long, not too big, not too expensive."[118] Of the inevitable comparisons with *generations*, which came out earlier in the same year, Clifton was gracious, saying, "The difference between the two books is simply the difference between two names—Haley and Sayles, both names illuminating the who. I hope that *generations* has helped in Alex Haley's knowing, certainly *Roots* has helped in mine."

In fact, *generations* creates particular pictures of Clifton's great-great grandmother Caroline, her great-grandmother Lucy, and her own parents that are sometimes later belied by poems about them which appear elsewhere in her body of work. Additionally, the memoir offers clear biographical sketches of various other members of Clifton's family. Its structure is very formal and specific and one might best characterize its language as an extended prose poem rather than the discursive language typical memoirs and autobiographies used at the time it was published. Of course, in the contemporary moment the field of what is now called "creative nonfiction" has experienced a sea change: memoirs now appear in various forms, including fragments, as autofiction or autotheory, investigative memoirs, memoirs-in-essays, and even in the form *generations* anticipated by more than twenty-five years, more poetic memoirs characterized by highly charged, lyrical language, and a poem-like structure. It is possible that a memoir retrieving memories erased by the violence of slavery required such innovation. As scholar Cheryl Wall wrote of *generations*, "Representing a past that is largely unwritten, caught in photographs, and remembered only in fragments of music demands of writers both a visionary spirit and the capacity for dramatic revisions of form."[119]

The book is built in five parts; the first four of these each covers one generation of Clifton's patrilineal family beginning with her great-great-grandmother Caroline, followed by sections treating her great grandmother Lucy, her grandfather Gene, and her father Sam. While each chapter is normally titled after the person whose story it tells, the initial chapter is called "Caroline and Son." Who the "son" of this title is we are not told, but it could refer to either Caroline's grandson Gene or her great grandson Sam, both of whom she raised. The final chapter is called "Thelma" and depicts both the early life of Lucille Clifton's mother and then the family's life in Depew and Buffalo, as well as Lucille Clifton's time in Howard University. "Thelma" recounts the family's life up until Thelma's death and then, very briefly, recounts the birth of Lucille Clifton's six children. While the book moves from history to the present moment, the present continues to appear in the past and the historical tales continue to recur throughout the book as well. Often, throughout the memoir, we are told the fate of a person before their stories are recounted. Holladay calls this narrative motion "concentric circles."[120] In a way it seems that Clifton shows the "past" is *always* part of the present and the present gives meaning to the events of the past, such as Caroline's enslavement or the death of Lucy. The past, for Clifton, might even explain (though never justify) Sam's abusive behavior toward his family that comes to light rather obliquely and late in the book.

[G]enerations feels like an oral document, and indeed Lucille Clifton explained that when she felt unable to begin, "Toni [Morrison, then a junior editor at Random House] said perhaps that I might want to talk into a tape recorder."[121] True to this origin, the text follows the various speech patterns of the family, from Sam's frequent use of "Oh" when beginning a story to Lucille's sister Elaine's paragraph-long and nearly punctuation-less recounting of Sam's death. Most chapters begin with Clifton's account of Sam telling her family stories ("My Daddy would say..."); a couple chapters begin with someone else speaking—the old white woman in the opening chapter, or Elaine. The final chapter, "Thelma," begins with Clifton's own colloquial opening, "Well." In 2017, the orality of this text was brought full circle when Clifton's daughter Sidney, a television producer and actress, narrated an audiobook version.

The familiar and intimate tone the book's narrators establish with the reader is also heightened by the family photographs that punctuate the text: each chapter begins with one, drawing the reader into a relationship with the person whose life Clifton is about to recount. Cheryl Wall has written extensively about the relationship between the photographs and the texts, quoting bell hooks in commenting, "For African Americans, for whom illiteracy was one of slavery's legacies, photographs became a way to document a history that they could not write down. Preserved not only in photograph albums but on the walls of the most humble homes, these 'pictorial genealogies' were one means by which black people 'ensured against the losses of the past.'"[122]

The many epigraphs in the book also situate it within certain literary and historical traditions. The opening pair of epigraphs (one from the Book of Job and the other attributed to "the woman called Caroline Donald/born free in Afrika in 1822/died free in America in 1910") not only anchor it as a text informed by history, but also, as Wall points out, their pairing "establishes an equivalence" between Caroline Donald's words and the scripture.[123] She, too, is not identified by the European name given to her upon enslavement, but rather, in recognition that she had a previous unknown name, she is referred to as "the woman who was called Caroline Donald," and the important further information notes that she both lived and died "free."

The individual chapters of the memoir are further framed by epigraphs from Walt Whitman's "Song of Myself." As scholar Edward Whitley explains, for Clifton, "Whitman becomes a site for responding not only to the tradition of male autobiography but to the whole of American literature."[124] Whitman, in the particular poem Clifton quotes in the epigraphs throughout *generations*, staked a claim to an American idiom as part of poetry in English. By placing these epigraphs and photographs before each chapter, Clifton situates her own family's story, even when marginalized and suppressed, as part of the tradition of American literature. There may be some irony in her invocation of Whitman, since, as Wall explains, "although Whitman stood apart from most white Americans in his recognition of black people's humanity, his egalitarianism was tinged with the racism endemic to his time."[125]

The text begins in conversation between Clifton and a woman she has contacted through a newspaper advertisement looking for information on the Sale/Sayle family, the original forms of Clifton's maiden name Sayles. There is a moment of confusion because the woman on the phone, who is white, does not recognize the first names Clifton is reciting to her, until she comes to the name Caroline, whom the white woman does recognize: she knew her as "Mammy Ca'line." "Who remembers the names of slaves?" Clifton asks herself.

When she explains to the woman that her family were enslaved by the white Sale family, the woman reacts immediately with pity, "and there is silence." She promises to send Clifton the written history of the family, "But I never hear her voice again."[126] This emotional reaction coupled with the (useful) provision of written archive from the white woman plus her ensuing silence speaks to the dual problematic condition of Black history: scantily recorded or ignored or erased in the first place, but also fundamentally unable to be meaningfully contended with by the white people whose ancestors were such an integral part of it.

Clifton, denied a chance for dialogue or any possibility of communal reconciliation, is instead left to process the written documents she has been sent on her own. Strikingly though, and perhaps unsurprisingly, the written history Clifton has been sent by the woman is never mentioned again in *generations*, except for an early off-hand remark from Clifton about the woman, "I see she is the last of her line. Old and not married, left with a house and a name." It is a remark of pity for the older woman as Clifton follows the comment by saying, "I look at my husband and our six children and I feel the Dahomey women gathering in my bones."

This tension between what is remembered and what is forgotten in history continues throughout the book, accompanied by a tension around who is doing the remembering. Clifton receives the written history of the Sale family (the "y" was added by Lucille's namesake, her great-great-grandmother Lucy, upon the birth of her son to distinguish him from the people who had enslaved his ancestors) from which her ancestors are absent. Sam, who was raised as a young boy until the age of eight by his great-grandmother Caroline, recounts to Lucille an argument he had with Caroline when he expressed a desire to know her African name. She will not disclose it. "But it'll be forgot!" the young boy yells, in distress. "Don't you worry, mister," Caroline says, calmly, "don't you worry."[127]

The argument calls to mind the conversation at the beginning of Dionne Brand's book *A Map to the Door to Nowhere*, in which a young Brand is trying to get her great-uncle to remember the name of the African nation from which their family was taken and has descended. The great-uncle cannot remember. He claims it is on the tip of his tongue and he will remember it when he hears it, and so the young Brand starts reeling off names. They do not arrive at the name.[128] This obliviation of the past is characterized in metaphor by Brand in her invocation of the "door to nowhere," the portal through which African people passed into bondage on the slave ships. There are actual portals in castles across the West African coast, perhaps the most famous being the Portuguese castle in Elmina, Ghana. Brand positions the door as a stark barrier between the past, forever gone and erased and inaccessible, as African people crossed the Atlantic, forcibly enslaved in bondage.

This unsolvable quandary of the past as obliterated and unrecoverable and yet materially present in the bodies and memories of living people continues throughout *generations*. Although Clifton never again hears the voice of the woman with whom she shares so much history, the history of the family continues to resonate against the unfolding events of the death and funeral of Clifton's father Sam Sayles (Sam had since added an "s" to the family name, reasoning "there is going to be more than one of me.") This rupture from the past is heightened by the fact that Sam's voice recounting the family stories is interspersed with scenes from the journey north, the burial, and the days after. Of course, as Brand discovered when trying to jog her uncle's memory, the history of enslaved people is difficult to tell. In the case of Lucille Clifton's father Sam, trying to recount the life of Caroline Donald, "history becomes what eight-year-old minds can retain."[129]

While the Cliftons pack up their car and prepare to drive north for Sam's funeral, Caroline's travels—by sea from Africa to New Orleans, and on foot from New Orleans to Virginia—are mentioned again and again like a kind of refrain. History is closer than we imagine, Clifton seems to be saying, and in a sense, through the body of Sam Sayles, it *is*: Clifton is recounting the stories of a man who was raised by a woman who had been enslaved. In other words, Lucille Clifton is only one degree away from a person who had been enslaved. Those who knew her, including me, are only two degrees away. Slavery is so close to present American life you could touch it.

In Lucille Clifton's poems that mention Caroline, including "ca'line's prayer," the landscape of Africa is often invoked: "remember me from wydah/remember the child/running across dahomey/black as ripe papaya/juicy as sweet berries."[130] Often this landscape is juxtaposed against the American landscape to which Clifton feels less connection or no connection. For example, in the poem "driving through new england" she writes:

> driving through new england
> by broken barns and pastures
> i long for the rains of wydah
> and the gardens
> ripe as history
> oranges and citron
> limefruit and african apple
> not just this springtime and
> these wheatfields
> white poets call the past.[131]

She implies here that for the "white poets" the past is not only passive and plain, as described by "pastures" and "wheatfields," but also diminished or ruined, as in the "broken barns." When she says the gardens are "ripe as history," she claims that the land itself is more alive, but that also history itself is not faded, but fresh and full.

Of course, the drive the Cliftons take from Baltimore to Buffalo, while mirroring Caroline's long-before walk, also takes place against the backdrop of the green hills of Pennsylvania, including the fields of Gettysburg, whose restless ghosts Clifton has previously recognized as hostile (in "l. at gettysburg"). To be sure, American highways and back-roads were never safe for Black drivers, so much so that for many years, a guidebook called "The Negro Motorist Green-Book" was published for Black motorists and travelers to know which roads, towns, restaurants, and hotels were acceptable and safe for them to frequent during journeys and vacations. Samuel Sayles died in 1969 and by then the Civil Rights Act of 1964 had seemed to diminished the immediate need for the *Green-Book* in providing information on restaurants and hotels.

While it ceased publication a few years later in 1966, American roads remain a hostile place for Black people, who are frequently killed by police during routine traffic stops, including very recently: just some examples include Philando Castile, Sandra Bland, and Patrick Lyoya; Black travelers seeking assistance or even being present on business in certain neighborhoods are in equal danger from white citizens, as the deaths of Renisha McBride and Amaud Arbery show, or the recent attempted murder of FedEx driver D'Monterrio Gibson.

As Sam drew wisdom throughout his childhood from Caroline, Clifton would later recount folk wisdom in little poems named for Aunt Margaret Brown, Caroline's sister from whom she was separated when they were sold to different white families. Any knowledge Clifton had of Aunt Margaret Brown's "wisdom" would be intuited, or divined by other spiritual means, since Brown would have passed long before Clifton's birth. The scene Sam Sayles describes of the two sisters—Caroline Donald and Margaret Brown, who were permitted to visit one another occasionally, rocking on the porch and discussing events they had heard about during their childhoods, including Nat Turner's rebellion, John Brown's raid, and the Civil War—happened in the last half of the nineteenth century. Clifton's Aunt Margaret Brown later comments in poems on contemporary events such as the lunar landing, Lena Horne's beauty, and the critical difference between comedians Eddie Murphy and Richard Pryor.

Both of the poems in which Margaret Brown's wisdom is shared by Clifton, the early and uncollected "From the Quotations of Aunt Margaret Brown" and the later "from the wisdom of sister brown" are titled with the phrase "from the," which implies the poems we receive are mere excerpts from a larger canon of work. Indeed, there are several boxes of handwritten pages housed in the

Clifton Archives at Emory University's Rose Library, called in the archival note describing the collection "mostly illegible." The terming in the poems "from the" grants archive-like status to a corpus the casual reader has no access to, conferring respectability on Brown as an important thinker or philosopher. And when one reads the poems, one feels such an appellation is earned. The aphorisms of "From the Quotations of Aunt Margaret Brown" and "from the wisdom of sister brown" reveal a sharp intellect which formed a trenchant critique of white America.

Of the founding of America, Aunt Margaret Brown declares:

Talk about Columbus,
I tell you who discovered
America;
Martin Luther King
that's who.[132]

Of Murphy and Pryor, Margaret Brown perceptively explains:

eddie, he a young blood
he see somethin funny
in everythin   ol rich
been around a long time
he know aint nothin
really funny[133]

In many ways, the story of Lucy Sale, the ancestor Clifton was named for, forms a conceptual centerpiece for the book. Sale, Clifton's great-great-grandmother, died when her son Gene was just an infant. Caroline raised Gene, after the death of his mother, and also raised Gene's son Sam after Gene himself died at age thirty. Lucy, as Sam tells Lucille with a hint of odd pride, was the first Black woman to be legally hanged in the state of Virginia. The "legally" is the sticking point of course, as many unrecorded women had been killed in illegal lynchings before. Lucy, who had her child Gene with a white man named Harvey Nichols, killed Nichols one night—"shot him off his horse and killed him"—and then sat next to the body and waited for the gang of men who came looking for Nichols after his riderless horse returned.[134]

The story is told slowly in fragments—in fact it is first mentioned on the very first page in the initial conversation that Clifton has with the older woman who sends her the history. "Is the Nichols house still there?" Clifton had asked. "I hear the trouble in her voice," she says, when the woman answers in the affirmative.[135] By the time we get to the chapter called "Lucy," we already know that Lucy has killed a man, that he was white, that she was involved with him, that he was a carpetbagger from the north, and that she was tried for the crime rather than being lynched because of some kind of respect Caroline had earned as a midwife in the community.

This accretion of details of history is interspersed with descriptions of the Cliftons driving north from Baltimore for the funeral, arriving in Buffalo, and being welcomed by Clifton's two sisters, the older Jo, and the younger Elaine, called Punkin. By revealing Lucy Sale's story slowly in waves, Clifton shows the ever-presentness, not only of Lucy and her legacy, but in Sam Sayles' role as storyteller, narratively holding the family together even in the wake of his own death. Once Clifton has arrived and settled in, the sisters huddle together, afraid of being haunted by their father's spirit. "Not you, Lue," Punkin says, "you were always his heart."[136] For her part, Clifton is not concerned by the absence from the house of her dead father. In the bed of the guest room with Fred, her other sisters asleep in other rooms, Lucille lies awake in the night, thinking, "My Mama and Daddy were dead and their house was full of them."[137]

It is not until the fourth or fifth telling of Lucy's story that Sam even gets close to the reason Lucy killed Harvey Nichols, and even then he doesn't even really explain it other than to say it was after the baby was born, and that "oh, Lue, he was born with a withered arm." The odd implication that Sam is making is that Lucy was upset at the deformity of her son, though this is never stated outright. The child is named Gene Sayle, given his mother's name rather than the father's name since they were not married. As I mentioned before, at Gene's birth, Lucy added the extra "y" so that her son would be distinguished from the slave-owning family which bore the name "Sale."

Caroline employs a lawyer from the Sale family to defend her daughter in the trial, but since Lucy was found next to the body, holding the rifle used to kill the man, she is swiftly convicted. Sam once again points out that it was a "legal" trial, and cites Caroline's position in the community as justification for such due process. His unusual pride in the event is offset by Clifton's own imagined vision of what the actual execution was like: her description of the hanging of her namesake is fairly graphic, but what she fixates on is Caroline, standing there silent, watching the scene. "I know she made no sound," claims Clifton, "and I turn in my chair and arch my back and make this sound for my two mothers and all Dahomey women."[138] That sound is so compelling: a sound Clifton makes *through time* on behalf of her great-great-grandmother upon the loss of her daughter, whose neck is broken and who is asphyxiated by hanging.

Sam Sayles' pride in his grandmother's status as the first Black woman legally hanged in Virginia and Lucille Clifton's trans-generational enaction of grief are each unusual in their own ways as representative responses to this traumatic family history, but what follows is even stranger. Clifton writes:

> And there would be days when we young Sayles would be trying to dance and sing in the house and Sammy [Clifton's brother] would miss a step and not be able to keep up to the music and he would look over in the corner of the room and holler "Damn Harvey Nichols." And we would laugh.[139]

In the end, despite Lucy's dubious honor and Clifton's echoing grief, and the trouble in the voice of the old woman at the beginning of the tale, Harvey Nichols lived on in the Sayles mythology as the butt of some kind of unexplained joke. Clifton, accustomed to documents and historical records, wants to find out if the story as told to her by Sam Sayles is actually true, but her father dismisses her concerns, saying "Somebody somewhere knows."[140]

One is reminded that the histories of oppressed people often lack normally present archival documentation. When Lucille turns to Fred for advice, "fussing" and wanting "proof," he concurs with his father-in-law, telling her, "In history, even the lies are true."[141]

Some fifteen years later, in an unpublished poem called "great-grandmother lucy reads my poem about her," Clifton explains not the reason Lucy may have committed her crime, but what may have attracted her to Nichols in the first place:

> great-grandmother lucy reads my poem about her
>
> daughter,
> it was at first his eye,
> blue green as the atlantic,
> his hand,
> pale as the valley
> of the shadow of death
> and the thick must of his arm
> as he pulled me down.
>
> i thought of my mother
> rocking, longing for Africa,
> hungry for the grass of home,
> then weeping for the sweet release
> of death
>
> and as he rocked me, wept in me,
> hungry for Africa,
> he was not what i wanted
> but it was sweet in the grass
> to die a little, daughter,
> sweet at first.[142]

In this poem Clifton attributes Lucy's action to old-fashioned sexual desire, but also some kind of deeper instinctual desire for the kind of connection Lucy perceived Caroline as having for her lost home in Africa. The ambiguity Lucy feels at the close of the poem is prefigured in the odd image of Harvey's hand being "pale as the valley/of the shadow of death," an image which –along with Harvey's eye being "blue green as the atlantic"—calls to mind the "maternal armies" pacing the floor of the ocean in the poem "atlantic is a sea of bones" written only a few years earlier.

The Lucy of the poem is acutely aware of the power relationship that exists between her, a newly emancipated slave, and Harvey Nichols, the carpetbagger from the north. The recent echo of ownership hangs between them like the "thick must" of Harvey's arm pulling her down. The issue of consent between a poor Black woman and a rich white man in Virginia in the early years after Emancipation would have been vexed, and the poem expresses that, likening the sexual act—as in the French double entendre "la petite mort"—to death.

As recounted in the poem "lot's wife 1988," the concepts of property and ownership were important for Sam Sayles. As Sam changed his name from Sayle to Sayles in recognition of his hopes for a lineage, he also had specific set ideas about what he needed to accomplish as a man. "What is a man anyhow?" runs the Whitman quote used as an epigraph for the section titled "Gene," after Lucy's son, Sam's father.[143] Whitman may be thought of as speaking metaphysically, but he is also speaking at a time in the United States when the debate was practical and moral and religious and legal as well. Whitman first wrote the line in 1858, the year after the Supreme Court's affirmation of the compatibility of slavery with the US Constitution in the 1857 Dred Scott decision; it would be another five years before President Lincoln would issue a proclamation of emancipation, three years after that that the Constitution would be amended, and many more years still to pass before indentured bondage of various kinds would come to an end.

Clifton writes in an earlier untitled poem, "being property once myself/i have a feeling for it,/that's why i can talk/about environment."[144] Rather than this position of radical empathy engendered in his daughter, Sam Sayles views ownership, and specifically property, as a way of asserting his own personhood and of assuring his family's legacy, purchasing the properties described in "lot's wife

1988" "to hold our name forever/against the spin of the world."[145] The "Lucy" section closed with the execution of Lucy, an incident (no matter how "legal" Sam insists it was) that is still described by Lucille Clifton as the event it most resembled: a lynching. From this—hinged by the Whitman quote—we move to the opening of the "Gene" chapter which opens "Daddy had surprised us and bought the house."[146] Ownership of the house at 254 Purdy Street, along with his position as a tradesman responsible for fashioning the couplers that connected train cars, cemented Sam Sayles' position as a member of the bourgeoning Black middle class of Buffalo, NY. There are later scenes of purchases solely meant symbolically: Sam buys a dining room set that the family doesn't need, and Thelma buys a set of rings she neither wears nor is able to afford[147].

Sam had a set of goals for himself, he later announced. "I have had a son and now I own a house. All I got to do is plant a tree. And he would smile."[148] It is curious his erasure of the three daughters in his estimation of what makes him a man only because he constantly prizes Lucille over all the other siblings, including Sammy who had "begun the Black boy's initiation into wine and worse."[149] Lucille, meanwhile, is his "idol," the favorite that Elaine and Jo are sure his ghost will not haunt. When later Sam, only partially literate—Clifton explains that he could read but could not write—struggles and struggles to write Lucille a letter while she is away at Howard University, he addresses it to "Dear Lucilleman."[150]

At first glance, Gene's life does not have the impact on Sam—and by extension Lucille—that either Caroline's or Lucy's had. As Sam describes him, he is destructive and selfish, and he dies young at thirty. He describes to Lucille Gene's various destructive behaviors, including vandalism and womanizing, and taking his young son to bars and taking bets on him beating the sons of the other men in fights. When the young Lucille tells her father that Gene was "crazy," Sam gets pensive, saying, "No, he wasn't crazy. He was just somebody whose Mama and Daddy was dead."[151] As for his bad behavior, Sam added that because of his early death, "He didn't hardly get to be a man." About the circumstances and cause of Gene's death, the text is silent.

After Gene's undescribed death, there is only one brief scene describing Sam's mother, Georgia Hatcher. Hatcher married again, a man named Luke whom Sam describes to Lucille as a "good man" though Caroline herself encouraged the children to be unkind to Luke. Sam recounts that Caroline advised him, "we didn't have to obey nobody," giving the boy that oft-repeated reason "you from Dahomey women."[152] The scene I refer to takes place before the remarriage. Georgia sits at the dining room table with a letter from some of her friends who had gone to New York City for work. Her friends were encouraging her to join them and she was crying because she knew she couldn't. When young Sam asks her why she wants to go to New York, she simply says, "I just want to see some things." Caroline, who as an eight-year-old child, endured that long forced walk through much of the South, is unimpressed when Sam recounts the story and asks her if she too wants to travel and see places other than Virginia. "I already seen it," Caroline says, closing the subject. Georgia Hatcher is not heard from again except by omission: Sam mentions several times that he was raised by Caroline.

The grief of Georgia at having her options in life precluded by the gendered expectations visited upon her by family life prefigure the later grief of Thelma Sayles, Clifton's mother. Thelma is perhaps even less ambitious than Sam's mother, mostly seeming content with her life as a domestic worker, raising the children and keeping house. But there's trouble at the edges of what Lucille Clifton describes to us; the couple fights often and on at least one occasion Sam beats Thelma, though it is treated in the text as an ordinary part of their relationship, and Clifton only comments on not being able to prevent it. She even remarks at one point, "Mama's life was—seemed like—the biggest waste in the world to me," though she quickly amends, "but now I don't know, I'm not sure anymore."[153] For her part, Thelma is desperate that Lucille should get away: "Get away," Thelma tells Lucille, "get away. I have not had a normal life. I want you to have a natural life. I want you to get away."[154]

There is a strand of silence that runs through *generations*. We witness Caroline's silence (in Lucille's imagination) at Lucy's execution and in Sam's recounting of Caroline's refusal to give her Afrikan name. Here, as well, the text is reticent about her reasoning. All we know about Caroline's life before slavery is that she was separated from her parents and her brother, though she and Margaret still have a chance to visit. The text also glides over trying to justify or explain Lucy's reason for killing Harvey Nichols. After all, shooting a man off his horse with a rifle at night requires extreme premeditation and probably a lot of target practice, along with a very steady hand and eye. The light implication that her motive was connected to Gene's withered arm is diminished somewhat by the larger context of Nichols being described as a carpetbagger and Lucy Sale as a newly liberated slave. In the end, (despite the much later poem "great-grandmother lucy reads my poem about her") Clifton does not try to explain her motive. She does honor Lucy in the earlier poem, "light," when she says that she "already" has an "afrikan name."[155] Of course, this framing of "Lucy" *as* an "afrikan" name also honors, and perhaps explains, Caroline, who deems her European name good enough when she refuses to disclose her own African name to Sam.

This reticence of *generations* is not accidental. Clifton, in a comment about Morrison's editing of the text with her, said, "I must pay tribute to Toni Morrison as an editor...she puts things in. I take things out."[156] Regardless of its brevity and the silences that exist within it, *generations* was clearly a very difficult text for Clifton to write. As early as 1973, senior Random House editor Nan Talese sent a note to Clifton on *good news about the earth*, with a handwritten note in the margins inquiring how progress on *generations* was coming along. In what can be taken as a sign of the times, the person to whom the letter is addressed is "Mrs. Fred Clifton," and the letter, though signed "Nan," concludes with the typed signature line reading "Mrs. Gay Talese, Editor." Both women's cursive handwriting, as might be expected of a generation who studied the art of Zaner-Bloser penmanship in elementary school, is nearly identical.[157]

While Jo and Elaine repeatedly declare throughout the text that Lucille would be safe from being "haunted" by Sam, the book itself demonstrates the opposite: it's his voice that dominates the book: he is the main conduit for all of the family stories in the first four sections of the book. It feels significant to me that Lucille Clifton's own birth and life are encompassed entirely in the final chapter, one ostensibly named for her mother, though considering that Lucille Clifton's own legal birth name is Thelma, one could see the chapter as being named for both of them, mother and daughter as a collective "Thelma." Though *generations* is an affirmation of the family's lineage, it is hard not to also see it as elegiac, since it mostly describes people who are already dead. Thelma Sayles' death is mentioned much earlier in *generations* and so by the time of her first appearance in her own chapter, we see her already as a ghost. Sam, too, is already dead before we ever hear his words or read his physical description.

The various silences in *generations*—Caroline's real name, Lucy's motivation for murder, the circumstances of Gene's short life and his death, Georgia Hatcher's fate—are revisited and compounded by a series of curious statements in the closing chapter of *generations*. Of Sam, the "hero" of this story, if there is one, in the middle of a passage praising him as a "strong man, a strong family man," Lucille Clifton writes, "Now, he did some things, he did some things, but he always loved his family."[158] The "some things" Clifton refers to here—twice—are likely both the domestic abuse suffered by Thelma and the sexual abuse Lucille Clifton recounts suffering at his hands in multiple later poems. She does not mention the sexual abuse here in *generations*, instead she goes on to say, "He hurt us all a lot and we hurt him a lot, the way people who love each other do, you know." The "you know" here makes it almost casual, conversation, something that would be said between friends or intimates.

She further describes the deleterious effect of his behavior on others in the family, including her brother Sam and her sisters Elaine and Jo, saying, "Punkin she has a hard time living in the world and so does my brother and Jo has a hard time and gives one too. And a lot of all that is his fault."[159] The framing in *generations* of Sam as a strong family man and Thelma as no more than a shadow of a woman is only briefly questioned in its closing pages. Both notions are revised and complicated by Clifton in the poems she later writes about her mother and father.

For her part, Thelma—whom Clifton refers to four times in the closing pages of *generations* as a "magic woman" or as having "magic"—becomes a powerful spiritual figure in Clifton's imagination after her death, visiting her often and dispensing advice in numerous poems, including the previously mentioned poem, "the message of thelma sayles." While *generations* mostly explores Clifton's patrilineal line, the predominant figures of that patrilineal line are women, Lucy and Caroline. Clifton further identifies her own spiritual powers as coming from her matrilineal line as in the physical form of the polydactyly that manifested in Thelma, in Lucille, and in her daughter Sidney. Surgeons removed each woman's extra digits in infancy—Clifton tried, but was too late, to tell the surgeon to leave Sidney's hands intact. [160] She invokes her twelve-fingeredness multiple times in her work as evidence of the "magic" that came through Thelma. In the late poem "hands" she writes of her own and of Sidney's digits snipped away, "i could no more ignore/the totems of my tribe/than i could close my eyes/against the light flaring/behind what has been called/the world."[161] Despite that her hands have been "regulated" by the surgeon's cut, "they were born to more/than bone.../i remain whole/alive twelvefingered."

In earlier poems from *The Two-Headed Woman*, Clifton is more critical of Thelma and forgiving of Sam. Of Thelma she says, "no man would taste you" and "madam, i'm not your gifted girl,/i am a woman and/i know what to do."[162] At first, she denies that Thelma has anything to teach her, but doubles back on this rejection mere pages later, saying, "i am not grown away from you/whatever i say."[163] As for Sam, she struggles with forgiving him, though she does not mention any abuse. In a poem called "forgiving my father" which follows these poems about Thelma, Clifton writes:

> there is no more time for you. there will
> never be time enough daddy daddy old lecher
> old liar.[164]

The "lecher" and "liar" here is being scolded by his daughter for being unable to account for his mistreatment of both Thelma and Lucille. Though the nature of the mistreatment is not explained, it's implied to be a lack of emotional attention and affection. Clifton goes on to literally forgive him for this, saying:

> but you were the son of a needy father,
> the father of a needy son;
> you gave her all you had
> which was nothing.

Later in the poem, Clifton despairs of ever being able to reconcile with her father, even through the writing of poems, a practice which she has recognized in the past—and will continue to recognize in the future—as powerful and empowering. She writes, "what am i doing here collecting?/you lie side by side in debtors' boxes/and no accounting will open them up."

By these kinds of invocations, both of Thelma and her lineage, she becomes an even more important figure than Sam, surrounding and lifting up Clifton's own work. If Thelma's ancestors are not named the way Sam's are in the book *generations*, one could consider her poem, "the lost women" from *Next*, in which she imagines all the lost and nameless ancestors:

> where are my gangs,
> my teams, my mislaid sisters?
> all the women who could have known me,
> where in the world are their names?[165]

At some point after the publication of *generations*, Clifton did attempt writing more about her mother in an unpublished prose manuscript called "Curiosities," which exists in several drafts. About Thelma Sayles' death Clifton wrote, "It is in the tradition of my sex, my race, my family to go on with life. In the spring of 1959 I visited my mother's grave carrying my baby girl in my arms for the first and last time. I went on with my life." The manuscript tells of Clifton's initial efforts at channeling her mother's spirit from the afterlife through automatic writing, and it was not an easy one for Clifton to write. As in *generations*, she is vexed by the problem of how to tell the truth of history. What appears to be the final revision of "Curiosities" opens, "This is the fourth first page I've started. I kept trying to be historic; a first page of dates and names and accounts, a first page of descriptions of our family, a day in the life, all starts, all wrong somehow."[166]

Eventually, she realizes, "My life is something more than my mother might have imagined. I am married still to the same man. My children are teenagers and I have written and published almost twenty books." In an automatic writing session following this moment, on the handwritten draft of this part of the manuscript, Clifton's pencil spells out in a long continuous loop, apparently in the voice of Thelma, "oh good baby good/you can keep going."[167]

Of course, most importantly to Lucille Clifton and to our discussion of her work here, Thelma was a poet. She wrote poetry in formal rhyme and meter and Clifton often recounted the story of showing Thelma some of her earliest efforts in poetry and Thelma dismissing the work by saying, "Oh baby that's not a poem! I'll show you how to write a poem!" at which point she would fetch paper and pen, recite Paul Laurence Dunbar, Leigh Hunt, or Sam Walter Foss, and start to teach her iambic pentameter.[168] Because of this, Clifton says, her earliest poems were sonnets such as those written by Edna St. Vincent Millay or Thomas Wolfe. Clifton would sometimes tell this story about Thelma in her readings. The audience usually laughed when Lucille told the story, and by the way she would tell the story maybe Lucille meant for that to happen, but then she would follow the story up by reading the poem "fury" from *The Book of Light*.[169] When Thelma burns the poems she has been refused the right to publish, Lucille understands in the core of her being the depth of the tragedy unfolding: "she will never recover."[170]

The juxtaposition of the two moments in Clifton's public readings seems critical: the comic patter and the tragic poem that followed. There is a powerful and dynamic teaching moment in this contrast between the assertion of personhood of Thelma's self-identity as a poet in the first, seemingly light-hearted, anecdote about the creation of poetry and then a dire and intense poem about its destruction. The woman with eyes like "animals" feeds the "jewels" of her poems into the "rubies" of coal. Even the moment of ruin is sanctified. And is the story of Thelma dismissing Lucille's juvenilia that light-hearted really? Here we see the elder poet asserting her expertise and attempting to teach the younger poet technique and traditional form. It sounds pretty serious to me. And, as we will come to learn, Clifton was indeed extremely attentive to both sound, meter, and prosodic rhythms in her work, aspects of poetic craft that by her own repeated admission she learned from her very first poetry teacher, the very first poet she knew, Thelma Sayles.

In fact, at some point in the past, Lucille recounts, St. Mary's College of Maryland was considering endowing a chair in poetry and naming it the Lucille Clifton Chair. Clifton was neutral. What if we called it the Thelma Sayles Chair, someone suggested; Clifton responded, "I'm not going to say no to that."[171]

It took many more years before Clifton began to tell more of the truths about her family, including her parents. The silences in generations were reinforced by the fact that Clifton did not actively seek publication for "Curiosities," even after the manuscript appeared to have been revised to completion after multiple drafts—at least four versions exist in the archives. There were other reasons: most of "Curiosities" recounts Clifton's growing interest in channeling, automatic writing, divination through Ouija board, and past life regression, describing her experiences with these practices, and this was a story Clifton was as yet unready to tell; it would not be until her 2004 volume Mercy that she would publish any of her automatic writing, though she did refer to the practice occasionally. The hundreds upon hundreds of manuscript pages of her copious automatic writing experiments are available for viewing in her archives.

Despite the cryptic references in the close of generations to the "hurt" caused by Sam Sayles, it was not until "shapeshifter poems," a multi-part poem in 1987's Next, that she actually mentions the abuse, though obliquely and in third person, describing it happening to "a pretty little girl;" a similar strategy is adopted in the poem "night vision" from 1993's *The Book of Light*, which appears one page before "fury." In that poem, once again in third person, "the girl fits her body in/to the space between the bed/and the wall."[172] Clifton does not name the abuse, nor describe it in any way, saying only that the girl "will train her tongue/to lie still in her mouth and listen," and that "she will do some/thing with this." There is an implication at the end of "night vision" that the terror the girl has undergone will lead her to a life of creative expression: "she will remember/to build something human with it."

In the poem "what did she know, when did she know it," which appeared three years later in *The Terrible Stories*, Clifton again talks about the abuse in third person, but makes it very clear to the reader that the abuse is happening to her. The image of the girl pressing her body against the wall is again repeated, but this time it is followed by a graphic description of digital penetration. Not until the poems "moonchild," which appeared among the new poems in *Blessing the Boats: New and Selected Poems,* and the poem "mercy," in her 2004 collection of that name, does she speak of the abuse in first person, actually name her father as her abuser, and begin to describe the abuse in more graphic physical terms. Her feelings toward her father remain complex and unresolved through her writing life, as many poems sympathetic to him appear in all of these collections, some of them juxtaposed with the poems about the abuse. In a trio of poems published in her last collection, *Voices,* "my father hasn't come back," "dad," and "faith," she considers the full range of her reactions and responses to him.

"[S]hapeshifter poems" describes the mythical creatures who were once men but were changed by the moon, saying, "they wear strange hands/they walk through the houses/at night   their daughters/do not know them."[173] The "little girl" in the poem thinks that if she lies "still enough/shut enough/hard enough" that the shapeshifter will not find her. This image of hardness in the body of the little girl as defense against the abuse will recur in later poems. As specific as Lucille Clifton was about the geography of the streets of Buffalo in earlier poems, one learns here—with devastating clarity—the layout of her childhood bedroom from these poems: the bed was pushed against the wall, we know where the window is, where the door is. While we know the shapeshifter is abroad and that it is the father of the "prettylittlegirl," what happens in the room is not described. There is a silent space in the poem that none-theless speaks volumes. By the end of the poem, the girl with the "scarred tongue" is breathing into her pillow the poem "she cannot tell   the one/there is no one to hear."[174]

Three poems about Sam Sayles appear in *The Book of Light* and the earliest of these, simply called "sam," does not mention the abuse and is sympathetic to the difficulties Sam faced in his life. Clifton says of him, "if he/could have gone to school/he would have learned to write/his story" and that "if he could have done better/he would have."[175] It is a remarkably equanimous view considering the later poems Clifton wrote about her father, though as I mentioned earlier, she continues to write poems honoring him even as she eventually exposes the abuse in more explicit terms. She is open about the fact that she believed Sam Sayles wounded and compromised by the complicated legacies of slavery and struc-tural racism: "oh stars/and stripes forever,/what did you do to my father?" He remained, throughout her young life, important to her. In fact, the very first letter she wrote after moving into the house on Talbot Road in Baltimore was to Sam, in which she included several pictures from several angles of the house. "I am the worst picture taker in the world," she confesses, and goes on to try to describe the pictures themselves: "The trees are white and pink dogwood and there are lilacs and red azaleas."[176]

Entirely in third person, the focus of the poem "night vision" is on the girl herself and her survival strategies. When she says, "she will remember/to build something human with it," the pronoun "it" has no antecedent in the poem other than the action of the girl wedging herself into the space between the bed and the wall—we are not told what this action is in response to. The action itself is again excluded from the poem. And, as mentioned, this poem of the girl's survival is followed immediately by the poem "fury," in which Thelma Sayles burns her poems. Fire dominates the very next poem as well, the third poem about Sam Sayles, called "ciga-rettes." Now having presented two examples of the ruin wrought by Sam, Clifton starkly declares, "my father burned us all."[177] While she describes the fire as coming from the ashes of his cigarettes, she also says the flames were "the glow of his pain." Sam does not recognize Lucille's "charred pillow" or that the halls of house are "smoldering."

Three years later, in *The Terrible Stories*, Clifton published "what did she know, when did she know it."[178] Once again, this poem mentions and describes the abuse but does not name or describe the abuser except by part, referring to "the fingers;" there is not even a pronoun to say whose fingers they are. A very astute reader might have recalled that Sam Sayles' fingers are often mentioned in Clifton's poems about him, including "my daddy's fingers move among the couplers" asking in that poem, "what do my daddy's fingers know about grace?"[179] The fingers are again mentioned in another early poem, this one from *Quilting*. In "to my friend, jerina," Clifton writes of there being "no safety/in my father's house."[180] She talks, again in third person, of a "girl/wallowing in her own shame/.../not willing to be left to/the silent fingers in the dark." Later still, somewhat more directly, in a poem called "june 20," she talks of her birth to "a frowned forehead of a woman" and "a man whose fingers will itch/to enter me."[181] In this way, Clifton was talking about the abuse in the way she could, and in the time that she needed.

The poem "what did she know, when did she know it" begins with a single phrase line, "in the evenings," but this is quickly disrupted by the second line which contains not only an inverted verb, but also a disrupted syntax of the declarative: "what it was the soft tap tap." This move from inquisitive to declarative is highlighted by the rhythmic shift to three heavy stresses in a row of "soft tap tap" which is echoed a few lines later in "sheet arced off."

in the evenings
what it was the soft tap tap
into the room   the cold curve
of the sheet arced off
the fingers sliding in
and the hard clench against the wall
before and after[182]

Though the third line follows the tap grammatically "into the room," it is further disrupted by a midline (and visual) caesura before yet another pair of heavy stresses in "cold curve." We will look at Clifton's prosody more closely a little later, but notice here how the poem returns to lines that are nearly iambic single phrases (with the sole and disturbing interruption of "hard clench," but is unable to sustain this cool approach in light of the difficult subject matter and soon dissolves into fracture and fragment, a pyrrhic foot (two light stresses) followed by a spondee, a caesura, and another spondee, and then a return to the tentative inquisitive:

> all the cold air   cold edges
> why the little girl never smiled

The irony here is that the question ("Why did the little girl never smile?") seems not to have been asked in her actual childhood, nor does it manage to articulate itself in the poem. It's also a line that drops its initial trochees into the dark caesura between "girl" and the first syllable of "never" enabling once again an iambic sound from "never" into "smiled." Clifton immediately switches in the final lines of the poem to a more painful interrogation—because everyone by this point has realized "why the little girl never smiled." Though intimated as a question, it serves to point out to the reader that there is something no one is talking about, but that everyone—most pointedly here the mother—knows.

The two final questions are similarly asked without the normative punctuation of a question mark, perhaps symbolic of the fact that these are questions asked of a woman no longer alive, questions that skim the rawest surface of the child-as-adult's anger, questions that will never be answered:

> they are supposed to know everything
> our mothers   what did she know
> when did she know it

This poem continually switches between declarative and inquisitive, but the switch is not accompanied by either the punctuation or the normal grammatical constructions that would enable the reader to be accustomed to the new rhetorical mode. As a result, it more closely imitates the mental structure of a child who does not understand the causal relationships, unable to understand why the father is acting against her in such a way, unable to understand why the mother does nothing, acts like she knows nothing. It's the chilling realization of the adult Clifton that whether or not her mother knew of her abuse, she was "supposed to know." In other words, she was either ignorant or she ignored the truth she did, at some point, discover. These realizations are equally painful. In the end, the poem seems like less of an indictment of Sam's abuse, but of Thelma's inability to prevent it.

It is not until the new poems published as part of *Blessing the Boats: New and Selected Poems*, a collection that would bring Clifton the National Book Award for Poetry, that Clifton finally names her father as her abuser. In a poem called "moonchild" (there is another unrelated poem with the same title in the collection *Quilting*) Clifton writes of playfully bragging with her girlfriends as they stuffed tissue in their undershirts to pretend they were growing breasts: "jay johnson is teaching/me to french kiss, ella bragged, who/is teaching you? how do you say; my father?" There's no answer in the poem, though the child Lucille knows that "the moon understands dark places./the moon has secrets of her own./ she holds what light she can."[183]

Despite this long-awaited identification of the "shapeshifter," Clifton goes on, only a few pages later in the same collection, to include in a poem called "what i think when i ride the train," an evocation and honoring of her father's manual labor as a maker of the couplers between train cars. She once again describes his life as a working class person of color writing, "his hands were hard/and black and swollen/the knuckles like lugs/or bolts in a rich man's box." In an America that requires his manual work to run smoothly, she assigns to him a place of honor when she writes, "there's my father,/he was a chipper,/he made the best damn couplers/in the whole white world."[184]

Though she continued to recognize the stresses, pressures, and duress that Sam Sayles contended with (for example, in a poem from *Mercy* called "the river between us"[185]) she finally opens up about the damage he caused her mentally and physically in a pair of poems later in that collection called "a story" and "mercy." The first of these is told more like a fable bemoaning the lack of a father who would protect and watch out for "beasts and ogres." As in the "shapeshifter poems," it is the father himself here who is the enemy who "loomed there in the half/shadow of a daughters room/moaning a lullaby/in a wolfs voice."[186]

Everything that happens next is covered by a single word—"later"—and the impacts are grevious: "our mothers went mad and/our brothers killed themselves/and we began this story-telling life." The poem tells a collective story, not an individual one, and the lives that are told (insanity of the mother, suicide of the brother) are more figurative than autobiographical, though we know that Thelma always worried about Sam thinking she was "crazy" and that, as we already know, Lucille's brother Sammy had at some point succumbed to "wine and worse." In fact, in a later poem, Clifton *does* say Thelma "went mad...for want of tenderness," concluding, "this is why i know/the gods/are men."[187] The survivors of the dark fairytale told in "a story" do not know how they made it through: "how did we survive/to live not happily perhaps but//ever after."[188]

Sam is present in both of the poems "mercy" and the poem "my father hasn't come back." These two poems finally describe the physical abuse without eliding it or casting it in metaphorical terms or disassociating it into third person. Clifton says in "mercy":

> how grateful I was when he decided
> not to replace his fingers with his thing
> though he thought about it was going to
> but mumbled "maybe I shouldn't do that"
> and didn't do that and I was so
> grateful then and now grateful
> how sick   i am   how mad[189]

This poem is doubly significant. Lucille Clifton finally describes the moment of abuse in physically explicit terms and also speaks in first person about her feelings both while it was happening and in the present moment, and Sam himself speaks and acts in the poem, pausing and reconsidering his actions. Of course, Lucille declaring herself "sick" and "mad" in the closing of the poem has multiple meanings. Being "sick" means both a metaphorical sick with grief, but also a manifestation of the real physical and psychic wounds that have attended this childhood trauma. Being "mad" first calls to mind the mental health connotation (following "sick" as it does), but easily and nearly triumphantly (after such a long period of repression and silence) calls to mind, instead, real anger.

Lucille Clifton writes about Sam again in three more poems that appear back-to-back in the last collection she published in her lifetime, *Voices*, which appeared four years after *Mercy*. In the poem "my father hasn't come back," she calls back to the earlier poems in turn, and Sam speaks again:

> my father hasn't come back
> to apologize   i have stood
> and waited almost sixty years
> so different from the nights
> i wedged myself between
> the mattress and the wall
>
> i do not hate him
> i assure myself
> only his probing fingers
> i have to teach you
> he one time whispered
> more to himself than me[190]

She once more disassociates him from his crime, trying to convince herself that she does not hate him, "only his probing fingers." While it appears at the beginning that this will be another poem of condemnation, extending the anger that bloomed forth at the end of "mercy," Clifton takes it in another direction, rather than back to the hurt of the past, forward to her children and grandchildren:

> i am seventy-two-years-old
> dead man and in another city
> standing with my daughters   granddaughters
> trying to understand you
> trying to help them understand
> the sticks and stones of love

So that small phrase—"how mad"—is really all we get of Clifton's anger. She still seeks and strains to understand her father, not to forgive him, but to process the conflict both she and he felt. It took Clifton thirty-two years from the publication of *generations* to address her father directly, to say, "[i am] trying to understand you." It is a remarkable moment after a lifetime of contending with the secret she carried, the damage he did, one that bears out Alicia Ostriker's opinion that what Clifton excelled at was exploring "the awful complexity of our connection to others."[191]

Whenever she read any of these poems, and I myself heard her read them often, she would say to the audience, "Every time I read these poems, after the reading someone comes up to me to say that this happened to them too." She would pause and cast an eye around the audience, and then reiterate, "Every time." What I now realize that she was silently saying was, *I know this has happened to someone in this room. And I am here for you.*

There is something clear-eyed about her vision of him in the two contrasting poems that follow. In a dreadfully honest poem simply called "dad" (the one and only time Lucille refers to Sam Sayles with the familiar, even affectionate, term), she finally condemns the long-ago incidents of domestic violence against Thelma that she witnessed as a young girl: "consider the raw potato/wrapped in his dress sock/.../for beating her."[192] Perhaps because we already understand "the gods/are men," we shouldn't be surprised when Sam thinks to himself at the end of the poem, "the gods might/understand/a man like me."

The concluding motions of the 1976 memoir *generations* are troubled greatly by this later and ongoing revelation of the personal history going on behind the scenes, as it were. As secrets are divulged, the true history of a family comes to be known. The text of the memoir isn't as sure as it may at first seem to be. There are even contradictions within it, such as when Sam says to Lucille early on about slavery, "It ain't something in a book, Lue. Even the good parts was awful," and later on says, "We fooled em, Lue, slavery was terrible but we fooled them old people. We come out of it better than they did."[193] Thelma seems to agree with his second sentiment when she tells Lucille, "Slavery was a temporary thing, mostly we was free."[194]

Among the many family photographs that accompany the text of *generations* is one of Sam Sayles standing in the alley between the house at 254 Purdy Street and the house next door at 252 Purdy Street. He is in his shirtsleeves, but with a knotted tie, wearing trousers with an ironed crease in the front. He is wearing a suit vest on his left side, the right side of the vest thrown over the shoulder casually. He is smiling. It is this photograph that is the subject of the final poem of the trio in *Voices:*

faith

my father was so sure
that afternoon
he put on his Sunday suit
and waited at the front porch
one hand in his pocket
the other gripping his hat
to greet the end of the world

waited there patient as the eclipse
ordained the darkening
of everything
the house   the neighborhood we knew
the world   his hopeful eyes the only
glowing things on purdy street[195]

This vision of Sam standing beside the house that no longer exists, ready for anything, filled with hope, patient in the face of "the darkening/of everything," is the bittersweet last image we ever get of him in his daughter's poetry. None of the later unpublished poems or drafts yet discovered in her papers mention him. Though she writes about Thelma Sayles several more times, it appears that Clifton never again wrote of her father. It's as if she wanted to leave him there, at the beginning of things, before all the ruin and losses yet to come.

There is, however, a brief aside on the last page of *generations* that makes one optimistic for the future of the Sayles family, despite Sam's behavior. When Lucille is explaining Thelma's views on slavery she adds, "And she smiled when she said it and Daddy smiled too and saw that my sons are as strong as my daughters and it had been made right."[196] Sam acknowledges here that in Lucille's children's generation the boys are as strong as the girls. It's a powerful affirmation in a family that has been described as having strong and nuanced women—who were descended from the legendary Dahomey warrior women—and destructive and flawed men.

As Thelma had the last word in the conversation about history and Sam given the subservient position of smiling and agreeing with her, in the lineage Clifton gives at the close of *generations* it is Caroline Donald, and not her husband Sam Louis Sale, who is named as the ultimate ancestor of the dynasty. As the book closes, it is Caroline's voice echoing down through history that has the last word.

Chapter 6: The Light That Came to Lucille Clifton

Lucille Clifton's engagement with spiritual figures continued throughout her body of work. As Kevin Young points out, Clifton's concern with the spirit is not separable from her concerns with physical and bodily materiality. "For Clifton," Young wrote in his afterword to her *Collected Poems*, "there's no split between the body and the spirit and the intellect: no ideas but in the body."[197]

Although she sometimes used the rhetoric of prayer itself, she often wrestled with the big questions about the nature of god and the afterlife by making ordinary the scriptural figures about whom she was writing. One is reminded of her desire to "find the human in the mythic, and the mythic in the human." She actively wrote into scripture, sometimes revising it, sometimes subverting it. In addition to the sixteen poems of "some jesus," one of the sections of her book *good news about the earth*, she published four other major sequences on Biblical figures—an undesignated series (as were the "buffalo war" poems) of eight poems on the life of Mary that appears in *The Two-Headed Woman*, "tree of life," ten poems telling the story of the garden of Eden from *Quilting*, "brothers," an eight-part poem which appeared in *The Book of Light* and recounts a one-sided dialog between Lucifer and God, and finally, "from the Book of David," appearing in *The Terrible Stories*, which in eleven poems reimagines the story of King David.

Sometime after the publication of *The Terrible Stories*, when Lucille Clifton first started imagining that her follow-up volume might be a volume of new and selected poems, Clifton conceived two separate tables of contents, one labeled 'body,' and the other labeled 'soul,' collecting these sequences and a few other poems.

I assume Clifton eventually thought better of the structural and thematic dichotomy, as she abandoned the idea of the two separate volumes of selected poems and instead compiled and published *Blessing the Boats*.

Akasha Gloria Hull writes of Clifton's approach to traditional Biblical stories, saying, "Perhaps the simplest way to describe her transformative mode is to say that she (1) Africanizes, (2) feminizes, (3) sexualizes, and (4) mysticizes the original text."[198]

Besides these Biblical sequences, Clifton engaged in a kind of spiritualism, channeling the voices of ancestors through Ouija board, past life regression, and other methods. She published an early version of these channelings as ten poems, under the title "The Light That Came to Lucille Clifton," included in her collection *Two-Headed Woman*, and many years later, in *Mercy*, she published twenty-two poems drawn from a mostly unrevised transcript of a channeling she received in the early 1970s, called "The Message of the Ones." As Hull points out, this kind of spiritual channeling was common among many of the Black women writers who were publishing at the time, including the aforementioned Morrison, Naylor, Walker, and Cade Bambara. "Fitting generally into this movement," writes Hull, "Lucille Clifton is yet unique in her unclouded self-revelation and the meshing of personal autobiography with her art. Spiritually endowed, she practices her gifts in both her life and her poetry. Clifton hears voices, automatically writes, reads palms, senses realities, and speaks normally unknowable truths."[199]

In addition to these two channeled transcripts, Clifton also composed a set of poems, "Ten Oxherding Pictures," based on the classical set of paintings and accompanying poems in Zen Buddhist tradition. Finally, among the last manuscripts and drafts found in her work, she began a choral work, called "The Book of Days," in which humans, angels, and both God and the fallen angel Lucifer all speak. These various modes in Clifton's writing about the spirit and spirituality are intimately connected to each other and to her own physical embodiment as a Black woman. "Lucille Clifton belongs to a long and storied tradition of Black American women," points out Marina Magloire, "endowed with spiritual powers." Magloire claims, "Far from espousing postracialism, Clifton's theory of spirit is made possible by her Black womanhood."[200] She mentions other writers who depict Black Women characters as mediums such as Todi Cade Bambara, Gloria Naylor, and Alice Walker (who famously signed the end of her novel, The Color Purple, as "A.W., author and medium." Magloire even mentions figures in popular imagination such as The Color Purple star Whoopi Goldberg's iconic depiction of medium and seer Oda Mae Brown in the film Ghost.[201] One might also think of Phylicia Rashad's portrayal of Aunt Ester Tyler in August Wilson's play Gem of the Ocean, or Angela Bassett's turn as the legendary witch Marie Leveau in the television series American Horror Story.

As Clifton developed as a poet throughout her career, her usage and engagement with these scriptures from various traditions shifted and changed. In the earlier poems of "some jesus" and the series about Mary and her mother that appears in The Two-Headed Woman, she seemed to be engaged in a midrash-like practice, interrogating the received meanings of the stories, melding African mythology and contexts with Biblical stories to create a uniquely Black spirituality and reveal some of the hidden layers within. Later still, in "tree of life" and "brothers," she sought, through an affinity with her retroactive spiritual namesake Lucifer ("the bringer of light"), to wrestle with some of the most painful questions at the heart of any spiritual practice: what is the cost of knowledge? If there is a loving God, how does He allow monstrous evil to exist in the world? Who is responsible for the suffering of children?

In the end, Clifton, like Blake, seemed to assemble her own cosmology, her own array of ethical approaches to understand how humans are meant to behave in the universe. These spiritual writings themselves, together perhaps with the various revelations of Thelma Sayles and Fred Clifton from beyond their deaths that recur throughout her body of work, could be assembled as a new canon of knowledge for study and contemplation. In the earlier poems, she was responding to the stories she had learned as a child and young woman in church, but with new and alternative valences.

Her relationship to Christianity is catholic—in the original sense of that word. Marta Werbanowska argues that Clifton's conception of Christianity aligns with that of James H. Cone, renown Black theologian and author of *Black Theology and Black Power*, a work that posits theology as a tool of Black liberation. Cone inspired many, including Malcolm X and Jeremiah Wright, once pastor to Barack Obama. Werbanowska explains that Clifton's themes of "Black affirmation and liberation of the world's oppressed populations" that recur throughout her poetry "show close connections between Cone's and Clifton's understanding of Black Christianity and spirituality as discourses of emancipation from the oppressive system."[202]

Even after Clifton published "the light that came to lucille clifton," she was nervous about how the channeled writings would be received if she talked about their provenance; this was one of the reasons she waited until many decades later to publish "Message from the Ones." There were many other transcripts from this same time period that remain unpublished, as well as multiple prose pieces. In addition to "Curiosities," previously mentioned, Clifton also composed a manuscript she called "Visits/Illuminations," and another on Black astrology called "Soul Signs."

"Visits" was planned as a series of interviews she conducted with twenty-one channeled spirits, twenty of them widely known figures, including actors, artists, dancers, and other historical personages; the twenty-first was a mysterious collective entity known only as "They." Most of these interviews were conducted by automatic writing, once or twice by trance and oral questioning. On the table of contents in the archive, there is listed both Foreword and Afterword, but neither of these seems to have been written. Figures "interviewed" include criminal Clyde Barrow, musicians Billie Holiday and Bessie Smith, actor Jack Cassidy (to whom Clifton took a particular liking), poet Emily Dickinson, and to Clifton's own surprise, Jesus of Nazareth himself.[203]

The "Illuminations" section that follows includes more in-depth encounters with four different figures: Katy, an enslaved woman in the early nineteenth century, George, an actor in Elizabethan England, Karl, a German police officer and concentration camp guard, and Dr. Thomas Neill Cream, a Canadian physician and serial murderer. Clifton kept all associated texts in folders: often there were pages of automatic writing, summaries, diary entries, and several times pages in which Clifton would write a question and her divination partner would write the answer in a kind of call-and-response format. Clifton's book of Black astrology contained an analysis of Black communities around the world according to traditional western astrology and a series of categorizations of food, film, and even pick-up lines by astrological sign. The title of Clifton's work-in-progress, "Soul Signs," was a riff on Linda Goodman's *Sun Signs*, a bestseller at the time Clifton was working on her book.

By the time she was writing "tree of life" and "brothers" and "from the Book of David" it was obvious that Lucille Clifton saw herself as a thinker, a philosopher, and theologian of a fashion. It would be useful for readers to consider her poems about spiritual matters as serious texts worthy of study in that context. The language and diction of the King James Bible and the oral rhythms and music of Black church services are both present in Lucille's work. Mary Jane Lupton recounts that because of Sam's recitation to Lucille and her sisters of the poetry of Paul Laurence Dunbar and Langston Hughes, Lucille had mastered written forms of Black English by the time she was ten or eleven.[204] Clifton herself told Lupton that the orations of Reverend Merriweather of the Macedonia Baptist Church, to which the Sayles family and many of their relatives belonged, were her greatest childhood influence in literature, after her parents.

Masters were all around outside home as well: besides Thelma Sayles, Lucille's Aunt Timmie was also a poet and poetry lover, chanting poetry to herself in both Cherokee and Masai as she ironed. Aunt Timmie is, however, most unlike the poet described in "somewhere," who finds a pen between the cushions of the couch in order to write a poem called *good times*. Like Thelma Sayles, Aunt Timmie's poetic ambitions remain strictly private. In a later poem, Clifton describes how Aunt Timmie spent her life as a domestic worker, but nonetheless recognizes her as a "master," saying of Timmie's skill and potential and lost opportunities, "if you had heard her/.../you would understand form and line/and discipline and order and/america."[205]

One of the main revisions Clifton makes to Biblical scripture in the poems of "some jesus" is to cast the language of scripture into Black English. She follows a long tradition. As depicted in the Quran, as Lucille Clifton knew, many of the figures from the Bible, including Hagar and the Queen of Sheba, are Black. The old spiritual songs of Southern Black Americans—themselves haunted by the rhythms of traditional Islamic chanting, as elucidated by scholar Sylviane Diouf in her essay "What Islam Gave the Blues"—made an explicit metaphor of the Hebrew Exodus from Egypt and the plight of enslaved Africans in the American South. Clifton was also following in the footsteps of Zora Neale Hurston, whose novel *Moses, Man of the Mountain*, published in 1939, used Black English to depict the dialog and conversation of the Israelites in Egypt, in contrast with the Standard English spoken by the Egyptian ruling class in that book. Hurston's Moses, occupying a space between the two communities, speaks in both dialects.

Here is the brief poem "daniel" from the beginning of the sequence "some jesus":

> i have learned
> some few things
> like when a man
> walk manly
> he don't stumble
> even in the lion's den[206]

This poem demonstrates both Clifton's affinity and skill with the epigrammatic short form, showing the concision and clarity available in brevity. She also takes the Biblical story of Daniel and applies it to the Black American experience, characterized here as "the lion's den." In this way she is able to take a story that many have heard before and give it freshness and relevance to a contemporary political and social moment.

In the following poem, "jonah," she continues the project, going further by including elements of the African landscape and direct references to slavery and the Middle Passage:

what i remember
is green
in the trees
and the leaves
and the smell of mango
and yams
and if i had a drum
i would send to the brothers
—Be care full of the ocean—[207]

Jonah is already in America at this point, already on the other side of his nautical adventure. Unlike the Biblical Jonah, Clifton's Jonah has not been returned to his starting point; he is on the other side of the Door of No Return. We are told in the King James Bible that the great fish "vomited" out Jonah, and Clifton uses the same verb—as she did in "slaveships"—for the expulsion of African people onto the American shores.[208] Clifton's Jonah here is still exhibiting the same concern Jonah did for the people of Nineveh; though the prophet did not flee voluntarily, he still wishes to warn them of coming danger. Also Unlike Biblical Jonah, Clifton's Jonah does not later question their right to salvation. Clifton's characteristic split of the word "careful" into "care full" intensifies its meaning, but also adds a second dimension: in addition to being wary and aware, they are meant to *have* "care" for one another—care Jonah wishes he had had, or someone had had for him, earlier.

Clifton's poem is also a mournful sequel: the Biblical Book of Jonah has no ending. Or rather, it is more accurate to say, it ends on a cliffhanger. Jonah has been through enormous trials because of his refusal to do God's bidding against the people of Nineveh. Having thus been harried, he now questions God's willingness to forgive without condition the people of Nineveh, whom he former-ly required to repent. In response to Jonah's riposte, God asks Jonah a question:

Then said the LORD, Thou hast had pity on the gourd, for the which thou hast not laboured, neither madest it grow; which came up in a night, and perished in a night:

And should not I spare Nineveh, that great city, wherein are more than six score thousand persons that cannot discern between their right hand and their left hand; and also much cattle?[209]

Jonah does not answer or rather the scripture ends before any answer is given. Perhaps Jonah answered but the verses have been lost to history. Or perhaps it is a place a reader is meant to step into and provide meaning for themselves. Clifton's Jonah, on the other hand, has surmounted his own doubts. He does not question God to learn from whence his trials came, rather he remembers his home, and wishes he had the tool to save his brothers from the same bondage and trial he has endured.

In subsequent poems in the series, Clifton ties the figure to more contemporary moments. John the Baptist, predicting the birth of Jesus, conflates him with Martin Luther King, Jr., when he says, "the world be a great bush/on his head/and his eyes be fire/ in the city/and his mouth be true as time//he be calling the people brother/even in the prison/even in the jail."[210] In both the poem "mary" and the poem "joseph," Clifton sexualizes the relationship between the two figures, complicating the question of whether Jesus' own nature is human or divine. Mary says, "i feel a garden/in my mouth//between my legs/i see a tree," while Joseph talks of his sexual life with Mary, saying:

> when my fingers tremble
> on mary
> my mouth cries only
> Jesus   Jesus   Jesus[211]

Remembering Africa is also a key moment in the poem called "the raising of lazarus." The man that Jesus famously brought back to life does not speak of Jesus in the poem, but rather matter-of-factly believes that his resurrection is natural and is tied rather to the determination of enslaved peoples to remember their homes. His closing sentiments also seem to echo Caroline Donald's determination that her line is safe. Lazarus' stentorious declaration is another version of her "Don't you worry, mister."

the raising of lazarus

the dead shall rise again
whoever say
dust must be dust
don't see the trees
smell rain
remember africa
everything that goes
can come
stand up
even the dead shall rise[212]

It is an interesting poem to compare to its original publication in the collection *good news about the earth*, which like the other volumes Clifton collected in *good woman: poems and a memoir 1969-1980*, was originally stylized in traditional uppercase-lowercase as *Good News About the Earth*. In the original publication of "lazarus," the title was normatively capitalized, and there was a period at the end of the first line, a comma following "dust," another period after the capitalized "Africa," and another period after "come." Perhaps the greatest and most significant alteration is in the last two lines where the original had an exclamation point after the exhortation "stand up" and a period at the concluding line, i.e. "stand up!/even the dead shall rise." The revision makes the closing line feel much more inevitable somehow, and much more in the realm of mystery, less logical, less explainable.

Punctuation and typography became more important to Clifton when she collected the poems of her earlier five books and republished them as *good woman*. She made two very important design decisions that influenced how the poems were seen on the page and received ever after: Firstly, she eliminated most, if not all, punctuation, as well as lowercased nearly every proper noun, including the person pronoun "i" and the word "god" (with few, but notable, exceptions). Even when drafts of the poems are normatively capitalized and punctuated, the final book versions were revised to remove these.

But secondly, and perhaps most impactfully, was the design decision to publish the poems in a san serif font, Optima, which was popular in books for children, and which several of her own books for children published in the seventies used, most notably *All Us Come Cross the Water*. Fred Clifton's single book, the young adult novel *Darl*, also used this font. Clifton continued to use Optima for her books throughout her publishing career. Her posthumous volumes from BOA Editions, her primary publisher, continue to honor this design choice, and in fact, in the *Collected Poems* and her selected poems *How to Carry Water*, only the poems are set in Optima—the introductions and afterwards use different serif fonts, though notably, the quotations of poems therein are also set in Optima. This design highlights the essential role of the sans serif Optima in setting the mood of the poems.

The poet Richard Foerster, who worked as a designer for BOA for many years, including on *The Terrible Stories, Mercy*, and *Voices*, commented that Clifton perhaps opted for the simpler design, "to establish her identity and ground her distinctive voice in this spare, bare-boned font."[213] Hermann Zapf, the designer of the font Optima, wrote of its creation in his book *About Alphabets: Some Marginal Notes on Type Design* (itself set in Optima) that the font had its origins in sketches Zapf had made after inscriptions on the Arch of Constantine and on gravestones in the Santa Croce cemetery in Florence. Of the design, Zapf wrote, "the unserifed forms delighted me by their simple, vigorous forms." He describes the font as "austere," "practical," and "impersonal."[214] All of these qualities heighten the impact of Clifton's own magisterial and highly tuned lyrics; the restraint of the font and minimal punctuation give a cool surface to what are highly passionate, deeply felt poems.

Both "jonah" and "the raising of lazarus" may call to mind the poem "atlantic is a sea of bones." The ocean itself appears in the Jonah story as a bardo space between life (Africa) and death (enslavement). For Lazarus, returning from the dead is seen as liberation, so long as he can "remember africa." Memory is a critical tool as we will see in the later poems "aunt jemima," "uncle ben," and "cream of wheat," which we will discuss in Chapter 9.

In the series "some jesus," it is not until the thirteenth poem that Jesus himself speaks. In "palm sunday" and the two poems that follow it, "good friday" and "easter sunday," we hear from him. As he enters Jerusalem in "palm sunday," the people surround him:

> giving thanks
> glorying in the brother
> laying turnips
> for the mule to walk on
> waving beets
> and collards in the air[215]

The diction in the line "glorying in the brother" gives this entry of Jesus into the city in triumph after the raising of Lazarus a specifically Black context, further reinforced by the greens the people lay in his path. In three of the gospels telling of Jesus' entry into the city, the crowd lays down branches cut from their trees, as well as their own cloaks. In the gospel of John, it is palm leaves laid down in the road, typically used in the Roman Empire to honor conquerors and generals. Here, instead of the martial palm or the cloaks and branches of history, we have the people laying greens in the road, and not only any type of greens, but beet greens and collards, both commonly associated with Black American cuisine.

Jesus speaks again in "good friday":

> i rise up above my self
> like a fish flying
>
> men will be gods
> if they want it[216]

The first couplet of the poem offers an interesting separation between personhood: the one that rises, and the "self" that is risen above. On the one hand this may speak to the dual nature of Jesus in Christian traditions, both human and divine, but it may also speak to more ancient Vedantic traditions, which Lucille Clifton was very familiar with due to Fred Clifton's study of Yoga and Vedanta. In the Vedanta, there is a small individual "self" or *jivatman* which is just a reflection and part of the unifying whole Self, the *Atman*. In this view, what may be happening at the beginning of "good friday" is Jesus transcending the limiting nature of his human form to join with the divine, a notion that is borne out by the second couplet. When Jesus says, "men will be gods/if they want it," Clifton suggests that it is up to the individual human to desire such transformation and to work to make it happen. The passion may be a kind of process that every person can choose to go through in order to achieve spiritual release. She is describing the ancient practice of Yoga.

In Buddhist philosophy, once one has attained enlightenment some choose to remain on the earth among humans as *bodhisattvas* rather than ascend to Buddhahood in order to help others attain enlightenment. Clifton casts Jesus in this role, explaining why he chose to return in the poem "easter sunday." She also attributes this decision to Jesus' understanding of injustice due to racism against Black and Indigenous people, here characterized as "red stars and black stars":

> while i was in the middle of the night
> I saw red stars and black stars
> pushed out of the sky by white ones
> and i knew as sure as jungle
> is the father of the world
> i must slide down like a great dipper of stars
> and lift men up[217]

The opening lines here reflect the closing lines of the poem "the bodies broken on," which appeared earlier in this same collection. In those lines, "the waters pulling white men down/sing for red dust and black clay/good news about the earth."[218] This Jesus uses the jungle as a metaphor, a feature of nearby Africa, but not of the Palestine in which Jesus lived, then or now. Finally, in Jesus' declaration of his mission to save others, Clifton invokes a traditional image of the Black flight to freedom on the Underground Railroad when she refers to the constellation of the Big Dipper, known in the coded Black spiritual of the same name as the Drinking Gourd, meant to remind people fleeing to freedom that they must always continue north.

If the earlier sequence of Biblical poems becomes a way for Clifton to create solidarity among the oppressed Black communities of the United States, her later sequence of poems focusing on Mary are very different. Though they too use a Black dialect—more specifically indo-Caribbean in these later poems—the Mary in them is more ambiguous about the role she has been thrust into, and the people in her life are less invested in this surrendering of her human experience to the large historical role she has, in their view, been condemned to. While these poems are immediate and personal in scope, they are not unrelated to larger social conditions. Magloire sees Clifton's positioning of Mary as a direct counterpoint and reflection of issues and conditions facing Black women in contemporary America:

> Mary's immaculate conception is an ambiguous blessing that could afflict future generations of women, robbing them of their ability to make decisions about their own bodies. Even the purported gift of divine conception cannot be construed as an unambiguous blessing of a fully consensual relationship when it is folded into a long and dark history of medical violence and reproductive injustice directed toward Black women.[219]

The poems begin with Anna, the mother of Mary, herself a saint and important figure in the Bible. Like Sarah, she is childless in old age and prays for a daughter. She appears in the Quran as well, though is not named there (though her traditional Arabized name is "Hana" or "Hannah"). Unlike in the Bible, the Quranic Hana does not give birth in immaculate conception, but more importantly this version of Anna is a mystic who sees the future when her daughter is born. It is this version of the story that forms the basis for the opening poems of the sequence in *The Two-Headed Woman*.

In Clifton's poems, it is not the mother of Mary, but an astrologer who has made predictions at Mary's birth foreseeing both the Incarnation and the Crucifixion: "at a certain time she will hear something/it will burn her ear/at a certain time she will see something/it will break her eye." Upon hearing the news of her daughter's unique fate—and unlike the figures in "some jesus"— Anna's concern is not epic but immediate; it is not communal or social, but local and individual. She does not see the grief of Mary at the death of her son as an event in a grand narrative, and she does not see the girl as the archetypal "Mother of God" or the "Mother of Sorrows," but rather as a simple girl she must protect from the horror she has predicted.

And what is Anna's solution? What can she do to keep this girl from her destiny? In the poem "anna speaks of the child-hood of mary her daughter," Anna says, "work is the medicine/for dreams."[220] She is determined to save the girl from her recurrent dream, and it's important to say that Anna understands her daughter is bound for a position of honor, but one she will only obtain through great personal cost: "she washed in light,/whole world bowed to its knees,/she on a hill looking up,/face all long tears." Clifton, while writing in Black Caribbean dialect, is using full and grammatical punctuation here. In some way this eliminates the stark and stentorian distance the lack of normative punctuation engendered in "the raising of lazarus." By including the punctuation of commas and semi-colons and question marks, she brings the story of Anna out of scripture, the formality of declaration, and into the ordinary and every day.

Rather than seeing Mary's future role as heroic or magical or beautiful or sanctified, Anna sees it for what it is: a mother losing her son. It is a tragedy she is determined to prevent from happening, but of course she has no resources, not even the ability to prophe-size a different future. So she digs in with the only tool she has:

and shall i give her up
to dreaming then? i fight this thing.
all day we scrubbing   scrubbing.

And here you see something you will see over and over again in Lucille Clifton's system of spirituality—not a results-oriented spirituality meant to earn you heaven or hell, but rather a spiritual system that is an ongoing practice of living in the world, one that is connected intimately to social and material conditions of people in their own lived lives. Anna is not asking big questions about where her visions are coming from, or the nature of God or what happens next. She is dealing very practically with what is right in front of her. The poem assumes tragic dimension because we, the readers, know precisely what is going to happen. We know Anna will fail.

Mary's agreement to the angels' offer, and the birth of Jesus itself, are both somewhat anti-climactic: "yes," she says simply, while the holy infant is described as "a pot turned on the straw," and as "a loaf/a poor baker sets in the haystack to cool," while the amorous Joseph of "some jesus" has become here merely "an old man/dressed like a father."[221] These poems depict the figures as ordinary people, not legendary or mythic as did the earlier poems, and the cycle skips over the main events of Jesus' life entirely, instead focusing on Mary's own life. From the birth the poems go straight to showing Mary as an old woman. She muses about her own childhood, longing for an ordinary life, "princes sitting on thrones in the east/.../joseph carving a table somewhere."[222] In the end, after her own too-eventful life, she is occupied with worry for "another young girl asleep/in the plain evening," hoping her fate will not befall anyone else.[223]

The final poem takes place, seemingly, at the Assumption, and borrows the form of the "Hail Mary" prayer. In this poem, Mary's traditional title of "Mother of God" is replaced by the not-quite-pleasant "mary astonished by God" and she is called by the name 'Marinka,' an African version of Mary's Arabic name Maryam. She is "split" by the seed of God and condemned to the role of "mother for ever and ever." Her fate is not seen as desirable and affection of the saints is called "awe full," splitting the word "awful" as in Jonah's earlier poem combining the meanings of both "awe-full" and "awful" into one:

> mary   mary astonished by God
> on a straw bed circled by beasts
> and an old husband. mary marinka
> holy woman split by sanctified seed
> into mother and mother for ever and ever
> we pray for you sister woman shook by the
> awe full affection of the saints.[224]

While the Anna we see here is committed to working against preordination, the Mary of these poems is a little more passive, observing and commenting. Both women are reluctant participants in their story. It is a reluctance continued in the poem "the light that came to lucille clifton," which immediately precedes the section of that title that concludes *two-headed woman*. In this prefatory poem, Lucille Clifton receives visitations that only come after "she understood that she had not understood/and was not mistress even/of her own off eye."[225] It is, perhaps, a common approach to spiritual knowledge: similar to the poetic notion of "negative capability," one must first arrive at ignorance in order to learn. In the Vedanta, it is the reason why Nataraj, the Dancing Shiva, can never slay the demon of ignorance—Apasmara must remain alive so that people can continue to overcome him and attain knowledge.

Clifton closes her eyes and is afraid to look, and then, as "a voice from the nondead past started talking," she tries not to listen. The voice, undeterred, spells out in her hand, "'you might as well answer the door, my child,/the truth is furiously knocking.'" What follows are nine poems.

Clifton begins the sequence with the same words that open the Gospel of John, "in the beginning/was the word," consciously placing her own text in the lineage of revelations. Though the spirits speaking to her speak in plural—"lucille/we are/the Light"—when Lucille Clifton answers, she speaks directly to one being, Thelma Sayles, saying, "mother, i am mad./we should have guessed/a twelve-fingered flower/might break."[226] She is ready to receive, saying, "i have managed to unlearn/my lessons." The mind, an "obvious assassin//the terrorist of voices," tells "miraculous lies."[227] It is not received wisdom taught by others that Clifton puts her trust in here, but in the knowledge she herself by intuition and self-reflection can obtain.

She writes to another visionary, Joan of Arc, in the poem "to joan." She asks Joan if when she heard voices, "did you never hear/ in the soft rushes of france/merely the whisper of french grass/.../ sounding now like a windsong/now like a man?"[228] She wants to know how and when Joan came to believe she was truly being visited by something of a different order. It's a question any spiritual person has asked themselves, or ought to have anyhow: how much of this is real? How much am I making up?

In the end, there's no conclusion. The matter is left open-ended. She turns not to a mother figure but to a father, saying, "i am not equal to the faith required,/i doubt "[229] Rather than the metaphysical world of the spirit, or the concepts of original sin or an afterlife, she has only "a woman's certainties;/bodies pulled from me,/pushed into me./bone flesh is what i know." There is no answering, no processing of any revelation, but an acknowledgment of the presence of ancestors "in populated air" present and singing. But if there is a revelation in "the light that came to lucille clifton" it is merely that. The poet makes no further claim to knowledge or wisdom, which is—as we have seen and understood—the beginning of both.

This hard-won insight is in stark contrast to attainment of knowledge in the foundational story of the Garden of Eden. There, of course, "knowledge" arrives in a lightning flash and it is easy: partake of the fruit, gain forbidden knowledge. The act also has immediate consequences: expulsion. While Clifton wrote a long sequence on the events in the garden in "the tree of life," published in 1991's Quilting, Adam and Eve are the subjects of several earlier poems as well. Of Adam, Clifton thinks little; she gives pride of place to Eve. In one poem she refers to "eve and her brother,"[230] while in another she refers to herself as "adam and his mother."[231] Although Adam and Eve are given their traditional roles in the first poem in which they appear (called "adam and eve," the opening poem of "some jesus") in later poems, it is always Eve who has done the naming. In the poem, "the birth of language," which appears earlier in the same book as "tree of life," Adam does name Eve herself, but under grave duress, described as being "fearful" and in a state of "astonishment." Only after the blades of grass in the garden draw blood on his tongue when he tries to eat them, "did he shudder/did he whisper/eve."[232]

In the ten poems of "the tree of life," the angels speak in chorus three times, Eve speaks twice, Adam once, and Lucifer, the hero of this story, or anti-hero as it were, speaks only once at the sequence's end. The other three poems, "lucifer understanding at last," "the garden of delight," and "the story thus far," are in an omniscient narrative voice. Lucifer, from the beginning, is a heroic figure, believed so by others precisely because he has defied God. In the original notes to the poem "brothers" from the *The Book of Light* (the notes are not included in the *Collected Poems*), Lucille discusses the Sufi interpretation of Lucifer's fall. God commanded Lucifer to bow to no one but Him. When Lucifer later refuses to bow to Adam, it is not because he was created out of fire and Adam of clay, but because he is being faithful to God's original command. He is called Iblis in the Quran, which has traditionally been understood to mean "The Despairing One," but some Sufi teachers say he despairs because God's command confused him. Clifton points out that Milton was apparently familiar with this Sufi interpretation of the fall of Lucifer when he wrote *Paradise Lost*.

As evidenced by Clifton's previous references, she sees Adam as more a passive participant in this most significant story— that of the end of union between human and divine, and the beginning of humans living with individual agency and responsibility. Taking a page from Milton's book, it is Lucifer who is the hinge between the human and the divine, and Lucifer—along with Eve— who becomes the character faced with the dramatic choices which drive all the action. Lucifer, as a mythological figure, also predates both Adam and Eve by millennia. Lucifer's ancient and pre-Christian roots are invoked at the beginning of the first poem of "tree of life" when the angels call him "son of morning" and "bringer of light," epithets that belong to both the Greek titan Prometheus who brought humans fire, and also to one of the two gods associated by the Greeks with the planet Venus: Phosphorus. Phosphorus' name, in Greek Φωσφόρος, meaning "bearer of light," was translated into Latin as "Lucifer."[233]

A brief aside: the second god associated with the planet Venus was Hesperus, bearer of darkness. There were two gods because the ancient Greek astronomers thought there were two different planets, one which rose in the morning and another which rose in the evening. It took half a millennium before Babylonian astronomers disabused them of the notion, showing them there was only one planet which could be seen in the sky at different times.

Lucifer's fall from Heaven into Hell manifested in various ways across ancient Mediterranean cultures, and may have come about first in Babylonian and Sumerian times in the tales of the goddesses Inana and Ishtar, both of whom also fell from heaven into the underworld. It reappears in Greek mythology, somewhat later conflated with the crucifixion of Jesus, when Prometheus is seized by the King of Heaven and punished for giving humans fire. He is bound to a mountain and an eagle comes down every night to tear out his liver. This ritual act is refracted in the Gospels into the story of the Roman guard at Gethsemane who wounds the torso of Jesus with his spear. Of course, Jesus had a more direct antecedent in Greek mythology than Prometheus: the god Dionysus wore a crown of thorns and his followers tore him apart each spring in order to eat his flesh and drink his blood; by doing so they hoped to be cleansed of their own sins. Not to worry, three days later, without fail, Dionysus would reappear whole and alive, ready to continue the party.

In the opening poem of "the tree of life," the angels left alone in heaven are mourning the departure of Lucifer to the garden. "[I]t is all shadow/in heaven without you," they sing, speaking to his central role among them.[234] Another figure is present of course, God, and he is described by Clifton in a curious appellation as "the solitary brother." By making Him a "brother," Clifton creates Him as equal to the angels, and, more importantly, equal to Lucifer, an appellation she will extend in her later poem about God and Lucifer, called "brothers." The "solitary brother" sits on a "seat/of stones   he is holding/they say   a   wooden stick/and pointing toward/a garden." The "they say" is interesting here, because it brings external viewers into the scene: later viewers and interpreters. One could imagine Clifton means the "they" to be readers of scripture, which naturally includes "us," the readers of this very poem. The angels are aware they will be written about.

What Lucifer does in the garden is not shown, but we do see that "light breaks/where no light was before/where no eye is prepared/to see."[235] The wording here is very reminiscent of the earlier poem (published more than a decade before) about Mary: that she will see something that will "break her eye." This is the critical issue: that humans—Mary, Eve, others—were unprepared to see, unprepared to know, that knowledge itself is dangerous. In fact, the normal interpretation of the Eden myth is that knowledge, carnal knowledge, is a sin. It's a concept agreed upon in multiple cultures: the Greek Semele, mother of Dionysus, spontaneously combusts when Zeus reveals his true face to her; Arjun of the Pandavas has a very close encounter, indeed with his sanity hanging in the balance, when the god Krishna, after much inveigling by Arjun, reveals his true form to the prince. Pip, the cabin boy of the Pequod in Melville's *Moby-Dick,* loses his own sanity after a day and night on the open water, clinging to a life boat, because in his vision of the endless horizon he has seen "God's foot on the loom" of Creation.

As Mary's birth and Jesus' birth each gives significance to their lives, Clifton next tells of Lucifer's birth, and as Eve was fashioned from Adam's rib, Lucifer breaks off "from the littlest finger/ of God" (which image calls to mind, of course, Clifton's own littlest magical fingers broken off by surgeon's scalpel) with a "flash of light" and a "bright shimmer" and a "flush in the tremble of air."[236] Lucifer is given the epithet "six-finger," [237] which further links him to the polydactyl Clifton and her previously mentioned "off eye."[238] Without Lucifer in heaven, the angels feel "less radiant" in "perpetual evening." Heaven is less heaven without its most dangerous shining bad boy Lucifer.

After this chorus of angels speaking, and before the entry of our romantic lead, Eve speaks. She is not worried, but intrigued. The "smooth talker/slides into my dreams/and fills them." She describes the apple as "snug as my breast/in the palm of my hand" and one must cheekily imagine the circumstance in which a woman's breast is snug in the palm of her hand while she is lying in bed. The apple itself is described in a simple yet sensual line, "apple sleek apple sweet" and then, in an echo of the "flush" in the air at Lucifer's birth, he reminds Eve that her real hunger is for her "own lush self."[239] We will talk later on in Chapter 8 about Clifton's fondness for using the triple heavy stress for heightened dramatic impact, but one can pause and see it used effectively here, linking Eve's possession of the apple with self-love.

Lucifer's activity in the garden is described in the poem "lucifer understanding at last":

thy servant lord

bearer of lightning
and of lust

thrust between the
legs of the earth
into this garden

phallus and father
doing holy work

oh sweet delight
oh eden

if the angels
hear of this

there will be no peace
in heaven[240]

Lucifer is addressed in the poem as "servant lord" implying that in the moment he has both roles, and his traditional epithet of "light bringer" is expanded when he called the "bearer of lightning/and of lust." What follows seems to reference Mary in the earlier poem looking between her legs and seeing the tree, a phallic symbol of both God impregnating her, but also the tree in the garden at the beginning of the end of things, or at the end of the beginning, depending on your point of view. Regardless, what happens in the garden next—a scene of conceptual copulation between Eve and Lucifer—is considered "holy work." The reader is left to imagine what it might mean for the other angels to discover what has happened: will they too revolt in order to experience this bodily human pleasure?

Clifton presents the drama in the garden of Eden without traditional morality, but rather as an allegory about both the price and reward of knowledge. In the following poem, "the garden of delight," she presents the various versions of Eden that haunt the human race, which has been sent forth from it. The departure of humans from the garden is not really presented as an expulsion. Some people think of "Eden"—a figure for Heaven itself, at any rate—as "stone/bare smooth/as a buttock" while others imagine it "extravagant/water," some merely thinking of "fire" or "air." It is telling that Clifton imagines both a Muslim conception of Heaven (with its rivers and islands; a suitable Heaven for a desert-bound people) and also what is normally thought of as actual "Hell"—"fire"—as a form of Heaven for some. Others, she says, "certain only of the syllables," search for "heaven" their whole lives, not knowing what they are really searching for. For all of these people that Clifton cites, she seems to believe, it is the searching that is the test.[241]

Adam and Eve each speak in the following poems. Adam, consistent with earlier appearances, and like the Sufi Lucifer, is confused, even perhaps in despair. He refers to Eve as being "stolen from my bone" and he experiences some kind of psychological trauma from this loss, wanting to "tunnel back/inside" and "reconnect the rib and clay/and to be whole again."[242] He is unable to formulate the words to name things—his primary task—and has no access to acts of creation, which women have mastered. Rather than be the "first man" he wishes instead he could have been "born," i.e. come from a woman and be mothered.

In Clifton's earliest poem about Adam, "adam and eve," Adam says, "the names/of the things/bloom in my mouth."[243] Later, in the poem "the birth of language," Adam finally does whisper "eve,"(while shuddering, whether in pleasure or effort we are not told), but does not speak of naming anything else.[244] It is not until the poem "eve thinking" that Eve takes credit for giving things their names, describing the moment thus:

> i wait
> while the clay two-foot
> rumbles in his chest
> searching for language to
>
> call me
> but he is slow
> tonight as he sleeps
> i will whisper into his mouth
> our names[245]

Adam is crudely described as a "clay two foot" here, and "slow" besides. Eve takes decisive action, as she does in the following poem, "the story thus far," which describes the actual expulsion, again not feeling as dramatic an event as normally framed. The two, Adam and Lucifer, are described as "clay and morning star" and they are following Eve's "bright back" as she leaves the garden and walks in the world, "unborn" as Adam was. The cherubim are present with their requisite fiery swords at the gate, but Eve barely notices them as she leaves. In fact, once she leaves the garden, "chaos fell away/.../and everywhere seemed light."[246] For Eve, it is the external world, and not the garden, that "seems very eden."

Finally, at the close of the sequence, Lucifer speaks. It is a defense of sorts, but a defiant one. I have often recited this poem, and eventually from memory; and in the way that memory warps, in my mind the title has always been "lucifer speaks in his own voice at last" which is not, in fact, the actual title of the poem:

lucifer speaks in his own voice

sure as i am
of the seraphim
folding wing
so am i certain of a
graceful bed
and a soft caress
along my long belly
at endtime   it was
to be
i who was called son
if only of the morning
saw that some must
walk or all will crawl
so slithered into earth
and seized the serpent in
the animals   i became
the lord of snake for
adam and for eve
i   the only lucifer
light-bringer
created out of fire
illuminate i could
and so
illuminate i did[247]

The opening lines of the poem are sinuous and rhythmic; their music is both pulsing and calming; they are nearly hypnotic like the movements of a snake. There is a pause and accusation when he says "it was/to be/i who was called son" hinting at his continuing resentment and jealousy of Adam and prefiguring the arrival of the *other* "Son" of God (yet another brother for Lucifer), though he does recognize he would be son "only of the morning," a wink to his previous life as the ancient morning star.

Like Prometheus, he cites the welfare of both Adam and Eve as his motivations, and his actions in line with Prometheus was well—to bring fire and light and life to humans, associating (as Eve did in the previous poem) Eden and life with God as darkness or occlusion. He invokes his own name, referring to himself as "the only lucifer/light-bringer," becoming in Clifton's mind a figure of illumination and liberation, though, of course, as she notes in the poem "evening and my dead once husband," such an independent life comes with mortality and its attendant disasters, "cancer and terrible loneliness/and the wars against our people."[248]

We, as readers in history, know the ending: that humans were indeed unprepared for Lucifer's gift, that the other "son" would have to appear and complete the task and close the circle.

Clifton revisits the aftermath of both of these tales—that of Lucifer and that of Jesus—in her sequence "brothers," which imagines an aged Lucifer and God having a conversation. The time is given as "long after," meaning perhaps in the present day or some mythical time in the future. The epigraph of the poem makes clear that "only Lucifer is heard," but the implication in the text of the poem itself is not that God is speaking but the reader does not hear Him, but rather that God *does not answer*. As the poems progress, Lucifer becomes aware of, and then agitated by, God's silence and tries to wrestle with the implications and meanings of that silence.

Clifton's conception of Lucifer and God is radical for more than one reason. Rather than Lucifer being the only "adversary," both are imagined as stubborn old "brothers," (as in the opening poem of "tree of life"), i.e. they are presented as equals in agency and understanding. Each is part of the other, though it is Lucifer who is in the position of supplicant, the younger brother, cast out of Heaven, excluded from God's company. Clifton's Lucifer here is neither "Satan" nor "devil" and this Lucifer even believes himself at times—perhaps his ongoing "sin"—to be superior to God, but for the most interesting of reasons: that God turned his back on Creation when he expelled Adam and Eve, while Lucifer accompanied them into exile.

This type of interrogation or revision—one could think of it as "wrestling with the angel" perhaps—is central to contemplative traditions in all major religions and spiritual traditions, where the text in question is meant to be wrangled with, argued over, and explored in order to yield its meaning. Contrast this with most mainstream orthodoxy in which a story is received, and its meanings are all known and agreed upon by the followers of any particular tradition. In the vein of the more contemplative tradition, Clifton's Lucifer begins with an invitation to his brother to reflection and discourse:

> come coil with me
> here in creation's bed
> among the twigs and ribbons
> of the past.[249]

This Lucifer imagines that God is not quite omniscient in a traditional sense, but that the two are equal "participants" in the act of Creation, entitled to rest together:

> like two old brothers
> who watched it happen and wondered
> what it meant.

When Lucifer refers to himself and God together, the pronouns ("we," "us") are lowercase, but when he addresses God alone the pronoun is uppercase, uncommon in Clifton, as we have come to know, making God even more lonely and distant and distinct, separated through this not-altogether pleasant mark of respect. Indeed, when Lucifer is not answered he grows a little tart, saying to God:

> listen, You are beyond
> even Your own understanding.
> that rib and rain and clay
> in all its pride,
> its unsteady dominion,
> is not what You believed
> You were,
> but it is what You are;

in Your own image as some
lexicographer supposed.
the face, both he and she,
the odd ambition, the desire
to reach beyond the stars
is You. all You, all You
the loneliness, the perfect
imperfection.[250]

Clifton moves past mainstream ideas about divinity into a realm where it is possible for the divine to misunderstand not only humankind, but itself. It is Lucifer who has to explain to God that He is not separate from what he created ("rib and rain and clay"), and that the very notion of human failing—"both he and she,/the odd ambition, the desire/to reach beyond the stars/.../the loneliness, the perfect/imperfection"—is an essential part of God Himself. And curiously, by implication, this God does not know Himself.

In "brothers," Lucifer further challenges God, declaring the distinctiveness his separation has offered both him and Eve, intimating God's jealousy:

as sure as she,
the breast of Yourself
separated out and made to bear,
as sure as her returning,
i too am blessed with
the one gift you cherish;
to feel the living move in me
and to be unafraid.[251]

When Lucifer talks of his actual superiority, the unchanging God (for the first—but not the last—time in the poem) becomes lowercase. Clifton uses Eve, even Jesus ("he returning") as examples of what is possible in a sacred world. She, through Lucifer, rescues (rehabilitates?) femininity and womanhood (through "bearing children") as an elevated spiritual position. Of course, that final image of the "living move in me" is also a form of threat when you are talking to a serpent: when a snake feels something living move in them, they may be talking about being stirred to life by deep emotion, but it is equally possible that what they feel moving in them is something they have just devoured.

In Section 4 of "brothers," called "in my own defense," Lucifer casts God as a lowercase parent and asks:

> what could i choose
> but to slide along behind them,
> they whose only sin
> was being their father's children?[252]

Here we see that Lucifer *chooses* his exile. His true "sin" is the exercising of free will, but with such choice comes the very human possibility of redemption:

> as they stood with their backs
> to the garden,
> a new and terrible luster
> burning their eyes,
> only You could have called
> their ineffable names,
> only in their fever
> could they have failed to hear.[253]

Lucifer blames God here for not calling out to his children, but says further, "only in their fever/could they have failed to hear." It is an odd construction, because even though Lucifer has just accused God of not speaking, the grammar of the second clause implies that he did call out but that those departing the garden did not hear him. It is possible therefore that it is God's silence that the humans cannot yet read. The choice between the fallen humans and the silent God is clear to Lucifer: only through the experience of separation can he truly experience understanding and union. He exits the garden.

In the new world, Clifton's Lucifer never makes his transformation into Satan, the "Great Adversary," he of the red skin and cloven hooves, horns protruding from his head. He remains an angel, entranced with pleasure ("vale of sheet and sweat after love") but aware that it is all a part of "the outer world," separated from the spiritual:

> ...the sharp
> edge of seasons, into the sweet
> puff of bread baking, the warm
> vale of sheet and sweat after love,
> the tinny newborn cry of calf
> and cormorant and humankind.
> and pain, of course,
> always there was some bleeding,
> but forbid me not
> my meditation on the outer world
> before the rest of it, before
> the bruising of his heel, my head,
> and so forth.[254]

Even though Lucifer meditates here on "delight," the poem ends with his grim foreshadowing of his end at the metaphorical hands of Jesus, mentioned only the one other time in the poem ("the bruising of his heel, my head,/and so forth"). Having engaged with the materials of the world, the pleasures of being alive, sex, the passing of time, "the sweet/puff of bread baking," Lucifer is compelled to ask: why does God allow suffering?

Lucifer's assault on the very nature of God, in section 6 of "brothers," is scathingly titled "the silence of God is God." Clifton sources it as a quote from Carolyn Forché's *The Angel of History*, but, in fact, Forché herself is quoting Elie Wiesel, who in *The Time of the Uprooted* wrote, "A Jewish writer said that 'the silence of God is God.' I say that God is not silent, although He is the God of Silence. He does call out. It is by His silence that He calls to you. Are you answering him?" Who was Wiesel himself quoting, I asked Forché once. She recounted to me that she had herself asked Wiesel that question and that Wiesel could not at that moment then recall.

Though Clifton attributes the quote to Forché, rather than Wiesel, Clifton does appear to be familiar with the full Wiesel quote, as Wiesel's admonition about God's supposed silence neatly answers the question in the previous poem of whether or not God called out and also addresses Lucifer's agitation in the single-sentence rant-like poem:

> tell me, tell us why
> in the confusion of a mountain
> of babies stacked like cordwood,
> of limbs walking away from each other,
> of tongues bitten through
> by the language of assault,
> tell me, tell us why
> You neither raised Your hand
> nor turned away, tell us why
> You watched the excommunication of
> that world and You said nothing.[255]

No question mark is used, though the sentence is in fact a question. Lucifer is in full-blown accusatory mode, and at last understands that God is not going to answer him. This knowledge allows him to finally touch the depth of his despair. Lucifer understands now that the language of questions and answers, the concept of God needing to justify Creation, is part of the separation, part of the exile itself. And this is the critical question, the one that any person of faith would have in the brutal twentieth century—a century no less brutal than the nineteenth or seventeenth or seventh in its intentions and motivations, but much more efficient, whether one thinks of the atom bomb (only ever deployed by one single nation—and *twice*, for good measure, one supposes), or the various genocides and wars that have raged.

Humans may ask many questions of themselves: Who are we? What are we doing here? What happens after death? But to God there is always, in the end, always ever only one: why? Lucifer is not—will never be—given answers of any kind. It occurs to him that the very fact of his existence, not just having fallen, but actually having been able to fall, is a form of grace:

> how otherwise
> could i have come to this
> marble spinning in space
> propelled by the great
> thumb of the universe?
> how otherwise
> could the two roads
> of this tongue
> converge into a single
> certitude?[256]

His split tongue that manages to both adore and decry his absent brother is a form of proof somehow. He also comes to terms with his role and relationship to his brother, rejoicing that he might.

> a sleek old
> traveler,
> curl one day safe and still
> beside You
> at Your feet, perhaps,
> but, amen, Yours.[257]

Clifton has spoken of finding the "Lucifer in Lucille," the petty part of us, the selfish part, the frightened part. Knowing those parts to exist, she reasoned, "There must be a Lucille in Lucifer."[258] This stand makes "brothers" the story of an individual's journey in search of integration.

The final section of "brothers" has the playful title ". . . . . is God," implying that there is a silence even beyond silence. Lucifer understands that God does speak, but in a million splintered tongues—including, he is shocked to realize, his own:

> so.
> having no need to speak

You sent Your tongue
splintered into angels.
even i,
with my little piece of it
have said too much.
to ask You to explain
is to deny You.
before the word
You were.
You kiss my brother mouth.
the rest is silence.[259]

In the opening conversational—and forgiving—"so," one is reminded of the opening of the final chapter in *generations:* "Well." There is a resignation in knowing that there will never be an answer. The sin is not in questioning God, but rather in seeing God as separate, as something to be questioned at all. If God is eternal then He must be internal, Lucille and Lucifer both suppose when they say, "to ask You to explain/is to deny You."

And if we are essentially alone and also essentially together, one, then there is nothing to ask, no one else that will speak back. "Brothers" closes without answering any of these questions, closes in fact with a sweet moment of ultimate chaste intimacy between siblings—a kiss on the mouth—which requires silence.

As Clifton used Biblical figures to explore larger social issues connected to spirituality in the poems of "some jesus," and looked at more personal dramas in the Mary poems, she combines both approaches in the sequence "from the Book of David," which appeared in *The Terrible Stories.* This phrase "from the" in the title allows Clifton to enter into the story of a figure who not only has spiritual importance as the traditional author of the Psalms, but also political importance as a historical king of Jerusalem whose myth and history has contemporary and materially immediate resonance to political realities in Israel to this day.

Clifton's David is neither warrior nor nation-builder, but an older David, vain and paranoid and full of lust and regret. Such a flawed figure proves a rich character for Clifton; she retains sympathy for her tragic hero, who, after a lifetime of violence and misdeeds, still wants to be loved by his people, and by God. In the opening poem "dancer," David is looking back on his forty-year reign, knowing that it was but precursor for what was to come. Like John the Baptist in the earlier "some jesus" poems, David imagines the coming of Jesus, "something to do with/virgins and with stars."[260] Interestingly, like Mary in the poem "Island Mary," he refers to the coming event as a "choosing." It is not clear who is choosing, the spirit yet to come, the people who await them, or the God who sends them forth. David is filled with questions: of the eleven poems in the sequence, four of them end in questions and of these four, only one is rhetorical.

As an old man, David looks back on his life, wondering whether his deeds will be remembered as more important than his own complicated life as a human with human feelings and emotions. "What matters to time," David wonders, "the dancer or the dance?"[261] The reader knows the answer. History will mostly forgive David his crimes, and in time, his exploits, even the bloody ones, will become praise-worthy.

The story of David in the Bible is action-packed: it has battle scenes—both epic clashes of whole armies as well as thrilling individual duels—as well as politics and espionage of the royal court, it has romance, love, and betrayal, and there's even a ghost or two whispering in the night. As with the earlier poems, the poems of Clifton's sequence do not have much narrative armature explaining the plot; Clifton assumes some familiarity with the scriptural stories on behalf of her reader and true to the "from the" in the title, she provides snapshots of individual episodes and does not try to build a narrative arc, as happened in "tree of life," nor even a dramatic arc as happened in "brothers." In place of such a structure, she creates a more collage-like assemblage of episodes from David's own reflections told out of chronological sequence. David, who has become King of Israel by killing other claimants, has to contend with pretenders to his own throne. In the poem "david has slain his ten thousands," the battle-weary king wonders what it is that God loves about him, "my wrath or my regret?"[262]

David, beloved by the people and betrothed to the daughter of Saul, the first king of Israel, fled his father-in-law's court after the old king became jealous and determined to do away with him. After much conflict, David finally reconciled with Saul by stealing into his tent one night during a battle and leaving his spear there to prove to the old king that he could have killed him. When he comes upon the man, Clifton writes, "in battle/.../we have become/ enemies//yet here/he is an old man/sleeping/or my father."[263] By sparing him, David remembers his old self a little, the writer of the psalms not a soldier, a poet rather than a killer.

In other poems, Clifton tells of David's disastrous love for Bathsheba—"whether i loved her/i could not say but/i wanted her"[264]—as well as the death of his son Absalom in a rebellion—"if you had stayed/i feared you would kill me/if you left i feared you would die."[265] At the end of this poem David asks, "what does the Lord require." The word Lord is capitalized, as Clifton often does when the deity in question is remote or removed or unconcerned with human tragedies, and the question has no punctuation: it is not a question David expects any answer to.

Goliath, David's most famous enemy, does not make an appearance until the penultimate poem, and even there he is not named. David is recounting the main themes of his life, reciting the names of five stones he gathered, one for each of them— hunger, faith, lyric, passion, and regret. Only the first did he use to slay the "giant," the others he "fastened under my tongue/for later   for her   for israel."[266] In the end, it was for his people that David acted as he did, even when he was being selfish. It is Bathsheba's son, Solomon, that he names as his heir, and not Saul's daughter Michal's son. David still seeks some answer from God or his fellow man. As conflicted as Lucifer from "brothers," though King of Israel, David is still that "unshorn shepherd boy" wanting to "love himself,/be loved," but knowing not how he could be, standing, as he is, "in the tents of history/bloody skull in one hand, harp in the other?"[267]

David's regret is different than Lucifer's. Lucifer, though fallen, finds some measure of acceptance in God's silence, and still speaks to God as a brother and finally, friend. David, on the other hand, human and troubled, is left with only his questions; questions made ever more relevant as the modern history of his country unfolds.

Chapter 7: The Picture Show

The stories Clifton drew from in her poetry were not only from myth or history or scripture, but also from the popular culture all around her. She wrote poems based on characters from comic books and movies, and even a set of poems based on the Black personae used to advertised various American grocery products such as maple syrup, rice, and breakfast cereal. In these poems, Lucille Clifton's sense of humor comes through, used to particularly painful effect when thinking about the legacies of slavery and the unhoming of African people. She always wanted to speak to as broad an audience as possible and her writing for children is ample demonstration that even when she wrote in a popular form or aiming to reach a wide audience, she never surrendered complexity or depth.

One poem we discussed earlier in the book, "whose side are you on?," has a kind of counterpoint in the poem "them and us." This poem also takes place on a late night public transit ride:

them and us

something in their psyche insists on elvis
slouching into markets, his great collar
high around his great head, his sideburns
extravagant, elvis, still swiveling those
negro hips. something needs to know

that even death, the most faithful manager
can be persuaded to give way

before real talent, that it is possible
to triumph forever on a timeless stage
surrounded by lovers giving the kid a hand.

we have so many gone. history
has taught us much about fame and its
inevitable tomorrow. we ride the subways
home from the picture show, sure about
death and elvis, but watching for marvin gaye.[268]

Here Clifton playfully invokes a classic 1980s tabloid newspaper headline staple, the "Elvis sighting": Elvis Presley, alive and
well, spotted at a local supermarket! Both the 1980s supermarket
tabloid and the Meryl Streep film *Death Becomes Her*, along with
many other 1980s cultural products, had references to Elvis' longev-
ity, spurred on by conspiracy theories about his gravestone which
misspells his middle name by one vowel. Clifton also slyly critiques
Presley's appropriation of Black music, fashion, and choreographic
style when she references "those/negro hips." The sharp distinction Clifton makes between "them" and "us" is similar to the one
made in "whose side are you on?" In this case, "something in their
psyche" wants to know that "even death" is conquerable, while
"we" are "sure about death."

The distinction quivers a little bit because even Clifton's
"we" is still hopeful, hoping against what knowledge history has
already taught. Despite being sure that Elvis is dead, at the end of
the poem, "we" are still "watching for marvin gaye."

Gaye died at nearly the same age as Elvis, and in curious
coincidence with Lucille Clifton's ancestor Lucy Sale, also added a
letter, the "e," to his birth surname, Gay, to distinguish himself from
the people he inherited the name from, in his case—unlike Lucy
Sale's—his own biological family. Legendary as a singer, he came
from a complicated family home in which his father had a long
history of violence and abuse. At the time of his death, Gaye was
living with both parents, sharing a bedroom with his mother, while
his father lived in another bedroom of the house. At the culmination
of a series of arguments over several days, Gaye was shot and killed

by his father during a physical altercation. The gun Gay used to kill Gaye was one his son had given him as a gift. Clifton uses the image of riding a subway home from the "picture show" to demonstrate that though the Black community has become intimately familiar with both social and domestic violence, she still remains painfully optimistic about the future. The complicating factors in Gaye's life (and his death) are not described by Clifton, but one is left hoping for him the same image that Clifton used to describe the vision of Elvis from "them and us": "it is possible/to triumph forever on a timeless stage/surrounded by lovers."

In four poems from *The Book of Light* Clifton uses the form of notes passed from a secret admirer, Clifton, to the object of her affections, in this case Clark Kent, the mild-mannered reporter who is secretly the Kryptonian superhero Kal-El, better known as Superman. These flights-of-fantasy exploring a young comic lover's loneliness and desire for love are made more powerful by their sequencing. the first two poems "if i should" and "further note to clark" appear followed by four poems about Clifton's parents and the abuse she suffered at her father's hands—"begin here," "night vision," "fury," and "cigarettes"—and then appear the two poems "final note to clark" and "note, passed to superman." The positioning of the painful poems about Clifton's childhood and family life in the midst of poems populated by characters like Kent, Lois Lane, and Wonder Woman calls to attention the necessary and healing escape that the comic books of her youth must have been for the "small imploding girl."[269]

The poem "if i should" is actually the origin point for the honesty in the poems about her father and mother that follow. She asks Clark Kent—secretly Superman, but always striving to hide that fact from the people around him—what would happen if she should tell the truth about her life. She refers first to the "darkest room" and wonders what will happen if she would "speak/with my own voice, at last" about "the randy/father" and "the mother bleeding into herself."[270] Clifton is girding herself for acting without any hero to come flying down and rescue her. She already knows that such a hero will not come.

The following poem "further note to clark" does not draw from the comics, but rather from the theatrical version of the film *Superman II*, which was released in 1980. In it, Lois Lane and Clark Kent (played with comics-worthy panache by Margot Kidder and Christopher Reeve) are sent undercover to Niagara Falls, posing as a married couple on their honeymoon. While investigating a case, a child falls and is rescued by Superman. Due to this odd coincidence, Lane finally wises up and puts it together that her bumbling partner has a secret identity. When he refuses to confirm her suspicion, she calls his bluff by jumping off a railing into the rapids rushing for the edge of her falls, daring him to rescue her. Even with Lane in grave danger, Kent refuses to reveal himself and manages to save her by surreptitiously using his heat vision to drop a branch into the river for her to grab. Lane is humiliated, though Kent eventually does confess his secret to her.

Clifton's poem plumbs an element of the encounter left unexplored by the film: Lane's feelings of betrayal that Kent was unable to be vulnerable enough with her to trust her with the truth. The poem's epigraph is a not precisely accurate quote from the original *Superman* film where Lois explores her feelings for Superman; here the epigraph imagines Lane trying to explain to Kent how difficult it is to bear the secret she has been asked to keep:

further note to clark

> *do you know how hard this is for me?*
> *do you know what you're asking?*

what i can promise to be is water,
water plain and direct as Niagara.
unsparing of myself, unsparing of
the cliff i batter, but also unsparing
of you, tourist. the question for me is
how long can i cling to this edge?
the question for you is
what have you ever traveled toward
more than your own safety?[271]

The poem's insistent questioning is heightened by a predominant pattern of a trochaic-dactylic tetrameter, with unstressed syllables beginning many of the lines. Trochaic (two syllables in one unit of rhythm, called a "foot" in prosody) and dactylic (three syllables in one foot) meters have their heavy stresses at the beginning of the word, as opposed to the most commonly heard iambic (two syllable foot) and anapestic (three syllable foot) meters which begin with unstressed syllables and have their primary stress at the end.

Often times, in English prosody, a line may have a general metrical pattern, but it might not have the same uniform poetic feet throughout. When one is scanning a line, one may detect an overarching pattern that sounds so strongly that individual syllables at the beginning of lines that have less content (usually connecting words like "the," "a" or "so") rhythmically don't impact the momentum of the line. The hanging syllable disappears in the rhythm. For example, one could read the opening line of this poem with the first syllable stressed or unstressed, but it doesn't change the rhythmic sense of the line.

> what **i** can **prom**ise to **be** is **wa**ter,
> **wa**ter **plain** and di**rect** as Niagara.

Whether "what" is stressed or unstressed, the trochaic/dactylic pattern predominates. The remainder of both lines in the couplet are trochaic/dactylic, specifically trochee-dactyl-trochee-trochee in the first line and trochee-dactyl-dactyl-dactyl. That chain of three dactyls closing out the second line imitates rhythmically the falling energy of the water. The regular rhythm through the following lines of the poem becomes its own kind of pattern within the context of lines that continue to have the primary structure, energy, and momentum of trochaic and dactylic lines.

A break occurs when Clifton lays two heavy stresses next to each other, creating a pause at the direct address to the "tourist." It's a double indictment because in the scenario, Kent, like Lane (currently hanging on to the edge of the cliff, hoping not to fall), is on the scene as an investigative journalist and is only supposed to be *masquerading* as a tourist. Clifton, in this poem about one person in love with another person who cannot allow himself to be vulnerable, is more directly confrontational than she is in any other love poem of hers. While the poem is mythic and fantastical in nature, Clifton told critic Hillary Holladay she was indeed writing about a former relationship of hers.

The first two lines of the final quatrain of the poem take a turn (after the line break on "the question for me is") into a couplet that alternates iambic and trochaic-dactylic lines. That hinge line is also a truncated line, only in trimeter (three feet) rather than tetrameter (four). The alternation between iambic-anapestic and trochaic-dactylic helps to create the contrast between the questions (iambic and so hopeful) and the answers (trochaic and realist).

The final two lines of the poem contain metrical inversions. In the penultimate line, the reader can choose to emphasize either "what" or "have" or "you;" each choice impacts the rhythm of the line and the subtlety of meaning. The close of the line sounds either trochaic or iambic depending on how the reader hears/reads the beginning of the line. The final line returns to dactylic-trochaic, but with the added emphasis on the word "own" occasioned by the laying of the heavy stress next to the word that follows.

> how **long** can i **cling** to this **edge?**
> the **ques**tion for **you** is
> **what** have you **ever tra**veled to**ward**
> **more** than your **own safe**ty?

From this fantastical and light-hearted poem that uses comic book characters to frame a sortie in favor of daring and bravery in emotional relationships, Clifton transitions on the next page to a poem of much more serious tone, "begin here." This small poem leads to the poems dealing with the abuse Lucille and Thelma Sayles both suffered at the hands of Sam Sayles. "Something in the girl/ is wakening," Clifton writes here, "some/thing in the girl/is falling/ deeper and deeper/asleep."[272]

In the poem "final note to clark," Clifton finally, in resignation, realizes that unlike the old comic books her Clark is "only clark kent/after all," confused at Clifton-as-Lane "taking chances,/.../

pointing out the bad guys/dreaming of your x-ray vision." The two old lovers trying to have a second chance are only "faithful readers,/not wonder woman and not superman."[273] Whatever potential might have existed in the risk-taking inherent in a relationship between the older people has failed. Mary Jane Lupton has identified Clifton's real-life love interest as a former administrator at St. Mary's College of Maryland, where Clifton taught. There is a letter in Clifton's files to him from this same time period, and far from betraying any personal feelings, it's all business: after advocating for the college to hire an Affirmative Action Officer to assist in diversity efforts in hiring and curriculum development, Clifton spends the rest of the letter making a case for the more respectful treatment of the college's maintenance staff, pointing out that the custodial and maintenance workers are primarily Black while their supervisors are primarily white.[274]

The final poem in the short series is addressed, not to mild-mannered Kansas-raised reporter Kent, but rather to Kal-Fl himself, the alien Superman. She begins in a jocular tone of camaraderie, "sweet jesus, superman,/if i had seen you/dressed in your blue suit/i would have known you." As opposed to "choirboy clark" Clifton knows the Man of Steel would be springing into action. After the serious entreaty of the earlier comic book poems, the deep vulnerability in the poems about Thelma and Sam that came in between, and the bittersweet resignation of the prior "final note to clark," Clifton opts to end on a note of humor and self-deprecation. Speaking to Superman she reassures him, "i understand the cape,/the leggings, the whole/ball of wax." After all, she reasons, "there is no planet stranger/than the one i'm from."[275]

Clifton's poems drawing from classical mythologies other than the Asiatic-African ones of the Bible are rarer, but she does write them. In addition to poems about the Indian goddess Kali in *The Two-Headed Woman*, in *The Book of Light* she also has a poem on the titan Atlas and a short series on Leda, the Greek woman impregnated by Zeus in the form of a swan the same night she also became impregnated by her mortal husband. The children Leda bore become very significant figures: two sets of fraternal twins,

Polydeuces and Helen, born of the immortal father, and Castor and Clytemnestra, born of the mortal father. The boys become the zodiacal Gemini and the girls grow up to have paradigm-shifting impacts on the politics of the mythological world: Helen occasions the Trojan War by her defection from Sparta, and Clytemnestra, in many ways, strikes its last blow, killing her husband, the Greek general who led the invasion.

In Clifton's books, the stories from various mythological canons lie side-by-side in the books—the Kali poems come right after a poem about Moses, poems about Biblical women Sarah, Naomi, and Ruth are sandwiched between the poem about Atlas and the poems about Leda. This sense of there being no difference between mythologies is heightened in the Leda poems, when Leda compares her own position—being impregnated by a god—to that of Mary. Here, too, a distant star "chooses," but the nativity scene Leda imagines is less pastoral than the one pictured in Jesus' nativity. The three kings for Leda are "dagger-fingered men,/princes of no known kingdom" while the animals are "battering the stable door."[276] In both cases, the "old husband"—Joseph or Tyndaraeus—is suspicious and "the fur between her thighs/is the only shining thing."[277]

Clifton takes Leda's complaint another step further into Christian legend by invoking Eve. Leda complains of "stars spinning into phalluses," and of "serpents promising/sweetness," phrases reminiscent of images associated with Eve's musings in "the tree of life."[278] The loneliness engendered in the Clark Kent poems finds new shape here, with these broader implications and callbacks to Clifton's earlier poems about Mary and Eve. Unlike Mary and Eve, Leda's frustration is not with the visitation itself, but with the "pyrotechnics." "You want what a man wants," she says to an uppercase God, "next time come as a man/or don't come."[279] The double-entendre on the word "come" in the final line introduces just a flick of levity and wit into an otherwise serious series of poems.

Another interesting point: seven years before she would publish the poem "moonchild," revealing her own abuser to be her father, Clifton seems to use the persona of Leda to identify her father as an abuser; after Leda gives birth, her children are taken away, her mother leaves, and her father "follows me around the well,/his thick lips slavering."[280]

The serpent promising sweetness makes another cheeky appearance in the poem "lorena." The title character of the poem, which appeared in 1996's *The Terrible Stories*, is Lorena Bobbitt, a woman who made headlines across the country in 1993. Bobbitt, whose husband John Wayne Bobbitt had been abusing her both physically and psychologically throughout their marriage, assaulted her husband one night as he slept, severing his penis with a kitchen knife. In something like a fugue state, Lorena then fled the house, jumped into her car, and drove away along the highway, steering with one hand, holding the penis in the other. At some point, erratic and endeavoring to keep steering steadily, she threw the penis out the window. When she calmed down enough, she pulled over and called 911 and reported the incident, including detailed instructions to the dispatcher as to where she was driving, when she threw the penis out the window, and where in the fields abutting the highway the appendage would likely be found.

John's penis was indeed found and successfully reattached in a long surgery, and he later tried to cash in on his notoriety by founding an unsuccessful band called The Severed Parts and star in two pornographic films the gruesomely yet wittily named productions *John Wayne Bobbitt Uncut* and *Frankenpenis*. Though acquitted by a jury of marital assault in the case brought by Lorena, he later accumulated a string of arrests and convictions, including for assault, marital assault, robbery, and battery. Lorena divorced John and went on to found an organization devoted to supporting those who have suffered domestic violence.

It is a horrifying situation, but Clifton saw the dark humor in it. She also, of course, as a descendant of Dahomey women and a warrior herself, saw in Lorena a powerful manifestation of feminist resistance against patriarchal violence. The poem functions as a sort of riddle poem because only Lorena's first name is given in the title. It's possible that readers of the poem in its earliest appearance may have more quickly identified the subject, the name Lorena is not overly common, and Bobbitt had been in the headlines, after all. The penis itself is represented only by the pronoun "it," never named in the poem outright. Often when I teach this poem, I remove the title and ask the students to think through what the poem might mean:

> lorena
>
> it lay in my palm soft and trembled
> as a new bird and i thought about
> authority and how it always insisted
> on itself, how it was master
> of the man, how it measured him, never
> was ignored or denied and how it promised
> there would be sweetness if it was obeyed
> just like the saints do, like the angels,
> and i opened the window and held out my
> uncupped hand. i swear to god,
> i thought it could fly[281]

After we read the poem together, I suggest various neutral titles such as "car drive" or "authority" and even a misleading one or two like "baby bird" or "little angel." Only after I give them the title and explain the context of this as a poem about a specific woman on a specific night do they normally understand all of the layers of meaning in a poem that is, at its heart, one more poem from Clifton about an individual person confronting a figure of authority and power.

The appendage itself, "soft and trembl[ing]," is vulnerable in Lorena's hand and whatever "authority" it once possessed seems small indeed. There is some wit in Clifton's characterization of "how it was master/of the man, how it measured him." Clifton humorously acknowledges that one must be forgiven for thinking, after learning of all the mythic qualities of this serpent-like phallus, that it is not a winged creature after all.

Lorena's power as dispeller of illusions (and castrator of violent men) is a power shared by mythic goddesses through the cosmos—Kali, Durga, and Artemis, among others—but Clifton neither mythologizes nor deifies nor demonizes Lorena Bobbitt.

Indeed, Lorena was eventually found not guilty in the matter of the knife assault, by reason of insanity. The court, despite John Bobbitt's prior acquittal on the charges of marital assault, did find that Lorena Bobbitt suffered from severe PTSD from years of abuse. Rather than dwell in the layers of causality and narrative, Clifton chooses instead to focus on the oddest moment, the ridiculous one that no one could really explain: Bobbitt flinging the severed penis out of the car window.

Behind the surface of such curious moments, things others may pass over, Clifton is able to summon deep meaning. In her last collection *Voices*, in addition to the voices of family members and history, she hears the unspoken stories behind the most ordinary and humble of items: foodstuffs on the grocery store shelves. In this case, she writes three poems about products featuring Black personae in the advertising, humanizing them into the people they once were, or might have been—complete with backstories, motivations, and hopes for their own future. Most Americans of my generation grew up quite familiar with the figures Aunt Jemima, who appeared on maple syrup bottles, Uncle Ben, who advertised parboiled rice, and the nameless Black chef who appeared, crisp in chef whites and hat, on the box for Cream of Wheat cereal.

Clifton's poem on Aunt Jemima gets at the heart of white nostalgia for a servant culture, exploring the historic "mammy" figure and its connection to the creation of Aunt Jemima as a character to advertise pancake flour in the 1880s. The "mammy" archetype was a racist caricature of a Black woman who catered to white children and was meant to be thought of as part of the family even though she was either indentured by her poverty and/ or forcibly and legally enslaved, as was Caroline Donald, known to all the white children of the Sale family as "Mammy Ca'line."

Early advertisements for the flour and syrup Aunt Jemima advertised talk about their "plantation flavor." Clifton's poem opens with the titular character remarking:

> white folks say i remind them
> of home   i who have been homeless

all my life except for their
kitchen cabinets[282]

When at the conclusion of the poem Aunt Jemima lists her
own hungers, she includes "my true nephews my nieces/my kitch-
en   my family." When Clifton performed this poem, she
emphasized the personal pronoun "my" to expose exactly what
had been taken from Jemima—personal ownership—concluding
with "my home."

The poem "uncle ben" continues the progression of reclamation through remembering the past by getting more pointed
about the fact that these brand ambassadors are bereft figures from
which much has been stolen. The poem is more specific about the
African origins of the three of them as former slaves taken from
their homes and pressed into bondage:

uncle ben

mother guineas favorite son
knew rice and that was almost
all he knew
not where he was
not why
not who were the pale sons
of a pale moon
who had brought him here[283]

It matters, in a way, that the food all three are marketing
is palliative food, soft and bland, "comfort food" meant for ease:
Jemima's syrup, Ben's parboiled rice, the nameless chef's soupy
tasteless slurry, rather than spices, or condiments, or culturally-spe-
cific cuisine. Black people in America were not meant to have
character, not meant to have roots to any other place. As Dionne
Brand pointed out, the Door to Nowhere was meant to obliterate
any identity, any past.

Aunt Jemima's original likeness was drawn from a caricature
of a white performer in blackface on a vaudeville poster in 1889,

though later she was redesigned in a composite form, based on several models. Black actress Nancy Green portrayed Aunt Jemima on road shows and at trade demonstrations on behalf of the brand. Uncle Ben made his first appearance in his waiter's uniform (said to be based on a waiter in a Chicago hotel) in 1946, while the Black chef graced Cream of Wheat boxes since the 1890s. Eventually these images were updated. Aunt Jemima was redesigned as a more modern woman, losing the head kerchief and receiving a stylish coiffure, in 1989, followed by Uncle Ben donning a suit and the persona of chairman of the board in 2007.

While in Clifton's poem Jemima considers herself "homeless" and includes as her greatest hunger the one for "my home," the poem about Ben identifies what part of Africa he came from—Guinea. The poet, if not the man himself, is well aware why he is in North America now, that he had been *brought* there to the place where he "worked the river,"

> worked as if born to it
> thinking only now and then
> of himself   of the sun
> of afrika[284]

The nostalgia for Africa from the earlier poems in *good times*, such as in the poem "i went to the valley," which concludes "my soul got happy/and stayed all day." [285] In returning to an ancesteral idea of Africa, Clifton returns Ben to a place where he can think, "all of my bones/remember."[286] "Remember africa," the speaker exhorts in "the raising of lazarus."[287] Clifton returns to her alternate spelling in Ben's poem to heighten the poignant connection to the lost and ancient originary home that Ben sometimes muses about "only now and then."

In the third poem in this little set, "cream of wheat," both naming and memory take on important roles. The poem is already different in that the name of the figure on the box is not given, unlike the poems featuring Aunt Jemima and Uncle Ben, and in fact the chef discovering his name is part of the poem itself:

cream of wheat

sometimes at night
we stroll the market aisles
ben and jemima and me   they
walk in front   remembering this and that
i lag behind
trying to remove my chefs cap
wondering about whatever pictured me
then left me personless
Rastus
i read in an old paper
i was called rastus
but no mother ever
gave that to her son   toward dawn
we return to our shelves
our boxes   ben and jemima and me
we pose and smile   i simmer   what
is my name[288]

First of all, we see Ben and Jemima as separate, walking ahead, as if the fact that they know their own names allows them to remember and reminisce, Jemima aware that she has other nephews and nieces, Ben not only knowing he was brought across the water from Africa, but also knowing the country he came from. The chef does not remember his name but learns it through reading an old newspaper. Historically, "Rastus" was a racist diminutive (of the Greek name "Erastus") that was often given to characterize and diminish Black men. The company that manufactures the cereal started using "Rastus" to refer to their Black mascot in the 19th century, but in the mid-20th century replaced the caricature with a drawing made from a photograph of a Black chef in Chicago.

In the poem the chef is struggling to remove his hat, the symbol of his role and bondage. He knows that "Rastus" is not his true name, that his mother would not have named him that, that he has another, but that it is lost to history. There is a powerful double meaning in the last line since the verb "simmer"—a synonym for quiet and unexpressed anger—is a typical part of the instructions for the preparation of the cereal. The chef's frustration and anger stem from his inability to know his own name or history.

On June 17, 2020—a month after George Floyd was murdered and in the context of the civil unrest that followed—the company producing Cream of Wheat announced it was reconsidering the use of the chef on its packaging. Hours later, Quaker Oats announced it was rebranding Aunt Jemima as Pearl Milling Company, the original producer of the pancake products, and Mars, Inc., announced that they were rebranding Uncle Ben's as Ben's Originals and removing the portrait from the packaging. In September of that same year, the chef was finally removed from Cream of Wheat advertising. Coincidentally, the Land O' Lakes butter company had already removed the "Indian Maiden" from their package earlier that year, after many years of criticism from Indigenous communities. These American corporations recognized, very late, that the use of racial stereotypes in their advertising did have real-world impacts. One hopes American sports teams will follow suit.

Clifton's playful-yet-serious treatment of the stereotypical Black figures in food advertising mirrors the way she approaches various types of complicated issues in her children's books. Her first book for children, The Black BC's, was published in 1970 and provides an alphabet for children incorporating Black history, long anticipating currently popular books like A is for Activist, My Feminist ABC, and An Asian American A to Z, teaching young children about politically progressive figures from American history. In The Black BC's, each letter is followed by a short descriptive epigram followed by a brief prose encyclopedia-like entry. The book opens, naturally, with a reference to Africa: "A is for Africa/land of the sun/the king of continents/the ancient one." The illustrations are by artist Don Miller, and are highly textured due to the fact that each is tempera painted on board.

In B (for "Books") Clifton pays tribute to important African American poets and writers. Besides the famed Phillis Wheatley, Clifton notes that the first published poem by a Black American was written by a young woman named Lucy Terry and was published in 1746, some twenty years before Wheatley's book appeared. Clifton also cites Jupiter Hammon and William Wells Brown. Among contemporary luminaries she includes well known writers like Brooks, Baldwin, Hansberry, and LeRoi Jones, but she also mentions lesser acclaimed writers, such as playwrights Lonne Elder III and Ted Shine. Some of the letters, like C ("Cowboys"), E ("Explorers"), I ("Inventors"), and P ("Politics") similarly highlight as yet undervalued contributions of Black people to American society. Other letters pay tribute to individual figures like Frederick Douglass, Martin Luther King, Jr, Sojourner Truth and Harriet Tubman (who share the "T"), Denmark Vesey, and Malcolm X. Other letters like F ("freedom"), M ("middle passage"), and U ("underground railroad") explore aspects of Black History. Some few chapters explore particular concepts of importance. In "N" (for "Natural") she discusses Black hair and talks about beauty standards of whiteness that denigrate or diminish Black peoples' own features. In the graphic a young boy is using a pick to style his afro:

> N is for Natural
> or real or true
> the you of yourself
> and the self of you[289]

Compellingly, for Clifton, "Q" is an important letter, accompanied by an epigram that could have found a place in any of her poetry collections:

> Q is for Questions
> the wise man's tool
> who cannot ask
> remains a fool[290]

Beginning in 1970, Clifton began a series of books with the same protagonist, a young boy named Everett Anderson. Illustrated by Evaline Hess in a style that combined line-and-washed geometric abstractions with gorgeous inked figural depictions, that first book, *Some of the Days of Everett Anderson*, presented a series of episodes from the life of Everett in little narrative fragments. Most, not all, of the poems are in quatrains and the episodic nonlinear form does feel reminiscent of the poems (and structure as a whole) in *good times*.

Clifton continued to tell the story of Everett Anderson—who aged, though slowly—in a series of books culminating in 2001's *One of the Problems of Everett Anderson*. We see Everett deal with an absent father, contending with life with his mother on their own, and then the introduction of a new man, Mr. Perry, who eventually becomes his stepfather. In *Everett Anderson's Nine Month Long* the Anderson family welcomes a new baby, Everett's sister Evelyn. Most of the later Everett Anderson books are illustrated by Ann Grifalconi, who unlike Evaline Ness in her highly stylized art, opted for a more realist approach. Grifalconi uses one of two modes for the books, the first a minimal line drawing, similar to a newspaper comic strip, and the second a more lushly shaped and textured crayon style.

A landmark book in the Everett Anderson series was 1983's *Everett Anderson's Goodbye*. In this book, dedicated by Clifton "to my sad friends," Everett goes through the Five Stages of Grief (included at the beginning of the book) upon the death of his father. In brief rhyming poems Everett deals with his sadness, ultimately concluding, "whatever happens when people die,/love doesn't stop, and/neither will I."[291] The book, published the same year Fred Clifton received his cancer diagnosis one year prior to his death, helped Lucille and her children cope with those traumatic events.

Clifton also wrote many books that were not part of the Everett Anderson series. These books also deal with issues of deep political and philosophical importance, but through the perspective of a child. They use logic and emotional responses that would be legible to children.

In *The Boy Who Didn't Believe in Spring* the very serious (and somewhat curmudgeonly) young King Shabazz—named, of course, for Black luminaries Martin Luther King, Jr. and Malcolm X/ Malik El-Shabazz—is skeptical hearing about "spring." Shabazz lives in a very urban setting and sees no evidence of spring anywhere.

He and his friend Tony Polito wander the neighborhood trying to find proof of "spring." After wandering past shops and restaurants and store-front churches they come to an empty lot in which sits a rusted out shell of a car. There, in the form of daffodils and birds and an egg-filled nest, they find the proof they were seeking.

Her use of Black English in this book, and in *good news about the earth*, published in the same year, engendered mixed responses. Of *The Boy Who Didn't Believe in Spring*, a Black graduate student in elementary education at Cornell University wrote a very critical letter to Clifton. The scholar was "appalled" at the children's use of Black English and told Clifton that the book would "further reinforce poor language patterns," and that the "language of the downtrodden and uneducated" would be a "grave handicap to carry with one through life." Ithaca-based bookseller, Helen Grow, from whom the student purchased the book, was carefully cc'd on the typed letter to Clifton and Grow wrote to Clifton separately, assuring her of the value of the book and its use of language, writing, "you and I remember when there were no books for black children at all."[292]

Clifton's use of Black vernacular in these books was equally praised, and sometimes from unexpected quarters. The white New Formalist poet Frederick Turner, who was raised in then-colonial Rhodesia (now Zimbabwe), wrote to Clifton, praising the language of *good news about the earth*, calling it a "synthesis of old myth, biblical literature, African heritage, and Afro/American idiom," saying that it was "as pungent, as beautiful as the fruits and colors you describe." Scholar William Fogarty has also discussed Clifton's particular blend of dictions, terming it her "oracular vernacular."[293] Fogarty also comments on the development of Clifton's vernacular throughout her published work, saying, "as Clifton's investment in inscrutable spiritual situations deepens over her career, and as she searches for language commensurate to those enigmas, explicit African American vernacular extends to broader evocations of speech. For example, her sequence about the Annunciation [in *two-headed woman*], in which the angel Gabriel announces to Mary that she will give birth to Jesus, is arranged in language that at times suggests Caribbean dialect but mostly mixes standard

English and nonstandard constructions that are colloquial, but not as specifically locatable as the American Black speech of the 'some jesus' sequence."[294] Fogarty goes on to usefully map the shifts in diction throughout Clifton's poetry; it would be equally illuminating to examine shifts in her diction in the writing for children.

The occasional disgruntled graduate student aside, Clifton's target audience for *The Boy Who Didn't Believe in Spring* was well pleased: she received a one-page missive in painstakingly penciled block letters from a young boy named Tony Polito, who expressed his excitement at having the same name as one of the characters in the tale. Further, young Tony told Lucille Clifton that he was white but his brother was black and they liked to imagine themselves as the two boys in the story. Tony Polito's final verdict? "IT'S A GOOD BOOK."[295]

1973 was a busy year for Clifton; she published three other books that same year, gorgeously illustrated by two young Black artists who were married to one another. Stephanie Douglas created intricate collages of photograph, drawing, painting, and fabric for the books *Good, Says Jerome* and *Three Wishes*, while husband John Steptoe illustrated Clifton's *All Us Come Cross the Water* with hypnotic paintings informed by surrealism, African design, and a highly modernist approach to the figure. Both use a dramatic and visually stimulating approach to color, though Douglas' illustrations use a dynamic push-and-pull perspective while Steptoe opts for a subtler, flatter plane. At the time they were illustrating Clifton's books, Douglas and Steptoe had a young son of their own, Javaka Steptoe, who grew up to follow in his parents' footsteps and become a renowned writer and illustrator of children's books, most recently the award-winning *Radiant Child: The Story of Young Artist Jean-Michel Basquiat.*

In these books, the protagonist needs help understanding things happening in their lives and has an older member of the community to provide them with guidance. *Good, Says Jerome*, like *Some of the Days of Everett Anderson*, is episodic and nonlinear. Jerome wonders about various things—moving, whether his new teacher will like him, even what happens when someone dies—and his older sister Janice Marie helps him tackle these issues with practical advice.

All Us Come Cross the Water is Clifton's first published book using the Optima font. She continued to use this font for her poetry for the rest of her publishing life, excluding *The Book of Light*. *All Us Come Cross the Water*, written in Black English, is dedicated "For Fred's Darl" (referring to the titular character of the YA novel Fred published that same year) "and John Steptoe's Stevie," the titular protagonist of Steptoe's own recent children's book. In *All Us Come Cross the Water*, the protagonist is named Ujamaa, after a Swahili word meaning "siblinghood." The word was used to describe a political ideology of African socialism by anti-colonial thinker Julius Nyerere, who became president of Tanzania. Ujamaa came to be adopted by Maulana Karenga as the fourth of the seven principles of Kwanzaa, a holiday he developed to celebrate and honor African American culture. Karenga described ujamaa as "cooperative economics," enjoining Black community members to found and patronize their own businesses, including grocery stores and other types of services for collective profit.

At the beginning of the book, Ujamaa, who is called "Jim" by his teacher Miss Wells, is asked to participate in a classroom history project. He does not say anything, even to correct her as to his name. The teacher, who is also Black, tells him, "we must not be ashamed of ourselves, Jim," and asks him if he knows he is from Africa.[296] This upsets him, though the reader is not told why. When Ujamaa talks to his older sister Rose about the encounter, she—unlike Jerome's sister Janice Marie—is not helpful. "Rose, where we from?" asks Ujamaa. Rose replies, "Mama was from Rome, Georgia, and Daddy from Birmingham." The answer is not satisfying to Ujamaa. He asks their origins before Rome and Birmingham. Rose explains a few generations further back, but Ujamaa says that he means "way back." Rose laughs, and says, "There's wasn't no way back before that. Before that we was a slave." Her answer makes him furious: "Rose make me sick."[297]

Rose, in her way, aligns with Dionne Brand's concept of the erasure engendered by the "door of no return"—that Black people in America have no "before"—that what was before, in Africa, has been irrevocably cut off. She also uses a curious grammatical construction: when she says, "we was a slave," she collectivizes the African experience of slavery, making the plurality of the "we" into the singular, "a" slave. Ujamaa tries talking to his father, but tired from working all day, his father snaps, "Boy, I'm too tired to fool with you. Go ask Big Mama them questions." Big Mama, Ujamaa's great-grandmother, is the one who gave him his name. The figure of the powerful elder recurs in Clifton's work, of course. In addition to Sam Sayles' great grandmother Caroline (who hid her own African name) we now have Ujamaa's great grandmother Big Mama (who *bestows* an African name), and later still in Clifton's YA novel, *The Lucky Stone,* the protagonist Tee will come to depend on her own great-grandmother Mrs. Elzie F. Pickens ("The 'F' stood for 'free'.").

Ujamaa really believes that Big Mama will be able to help him because "she see things cause she born with a veil over her face. That make it so she can see spirits and things." Big Mama, who drifts in and out of mental focus, is able to help him, telling him that her own mother was brought from Dahomey in 1855 when she was nine years old. She tells him that his father looks like Ashanti people. "That mean I'm from Ashanti people?" he asks. "Who are you, boy?" she asks him then, and at that point a reader may feel unsure whether she is having memory loss or if she is asking him a more pointed question about how he self-identifies. "I'm Ujamaa," he says and the answer satisfies the older woman: "Go on now then," she tells him. "I'm through."

Ujamaa has another conversation with Tweezer, an older man in the neighborhood, with whom he is friends, but of whom his family does not approve. Throughout Clifton's books, there are alternative familial and social arrangements, and not always explained in the book. There are ordinarily older adults, like Tweezer, who are not part of the family, but still part of the family's life. One of Clifton's other books, *My Friend Jacob*, features a young Black boy befriending an older developmentally disabled youth who eventually comes over to the narrator's house for meals and social visits.

Tweezer is another figure of authority and friendship for Ujamaa. Because he sits "with his wine in a cup" outside the Panthers Bookstore most evenings, Ujamaa always knows where to find him. Like Caroline Donald, Tweezer is unconcerned with the origin of his name and understands the reason why one might even hide it. He tells Ujamaa about his grandfather who was enslaved and refused to tell his enslavers his name: "Reckon he figure if they ain't got his name they ain't really got him...Long as your own give you the name you know it's yours. We name us. Everybody else just calling us something." It's the explanation Sam Sayles never got from his great-grandmother.

Tweezer's point is reminiscent of an argument that Fred Clifton's Darl has with his own teacher Miss Smith. *Darl* (1973) is an epistolary novel comprised of letters written back and forth between a young boy, Darl—one imagines him about ten or eleven—and his white teacher, Miss Smith. They go back and forth about many things, the young boy not meaning to be combative, but aways standing up for himself. At one point Miss Smith refers to Black people as "Negroes" and Darl answers, "Black people don't call themselves Negro no more." When she asks in response, "Do all Negroes call themselves black?" he claps back, "Don't you mean do all black people call themselves black?.".[298]

During his talk with Tweezer, Ujamaa finally articulates for us what upset him about the exchange with Miss Wills at the beginning of the book. "We all from different parts of Africa," he says. "How we gonna say what country we from?" What upset Ujamaa was not being told he was from Africa, but that Miss Wells diminished the specificity of his origin by lumping the entire continent together.

"We from all them countries," Tweezer tells him. "All us off the same boat." Ujamaa disagrees, saying, "We wasn't all slaves." Tweezer sets him straight, and it's easy to hear in the language of his rejoinder a poetic rhythm that would have been impossible to communicate in Standard English: "Wasn't none of us free, though. All us crossed the water. We one people, Ujamaa. Boy got that name oughta know that. All us crossed the water."

Ujamaa is transformed by the conversation, realizing a deeper and more nuanced significance to the unifying identification Miss Wells used. "All us come cross the water," he thinks, adapting Tweezer's statement about history into the present tense, and further understanding his own responsibility to collectivity, reinforcing for himself Tweezer's admonishment: "Someone name Ujamaa oughta know that." The next day at school he has found the courage to stand up and correct his teacher and ask her to call him by his true name.

Darl's arguments with his own teacher began around the question of spelling and spoken language. They evolve to views of history and the meanings of American holidays to different people. Eventually, as the novel unfolds, they begin to warm to each other and trust each other and even agree to a secret signal (putting a pencil behind their ear) to let the other one know when they are confused or unsure about something. Eventually Miss Smith invites Darl to a visit with her parents during Christmas and Darl helps her by giving her advice on how to handle a difficult situation with some of the students in the class. By the end of the book the two have come to a friendly relationship of mutual respect, and Miss Smith, who had been deciding whether or not to accept a job at another school, decides to stay.

Fred Clifton's book is a model of care between a student who has confidence in his own way of understanding the world on his own terms and a teacher who accepts the student as having wisdoms and intelligences she does not have access to, and who comes to see him as an intellectual equal. Though Fred Clifton also wrote poetry and performed it in venues around Baltimore, he did not publish another book before his death in 1983. Some of Fred's writing, including a handwritten essay on phenomenology, is in the Lucille Clifton archive at Emory University, and the Cliftons' son Graham told me that there are still some of Fred's files, papers, and audio recordings in the family's possession; perhaps in the future they may yield more of Fred Clifton's writing.

Lucille Clifton's 1979 novel *The Lucky Stone* uses a similar structure as *generations*. The story, written to a slighter older age range, 7-9, than most of Clifton's other books for children, tells the story of Tee, whose great-grandmother, the aforementioned Mrs. Elzie F. Pickens, has a "lucky stone." The book has two narrative frames. The first is Tee hearing the story of the lucky stone from her great-grandmother. When Elzie was a little girl she was walking down the street when her neighbors, a woman named Vashti and her mother Mandy, called out to her. The two neighbor women were sitting on the porch and Vashti told Elzie that if she fetched her a glass of water, she would give her a lucky stone. Vashti's recounting to Elzie the story of the lucky stone's origin is the second framing.

Vashti tells the story of her own mother Mandy, who, as a little girl, was enslaved on a cotton plantation. One day, Mandy ran away, evading her pursuers and hiding out in a cave. She scratched her initial onto a stone and was able to alert a Black passerby to her presence by tossing the stone out of the cave as he passed. Word spread that Mandy was alive and hiding nearby and so all the local African people would leave something for her to eat as they passed the cave. With their surreptitious deliveries, Mandy managed to survive in the cave until the emancipation. She gave the stone to Vashti and it saved Vashti too when she dropped it once and avoided being struck by lightning. The stone later helps Elzie meet the man who would become her husband. Clifton's storytelling style in *The Lucky Stone*, as in *generations*, uses narrative circularity to bring the times of slavery directly into the present moment and also imbues the ordinary with a belief in mysticism and miracle.

Clifton's only book of middle grade (ages 11-13) fiction, *The Times They Used to Be* (1974), is written in the same spare but stylized language in which *generations* is written. Though the language is unrhymed and has the rhythmic feel of a prose sentence, it is lineated like a long poem. "Mama, mama/tell us about when you was a girl," it opens, already cluing us in that we will again be hearing a story told about the past. The unnamed mother begins then telling a story of her past:

It is the story
of what happened to Tassie Scott
the time sin broke all out in her body
because she wasn't saved.
And also about me,
and how it was

the summer my uncle Sunny
followed the nun
back and forth,
across the Grider Street bridge.[299]

The two storylines of Tassie Scott and Uncle Sunny continue on parallel tracks throughout the book until they intertwine at
the conclusion. Tassie, the mother-as-a-child-narrator's best friend,
is very upset and ashamed by her "sin" and wants to run away.
What she has done we are not told and neither is the narrator,
but the girls make their preparations to help Tassie escape. Uncle
Sunny is home from the army and living with the narrator's family.
He had served in the 92nd Infantry, an all African-American division,
nicknamed the "Buffalo Soldiers Infantry" after the 19th century
Black cavalrymen (though naturally also invoking Tyrone and his
friends from Clifton's earlier poems). Sunny seems to be suffering
from some kind of PTSD and recounts to the family in increas
ingly manic episodes the ghostly nun he sees on the bridge but
cannot apprehend.

Tassie, whose father is in jail, does not have much guidance
at home. She argues with her grandmother about church. Tassie
wants to become a Baptist like her friends but her grandmother
insists she become sanctified instead, saying dismissively, "Baptists
shout on Sunday/and drunk on Monday!"[300] One night, before the
girls manage to run away, bad news comes: Sunny has driven his
car off the bridge and has drowned. The girls sneak into the funeral
home to view the body and it is there that we learn the source
of Tassie's shame. While they are looking at Uncle Sunny's body,
Tassie starts having her period. Having been too ashamed to tell
anyone, she doesn't know what is happening and has identified it
as "sin." The narrator runs to fetch her own mother, who is able to
comfort Tassie. She gives her a sweater to tie around her waist to
disguise the blood, and helps to walk her home.

The book ends on a curious note: it is the night before
Sunny's funeral and the narrator hears on the radio President
Truman's announcement that he is integrating the army. "The 92nd
was gone," she thinks.[301] The narrative does not return to the initial

framing of italic text depicting children asking their mother about "the olden days." History passes fleetingly away, the episodes of Tassie's shame and Sunny's delusion compounded by the wistful yet hopeful moment of social progress occasioned at the book's end. As in Stephen King's novella "The Body," famously adapted to film as *Stand by Me*, the rites of passage of the children play out against painful ruination, its climactic moment being Tassie's menstruation upon viewing the body of the deceased Sunny. One imagines that, with its cinematic events and subtle emotional tunings, *The Times They Used to Be* would make an excellent film as well.

After Clifton started receiving wider recognition following the publication of *good woman*, she published less for children and focused mainly on her poetry. Other poets who write for children, such as Naomi Shihab Nye and Marilyn Nelson, have pointed out how often their work for children is taken less seriously or is ignored. Nelson, in particular, often points out how she wrote her book *Carver*, on the life of George Washington Carver, as a book meant for children, but rather than publish it with that emphasis, gave it to the same press that published the rest of her poetry. She believes this is the reason that that particular book was taken more seriously as a literary work. This diminishment of children's literature as not as meaningful or serious *as literature* is the case with Clifton's writing for children as well. Most critics of her poetry do not discuss it and when they do (perhaps I am also guilty of this), it is with less attention and focus than is given to the "adult poetry." Clifton did take the vocation of writing for children very seriously; in fact, at one point in the mid-80s, she wrote to Jacqueline Kennedy Onassis, an editor at Doubleday known then for her support of Black writers, pitching a collaboration between herself and singer Michael Jackson, then at the height of his fame, on "the importance of self esteem and a positive inner self."[302]

In 2001, just after she won the National Book Award, she did publish one last and notable children's book, which fittingly features her frequent hero, Everett Anderson. He is somewhat older in *One of the Problems of Everett Anderson* and his little sister Evelyn has grown too, at least old enough to argue with him. It is possible that the publication of *Blessing the Boats* with its landmark poem "moonchild"—which revealed her father as her abuser as well as the nature of the abuse—allowed Clifton, or perhaps better to say *spurred her*, to write a book for children broaching the most sensitive topic of child abuse. One of Everett's friends Greg has come to school with bruises. Everett has noticed them before and even asked about them, but Greg told Everett that he couldn't tell him where they came from. Everett considers telling the teacher, but doesn't want Greg to get in trouble. Evelyn says its none of his business and he should stay out of it, but Everett's mother overhears and Everett is able to tell her what is happening. The reader does not learn of the aftermath of Everett's revelation to his mother other than Everett's own realization that his responsibility to his friend has not ended—he must still "hold" Greg and love him so he feels supported. The book ends on a hopeful note, with the boys off to join some friends from school to play baseball.

Perhaps it was the writing and publishing of *One of the Problems of Everett Anderson* which allowed Clifton to continue the disclosure she began in "moonchild" in the numerous poems in both *Mercy* and *Voices* that we looked at in Chapter 5 that address the abuse. Certainly, for Clifton, childhood was a complicated time that held both love and affection, as well as danger and violence. In some later poems, she is able to open up about how fairy tales and comics and movies of her youth helped her as a young girl contend with what was happening to her.

In one of these such poems, "after oz" (from *Mercy*), she contends with this difficult truth when she describes life on a farm in Kansas after a certain storm-tossed niece finds her way back home after being transported to a magical land of wizards and witches. Uncle Henry and Aunty Em slip into Dorothy's bedroom at night to "fill her pockets with stones/so that she is weighted down/so that storms cannot move her."[303] It does not work; the girl disappears anyway, coming back hours later. In the "disenchanted" kitchen the parental figures know they have lost their adoptive daughter; they recognize that she wants to get away from them. They must accept that for her, "home is no longer comfort/or comfort no longer home."

Chapter 8: Adam and His Mother

While Lucille Clifton is recognized as a poet of simple and clear diction, we have seen that she is as facile with the cadences of King James as she is with Black vernacular. She herself had much to say about this so-called "simple" expression. "I have never believed that for anything to be valid or true or intellectual or 'deep' it had to first be complex," Clifton wrote.[304] She contested that difficult language meant sophisticated thinking and that simple language meant ignorance. "I am interested in being understood not admired," she went on to clarify. "I wish to celebrate not be celebrated (though a little celebration is a lot of fun)."

Clifton's poems are marked not only by spiritual gravity, but by the humbler attentions of a working poet utilizing the various tools of poetic craft. Morrison was right when she said that critics working on Clifton at that time did not recognize or substantively explore what she termed Clifton's "risk-taking manipulation of language," with the exception of those who praised—or took issue with—her use of Black English as a literary language.

Clifton herself often discussed her roots as a poet educated in formal poetry and poetic form. In addition to her mother, Thelma Sayles, a poet who wrote in traditional iambic pentameter and rhymed forms, Clifton also cited William Blake, William Butler Yeats, Conrad Aiken, and Sonia Sanchez—another poet who marries colloquial oral speech to received form and poetic meters—as poetic influences. Omar Miranda, a scholar of Romantic poetry, has shown Keats to be an influence on Clifton as well, particularly in one of her most famous poems, "won't you come celebrate with me."

Clifton regularly uses elements of metrical rhythm in all of her poems, but rather than stick to a singular metrical pattern throughout a poem, she shifts meter line-by-line for oral or performative effect. Taking a cue from Sonia Sanchez, she uses the traditionally enjambed free verse line even while meter is at work behind the scenes. If you read a straight sentence through, the poem will sound truly like free verse, but if read with slight caesurae at the end of each line, one can clearly hear the rhythmic modulation. For example, her poem "moses":

moses

i walk on bones
snakes twisting
in my hand
locusts breaking my mouth
an old man
leaving slavery
home is burning in me
like a bush
God got his eye on[305]

Each line functions as a different poetic phrase and each has its own meter, the first line iambic, the second a heavy stress-trochee pair, the third an anapest, the fourth line starts in trochees and ends in an iamb—the rhythmic switch emphasizes the actual "breaking" going on—and the fifth line has a light stress followed by a spondee. Moses' human self and his human elements—his action walking, his hand, his mouth—are all iambic, small and delicate against the trochaic and elemental twisting, the locusts, slavery itself.

After a trochee-dactyl line and a trochaic line, the penultimate anapest leads into one of Clifton's favorite poetic strategies— multiple heavy stresses, in this case a spondee, a light stress ("his") followed by a second spondee. The interruptions of the line breaks force the ear away from hearing any regular pattern in the rhythm, and heightens the music of the interruptive incantation which puts Moses' human qualities in opposition to the immense forces of nature and God around him. He's once again iambic when he compares home to the burning bush before driving home the final line of the poem—God isn't the burning bush in this version of the myth, but its observer. Merely by watching something God causes it to flower, so too with creation, so too with Moses himself.

Clifton often uses a switch from trochaic intonation to a brief iambic energy build-up before deploying a series of heavy stresses that declaim with biblical fervency. This switch in meter brings emphasis through the sentence and allows the heavy stresses—sometimes as many as six in a row—to do their rhythmic work. Even when she provides the interlude of a light stress, as in "moses," she remains more or less symmetrical and musical in her use of the heavy stresses.

Like Sonia Sanchez, one of her acknowledged influences, Clifton sometimes deploys the sentence *against* the line to heighten a sense of drama or difficulty. As James Longenbach claimed in his book *The Art of the Poetic Line,* one can think of three different kinds of line breaks: end-stopped lines with punctuation, those that break on a grammatical phrase, and finally those that enjamb across a phrase for dramatic impact; Longenbach calls these last kind "annotating line breaks," after a term of John Hollander's.[306] Sanchez's poem "Personal Letter No. 2" is a good example of the line-breaks themselves torquing the emotional content of the poem. Allow me to demonstrate by first showing an incorrect version of the poem: I reassembled Sanchez's lines according to a break on the grammatical phrase and/or end stopped with punctuation, grouped the lines to give a sense of normative stanzaic pattern, and regularized the punctuation:

> i speak skimpily to you about apartments i no longer dwell in
> and children who chant their disobedience in choruses.
>
> if i were young i would stretch you with my wild words
> while our nights run soft with hands, but i am what i am:
>
> woman, alone amid all this noise.

The way this poem is lineated here causes it to flow musical-
ly, mellifluously even, somewhat at odds with the emotional turmoil
within. So here is Sanchez's actual poem as she printed it, with
irregular punctuation and very strategic line breaks that interrupt
and intrude on normal conversational rhythms of speech in order
to better convey the internal and emotional state of the speaker:

> i speak skimpily to
> you about apartments i
> no longer dwell in
> and children who
> chant their dis
> obedience in choruses.
> if i were young
> i wd stretch you
> with my wild words
> while our nights
> run soft with hands.
> but i am what i
> am. woman. alone
> amid all this noise.[307]

Lines here continually end with personal referents ("i",
"who", "you") suspending the action. In one dramatic case an
actual word is broken without hyphenation ("dis/obsedience") and
another "would," is compressed into the near gnomic "wd." It's the
penultimate line, however—"am. woman. alone"—that essentializes
the drama and demonstrates most clearly how Sanchez is able to
position the brokenness of the sentences against the poetic line to
represent the sense of loss and alienation felt by the speaker. As
in the Clifton poem, Sanchez closes the piece with a heavy-stress
packed line—double iambs (including "alone" from the previous
line) followed by three heavy stresses.

Clifton uses this scheme of sentences of various and irregular
lengths coupled with mid-sentence line breaks often. Since a traditional use of meter—that is, regularly recurring metrical pattern—is
clearly not her strategy, one must listen to the stresses line by line

in order to detect patterns in the poem as a whole. In "monticello," an epigrammatic piece about the suspiciously red-haired children of Sally Hemings, a woman enslaved on Thomas Jefferson's estate, Clifton deploys three different meters across four short lines:

monticello

God declares no independence.
here come sons
from this black sally
branded with jefferson hair.[308]

The first line of the poem, a complete sentence, begins with a heavy stress and ends in trochees, thus giving it a trochaic feel to it. Because of the switch in stresses there are three heavy stresses together in the middle of the line, making brief caesurae on either side of the word "no," offering the denial extra emphasis: "God declares no independence." This is immediately followed by two brief lines packed with six heavy stresses—a line of declaration against the dominant historical narrative: "here come sons/from this black sally."

The first of these has three heavy stresses in a row—"here come sons"—while the second, with its framing of light stresses at the beginning and end of the lines, seem to draw the ear and the eye to the word "black" and to Sally herself at the end of the line.

These symmetrically stressed lines are released into the rhythmic levity of the final line, a double dactyl followed by a heavy stress giving the end a light iambic sound: "branded with jefferson hair." This double-dactyl has a more folksy and humorous sound, like Mother Goose's famous double- dactyl heavy-stress line, "hickory, dickory, dock." The final line of "monticello" with its rhythmic switch seems to leaven the mood of the poem, making it a little bit more witty, even jocular in tone, rather than the more solemn declamatory tone of the second and third lines, though the word "branded" reminds the reader of Sally Hemings' status; even as the mother of numerous Jefferson children, she remained in bondage.

Hemings was a slave her entire life and Jefferson did not free her in his will; she and her children were passed on to new owners.

Although Clifton infrequently works in received forms, in her later collection, *Mercy,* she does include a senryu, a Japanese form of haiku that deals with human emotions rather than sublimating observance into nature imagery. Senryu are frequently darkly witty while traditional haiku traffic more in an earnest and wistful tone. Clifton's poem is called "sonku," a play on Sonia Sanchez's adaptation of the senryu which Sanchez termed "songku" for their focus on rhythm and music in addition to the bare observation that Japanese forms are well known for.

Clifton's "sonku" tells the story of the death of her son, Channing Clifton, at age 42 from an enlarged heart, a previously undiagnosed condition:

sonku

his heart, they said, was
three times the regular size.
yes, i said, i know.[309]

Once again, in a very short poem—the space of seventeen syllables as a matter of fact—Clifton switches poetic meters in each of the three lines of the poem. The very first phrase is an iamb, followed by a caesura, and then another iamb with an extra syllable "was" at the end, leading into the second line, and disallowing the kind of "inter-line" caesura that the rhythm of "moses" was so dependent on.

This line is followed by Clifton's characteristic spondee and then an iamb-anapest pair that nonetheless has a little bit of trochaic sound to it—specifically in "times the regular"— another example of the way Clifton's use of meter sometimes forces the sound of the line to an in-between action. The final line, iambs set up by an injunction "yes," then thuds with the sound of the dead man's heartbeat and the image's painful double-entendre of the mother's acknowledgement of both clinical and personal truths: "yes, i said, i know."

For those who may wish to explore some elements of basic prosody, Mary Oliver's *A Poetry Handbook* is a very nice and simple introduction. Her *Rules of the Dance* expands on the lessons of the earlier book, and includes a mini-anthology of metrical poetry in the second half. For those who wish a more comprehensive examination of English prosody, one might look at Annie Finch's *A Poet's Ear* or her *How to Scan a Poem*. Those who wish a very deep dive may like to look at Don Paterson's recent book *The Poem* or Finch's *A Poet's Craft*. Robert Hass' book *A Little Book of Form* is also useful for thinking about line lengths and stanzaic patterns, as well as other aspects of form.

On the page, Clifton's "sarah's promise," like Sanchez's poem, looks like an ordinary free verse poem without any particular unifying line length nor any stanzaic pattern or stanzas at all. If we look at it line-by-line we will see how, in shifting metrical patterns (somewhat reminiscent of the way preachers use varying oratorical rhythms—including pauses—to hold an audience's attention) Clifton uses prosodic rhythm to intensify the emotional impact.

The Sarah of the title is, of course, the wife of Abraham. In both Jewish and Christian traditions, she is the wife and Hagar is a concubine. In the Quranic tradition, you may know, Hagar (called Hajira) is the first wife and Sarah (pronounced with two long a's) is the second wife.

I say here "Jewish and Christian" as two separate traditions rather than using the typical term "Judeo-Christian" for two reasons. The first is that the term is inaccurate: it connects two traditions that are often at odds with each other. Besides, in terms of actual practices, Judaism and Islam are far more aligned to one another than either is to mainstream Orthodox, Catholic, or Protestant Christianities. But the second reason is more important: the term posits a chronological evolution of the "Judeo" to the "Christian," and so it inscribes a hierarchy of time, with the Christian as the modern, and Jewish as the older and historical, and by extension, perhaps, irrelevant. I suppose a third reason is that it excludes the

Muslim, which is from the same Abrahamic tradition, and posits the "Judeo" and the "Christian" as more intimately related, mainly because they're both seen as European dominant (regardless of the untruth of that), while the Muslim is seen as oriented around the Mediterranean, African, and Asian. In this sense, the term "Judeo-Christian" is racially coded as white, and politically coded as Western, and somehow hence more liberal and enlightened.

It feels relevant to unpack these concepts because Sarah's relationship to God in the Bible, as the mother of the sacrificed son, is very different than Hagar's relationship to God in either the Quran or the Bible. In the first place, as most know, the Jewish and Christian stories have God telling Abraham to sacrifice his son Isaac, the one who was born to Sarah at great cost and as a blessing from God. Muslim tradition, on the other hand, has God asking Abraham to sacrifice his first-born son, Ishmael. The stories are different in an even more significant way: Ishmael is told what is to happen in the thicket—in the traditional story, he assents by saying, "Do what you are commanded, father. You shall find me steadfast"—while the younger son is surprised. "But father," Isaac says upon arrival in the thicket. "Where is the ram?" The compliance of Ishmael and the shock of Isaac lead to very different interpretations of the story for the followers of each different tradition.

The two women are different as well. In the stories, neither woman is present at the sacrifice itself, but each has her own earlier encounter with God. Sarah, unable to bear a child and in extreme old age, is told by God that she will bear a son. Her response is to laugh. Much has been made, by scholars and poets both, of Sarah's laughter. Is it in joy? Disbelief? Despair? Gratitude? The reason for the laughter isn't relevant to the one who laughs: she does bear the miracle son.

Hagar too encounters God, or at least his representative. Her story, as recounted in the Quran, is direr: she has been left alone with her young son in the desert by Abraham. She prays for water but none is found. Hagar panics and starts running between two hills searching for water. In tradition, as soon as she put the baby down and ran, a spring opened at his feet, but she was in such distress that she ran back and forth between the hills seven times before she noticed. To this day, pilgrims on the Hajj follow her trail as part of their pilgrimage. Seven times they run between the hills Safa and Marwa, and at the end they drink from the spring, Zam-zam, which still runs, though piped and bottled now. As the story goes, the city of Mecca was originally built around this very spring.

What happens in the end of both versions of the story is that when Abraham takes the boy up into the thicket, binds him, and then turns to get his knife, he finds that the son has been substituted by a ram. Not as lucky as a human, the poor ram is sacrificed. Of course, this kind of animal sacrifice was common in the ancient Mediterranean, pre-Christian, pre-Jewish religious cults, and we already know that God preferred the sacrifice of animals that Abel the Shepherd offered, rather than Cain the Farmer's offering of grain. Interpreting the events which immediately followed God's decision, one might even suspect that Cain's ill-considered offering perhaps could only be rectified by the offering of his own brother, no ram being available that time, apparently.

The notion of the innocent animal as a sacrifice is also mirrored in the image of Jesus as the "Lamb of God." And certainly, an animal being substituted for an asked-for child sacrifice also has pre-Christian mythological roots, for example in the story of the Trojan War. Agamemnon was told that he had to sacrifice his daughter in order for the winds to rise so the fleet could sail to Troy. Clytemnestra is tricked, thinking she is bringing her daughter to marry Achilles, but she is taken and bound. In Euripides' version of the story, at the last minute before Agamemnon kills her, Artemis sends a doe to replace the girl. She is spirited away to Tauris by the goddess, and in a twist worthy of a contemporary soap opera plot, she eventually, and dramatically, reunites with her long-lost brother, who believed her dead.

In both the ancient myth and in Clifton's poem, the mother is enraged and acts to save her child. In the original myth, Clytemnestra's rage at the death of her daughter leads her to murder her husband. That strike of an axe by Helen's twin sister may have struck the last blow of the ten-year long Trojan War, but it also set in motion a whole other series of events. Coded deep within the canonical myths is the shift from matriarchy to patri-archy, posits Ursule Molinaro in her novel, *The Autobiography of Cassandra*. After all, Molinaro claims, the queens of *The Iliad* and *The Odyssey* are matriarchal and matrilineal queens. It was the husband of Clytemnestra who ruled in Mycenae, and the husband of Penelope who ruled in Ithaca. Helen departed for Troy by leaving her daughter Hermione behind, not abandoning her, but abdicating in her favor.[310] The efforts of the sisters and their cousin in the myths that follow could be seen as their attempts to preserve matriarchal power. Clytemnestra remarries immediately in Agamemnon's absence, while Penelope's refusal to do so marks her resistance to encroaching patriarchy and patrilinearity.[311]

In the end, the effort fails: Euripides tells of the downfall and domestication of the avenging Furies in his play *Eumenides*, in which Orestes is acquitted of the murder of Clytemnestra, judged instead as a legal execution for the crime of killing the king. Helen returns meekly home, reclaiming her throne, and drugs the men into stupor when they seek to remember the war occasioned by her previous departure.[312]

It is by considering these mythological contexts that we can see how Sarah, the enraged mother, is not content to allow the canonical events to transpire. God has commanded the father to kill the son, and the mother is enraged. She is unwilling to sit quietly by. We might find a contemporary equivalent in the enraged mothers of the Women in Black, an organization of Israeli women who are against the military occupation of Palestinian lands, and are trying to defend their sons and daughters from serving in active military.

In Clifton's poem, Sarah assumes the mythic role of the mother of the grieved and begins an argument with God, which is, of course, no laughing matter:

sarah's promise

who understands better than i
the hunger in old bones
for a son? so here we are,
abraham with his faith

and i my fury. jehovah,
i march into the thicket
of your need and promise you
the children of young women,
yours for a thousand years.
their faith will send them to you,
docile as abraham. now,
speak to my husband.
spare me my one good boy.[313]

Usually when one reads a poem, rhythm may follow a natural speech pattern. Certain words like "pattern" for example do have a particular way they are pronounced in English. "Pattern" is a trochee, two syllables in which the emphasis is on the first, i.e. PAT-tern. It may be possible if one is inflecting one's speech for particular emphasis, during the reading of a poem or giving of a speech, to pronounce this word as a spondee as well: PAT-TERN, but this would not be a normal speech pattern, and it would be very difficult to pronounce the word "pattern" as an iamb (two syllable foot with the emphasis on the second foot).

In a song or a rap, the performer can sometimes get away with emphasizing the wrong syllable, but even then, it can be clumsy. On the other hand, in English prosody a line is normally comprised of words of multiple syllables and one doesn't always scan word by word, but across the whole line. It is possible, as we saw earlier, for a line to begin with an unstressed syllable, but in the context of the whole scan trochaic, and the opposite is also true. Annie Finch contends that many so-called "free verse" poems have the "ghost of meter" lurking within them, and this is especially true of Clifton.[314] "[S]arah's promise" serves as a solid exemplar text to see Clifton's deployment of meter at work.

In an accentual-syllabic language like English, one can also scan lines in different ways; one can even deliver a line emphasizing different words for various dramatic effects. For example, return to "aunt jemima" with emphasis in the closing lines on the nouns rather than the repeated "my." You might not be able to pronounce the word "syrup" as anything other than a trochee, but you can vary emphases on connective words, and on monosyllabic words. Often, in song, one hears the performer stretch a single syllable across multiple measures. For example, in Ani DiFranco's song "32 Flavors," one verse with mostly decasyllabic lines closes with a truncated line:

> And God help you if you are a phoenix
> and you dare to rise up from the ash
> a thousand eyes will smolder with jealousy
> while you are just flying past[315]

One sees in the first three lines a close syllable count (10 in the first, 9 in the second, 11 in the third) while the fourth line has only seven syllables—DiFranco not only emphasizes the "ing" in the word "flying"—not the normal emphasis for that word—but also draws out the final syllable "past" across several measures. I bring all of these examples up to show how, in Clifton, one can make different choices as to which words and syllables to emphasize. More often, in poetry that is free verse predominantly, one tries to follow natural speech patterns most of the time, but we see Clifton often turning from more conversational rhythms into more formal and oratorial diction.

Let's see what we can make of the opening of "sarah's promise." I have bolded and capped what I see as the natural heavy stresses:

> **WHO** under**STANDS BET**ter than **I**
> (the) **HUNG**er in **OLD BONES**
> for a **SON**?
>
> (so) **HERE WE ARE**,
> **AB**raham with his **FAITH**
> and **I MY FU**ry.

You will notice that I put two syllables in parentheses. As in "further note to clark," we can see how individual syllables with less content (usually connecting words like "the," "a" or "so") rhythmically don't impact the momentum of the line. One *could* emphasize the "the" in the second line, but it doesn't make sense to, and once you see the pattern in the rest of the line, it seems less important as a whole. The matter of the "so" at the beginning of the second stanza is somewhat different in that the line *could* be pronounced "So **HERE** we **ARE,"** a little more conversational than the dramatic stressing of all three syllables—**HERE WE ARE**—a pattern I hear because of its matching with the line stresses of the middle line and the three heavy stresses in the third line of this same stanza. But I get ahead of myself.

What we have here in these first three lines is a regular metrical scheme disguised a little bit by the line break on "old bones," which Clifton uses perhaps to emphasize Sarah's condition. In scanning, one uses a slash to mark a heavy stress and can use a small "u" or "x" to mark a light stress (a spondee would typically be marked with two horizontal lines, but for ease I stick with slashes here).

Let me relineate the above, and divide the syllables, to show you the pattern:

> **WHO** un der **STANDS BET** ter than **I**
> (the) **HUNG** er in **OLD BONES**
> for a **SON?**

The stresses fall like this:

> / x x / / x x /
> (x) / x x / / x x /

You can now see that there is a pattern here of four beats which follows a metrical scheme: heavy stress-light stress-light stress-heavy stress, demarked as / x x /. This particular foot is called a choriamb, and if you imagined that it is not very common in English poetry you would be right. It is a stately rhythm, not one of the classical rhythms of lyric (sung) poetry in the ancient tradition. It is also a rhythm Keats was fond of—one hears it throughout his odes, particularly in "To Autumn"—but more about Clifton and Keats in a moment. The choriamb also does carry within it the feel of anapestic meter, the traditional rhythm of the chorus speaking in a Greek tragedy. In other words, it is the speech pattern of a background character who is trying to get the audience's attention. In this case, Sarah is indeed a background character, left out of the story of the impending death of her son. She does not mean to be ignored.

As Sarah speaks to God, one could consider her effort to make common cause with Him ironic: after all God too has "old bones," and will hunger for a Son; a Son that He Himself is willing to send into the thicket; a Son that He will not replace with a ram, but allow to be sacrificed. But Sarah means to make a deeper comparison, one between her and her husband, and she makes her point through *meter*:

> (so) **HERE WE ARE,**
> **AB**raham with his **FAITH**
> and **I MY FU**ry.

First, let us notice that Sarah begins with three heavy stresses (as in the first line of "monticello") to make her point. It's true, as I mentioned above, one could pronounce this line in many ways. One could emphasize the "so" or the "here" or the "are"—one might even emphasize the "we," though Sarah's commonality with Abraham seems less the point, as evident in the way she distinguishes them from one another.

"Abraham with his faith" might be scanned as: / x x x x /, whilst Sarah, presented in the line, "and I my fury," scans as an exact inversion: x / / / x .

In other words, Clifton is using the prosody to demonstrate the personalities of the characters in the story. Abraham's sonic life is more rhythmic and easier: he has agreed to the dramatic thing God is asking him to do. In a lilting line of six syllables, only two are heavy, the opening and closing ones, giving it a light and musical feel. Contrast this with Sarah's description of herself, the three heavy stresses—the same is in "this black sally"—hunching down, pulling inward.

Thus, situated in very different relationships to the task ahead and to God Himself, Sarah is going to pivot and introduce her ask. Once again, I will bold what I hear as the heavy stresses:

jehovah,

i **march in**to [could also be read as in**to**] the **thick**et
of your **need** and **prom**ise you
the **chil**dren of **young wom**en,
yours for a **thous**and **years.**
their **faith** will **send** them **to** you, [could also be read as "to **you"**]
docile as abraham. **now,**
speak to my **hus**band.
spare me my **one good boy.**

Now this passage actually starts out feeling more or less trochaic, but there is a disruption quickly followed by another—on the words "young" and "yours." Just as Clifton emphasized the word "black" in the line "from this black sally" we see/hear the word "yours" highlighted by its placement here.

As I did with the relineation of the Sanchez poem, I want to show you how regularly metrical this line sounds without those interruptions of "yours" and "young":

jehovah, i march into the thicket of your need and promise you
the children of women for a thousand years...

The promise is both powerful and horrifying. It's powerful because she's making a deal with God. That would be enough of a reason to marvel at it—and we know she wins because we already know the end of the story. But it is also horrifying, because she is giving away the lives of the children of other women, *young* women, unlike Sarah.

Sarah's promise leads us into an ending which contains both a rhythmic lightness and the triple heavy stress we have come to recognize as one of the meters in Clifton's toolkit.

One can read that line, "their faith will send them to you," in various ways. I highlighted the heavy stresses where they made the most rhythmic and dramatic sense to me, but one could interpret the line in a different way:

(their) **faith** will **send** them **to** you

By now one hopes a reader/listener will hear the line "docile as Abraham" and recognize a double dactyl. Docile as Abraham. The "now" which follows is another pause, an interruption, the speaker Sarah making sure her audience (God) is paying attention to her. Her opening sortie, "speak to my husband/spare me my," traffics in the same lilting dactylic feeling as the previous lines, but it belies Sarah's seriousness: she ends with the very stressed line, "my one good boy." One could emphasize the final three of these syllables or one could emphasize all four of them, but in either case she is hammering her point home.

Clifton used various types of poetic forms throughout her work. One might look at the stanza patterns of "my daddy's fingers move among the couplers," "the lost baby poem," "light," "there is a girl inside," or "the son of Medgar" to see the different structures she adopts. In other poems such as "OLD HUNDRED," "shadows," or "consulting the book of changes: radiation," she uses the call-and-response typical of Black church services. Various other poems use specific structures built around repetition, numbered parts following the same patterns of lines or rhymes, or list poems.

Earlier in her work, Clifton often used the ghost of a sonnet form. Daisy Fried recounted to me that she heard Alicia Ostriker, in a lecture, pointing out that Clifton's "miss rosie" more or less uses the scheme of a Shakespearean sonnet with three quatrain-like sections and a turn at the end (in three lines rather than a couplet) beginning with "i stand up." The shape of a sonnet lurks behind other poems as well such as "ca'line's prayer" and "if something should happen."

Let us take a look then at one of Clifton's most popular poems, one she frequently performed at readings, usually at the end, often asking the audience to recite along with her if they knew the poem, which they mostly did:

> won't you celebrate with me
> what I have shaped into
> a kind of life? i had no model.
> born in babylon
> both nonwhite and woman
> what did i see to be except myself?
> i made it up
> here on this bridge between
> starshine and clay,
> my one hand holding tight
> my other hand; come celebrate
> with me that everyday
> something has tried to kill me
> and has failed.[316]

While "sarah's promise" ended with the drama of three stressed syllables to drive its point solidly home, here were are welcomed into the poem, as Clifton did by inviting her audiences to recite with her. She returns to normative punctuation here, using periods and question marks, even though the line breaks vary between Longenbach's three kinds, some ending on a grammatical phrase, some end-stopped, and a few enjambments. After those three stresses one moves into an iambic rhythm, though it is a little disguised by the line breaks. This rhythmic opening then transitions into a bare statement, made more important because of the punctuation used to frame it (as in Sanchez's "woman. alone. amid")—"I had no model."

Clifton returns to an iambic rhythm over the next six lines, interrupting the music with the declaration of her own personal strength in the lines "my one hand holding tight/my other hand." In these lines we once more see a series of heavy stresses calling emphasis to the moment—the six syllable line "my one hand holding tight" contains in it five heavy stresses.

"Come celebrate," she extorts again, and then in the last three lines of this short poem continues the chain of heavy stresses. It's true that one could recite the ending of this poem more conversationally, like so:

> **with** me that **every**day
> **some**thing has **tried** to **kill** me
> and has **failed**.

One could also choose, as Clifton did in her performances, to bring a stentorian and oratorial emphasis to the ending by stressing both the "me" and the last three words:

> **with me** that **every**day
> **some**thing has **tried** to **kill** me
> **and has failed**.

Omar F. Miranda writes of this poem that Clifton "channels the Blakean imagination once again by tracking her personal creation myth" and sees her reference to the "bridge between/ starshine and clay" as a reference to Keats' "On Sitting Down to Read King Lear Once Again," where he writes of being "betwixt damnation and impassion'd clay."[317]

While Keats' bridge is between hell and earth, Miranda contends, Clifton's is between the earth and heaven. Rather than such a dichotomy between the material and spiritual—or human and divine—which Clifton has shown a reticence to espouse, I rather think of the opposition between "starshine" and "clay" meaning the two origin points of human existence, "starshine" in the actual and scientific world being the origin point of all matter on earth, and "clay" being the stuff God made Adam out of. It's an interesting irony that the more mystical and elevated element is the scientific origin of human flesh while the ruder and baser element is the spiritual origin.

Clifton seems to be, as Miranda goes on to explain, also adopting Keats' sonnet form in this poem, though it is a loose adoption indeed. Still there are three turns in the poem, as in the English sonnet, here at lines 3, 7, and 11, and the rough structure of quatrains and a final couplet/turn can be seen.

It ought to be clear by now that Clifton's poems can certainly be read on the page, but to read them aloud opens up new rooms of meaning. Her use of prosody and metrical elements, sustained and strategic, is sometimes counterintuitive, and requires a more careful and engaged ear than listening to the rhythms in a poet more obviously trafficking in regular meter. In Clifton, meter is all strategy, switching within the poem to create added tension, suspension, humor, or emphasis. She is as at home with a conversational tone as she is with those disconcerting trochee-iamb and dactyl-anapest switches. Paying attention to sound patterns in Clifton's lines, as well as the architecture of sound in the poems themselves, will greatly enrich understanding of her work's content and increase the aural pleasure of its music.

Chapter 9: Dark Lucille

"To speak is a great adventure," says Stanley Kunitz, in cautious—though perhaps privileged—optimism.[318] Lucille Clifton has always, from her earliest published work and throughout her career, tackled painful and difficult subjects, both personal and communal. And—as she has also written poetry about—she has a double burden: not only must she live through the painful and difficult experiences she has had in her life, but she commits herself to contending with these experiences in her writing, both the poetry and the writing for children. Kunitz praises boldness, but Lucille Clifton asks, nearly plaintively, in a short poem called "prayer," which concludes the opening section of *good news about the earth*, "why is your hand/so heavy/on just poor/me?"[319]

It is unclear in this question whether she is beseeching an answer from "God" or muse or some other force. Clifton's relationship to "God" throughout her work is what scholar Bettina Judd calls "atheological." The term "atheology" is from Ashon Crawley's critique of theology, namely that classical theology and philosophy "come together to target the object of blackness."[320] Clifton's own relationship to god-like figures or divinities, as we have seen, tends toward the pantheistic, even shamanistic. The monotheistic uppercase "God," in Clifton's work, is complicated, even untrustworthy. There's a reason why Black people distrust classical theological explanations for what 'good' is, and why God allows 'evil' to exist in the world, contends Judd. "Theodicy poses a particular problem for Black folks globally," Judd explains. "It is founded in a set of philosophies already designed to desecrate the body, mind, and spirit of a Black woman poet."[321] Still, what Judd recognizes as the most important prevailing through-line of emotion in Clifton's work is not despair, but *joy*. Regardless of the pain and duress and loss that characterized much of her experiences, Clifton continued to try to be brave and even joyous. In her famous poem "won't you celebrate with me," Clifton asks her readership and audiences to join her on that bridge "between starshine and clay" in order to celebrate that very survival.

In recognition of the deep vein of struggle, though never resignation, that tinges Clifton's work, Hilary Holladay even calls the second chapter of *Wild Blessings*, her study on Clifton's work, "Dark Blessings." The first chapter's title references "light," so Holladay is making a strong contrast very early on between what she sees as two primary elements in Clifton's work.

While one sees Clifton engaging with grief and trauma— "cancer and terrible loneliness/and the wars against our people"— it is not until a particular moment, the new poems included in *Blessing the Boats*, that she enters the period that I think of as "Dark Lucille."[322] As repeated illness strikes, and Clifton brings to full light the extent of her childhood traumas, the work undergoes a dramatic shift. Although "dark"—in its old racist connotations—conjures confusion, or ignorance, here I think of "dark" being a more subtle illumination: as one learns to "see in the dark," here in Lucille's later period, one gains greater and more subtle understanding of suffering, informed by painfully won wisdom and knowledge.

The work changes in three significant ways.

First of all, and perhaps most obviously, she published less new work. Clifton published five full length books in the period between 1969-1980 and fourteen children's books. Then, as mentioned earlier, she had a poetry publishing hiatus from 1980-1987, during which time she nonetheless published three children's books, including the important *Everett Anderson's Goodbye* and *Lucky Stone*, one of her two middle-grade novels. She had a second very productive period from 1987-1996: in these nine years she published four full-length collections, collecting some of her most important and anthologized poems. Throughout this period, her books are generally between fifty and seventy pages long; some longer, none shorter. In the last fourteen years of her life, she published only three new books, and each of her last three collections contained significant portions of previously published work.

As I have come to discover, it is not that Clifton was writing less, but that she was shaping the last three books very carefully—one was a volume of new and selected poems—and withholding many of the new poems she was writing during this period. When they worked in the archives, editors Kevin Young and Michael Glaser found thirty-four unpublished poems from this time period; I found nearly one hundred more in Clifton's digital files.

In the second major shift from her earlier work, the poetry is formally more varied in terms of language and diction, often using a longer and more sinewy line than the extreme pared down form she had become known for. The new poems from *Blessing the Boats*, *Mercy*, and *Voices* also rely less on the disembodied and oracular tone, less on the rhetoric of prayer to the other-worldly, and become more ordinary in voice, more daily in tone, as were so many of the unpublished poems she wrote during this period.

In a structure reminiscent of the circularity of *generations*, each of these collections include concluding sections of previously published work: *Blessing the Boats* includes selected poems, *Mercy* includes the twenty-four-page sequence "Message to the Ones," originally drafted in the 1970s, and *Voices* includes "The Oxherding Pictures," which had been published as a letterpress edition in the late 1980s. The new poems included in each volume were a smaller portion of the whole: *Blessing the Boats* includes nineteen new poems, *Mercy* includes twenty-four new poems (one of these is the seven-part sequence written in response to the events of September 11, 2001 in New York City), and *Voices*—with the largest percentage of new work—includes twenty-eight new poems.

The third shift is the most significant one. Clifton's daughter Rica passed away from cancer in 2000, even as Clifton herself was contending with the disease; but this shattering event was not the end of the trouble coming around: her son Chan passed in 2004 from an undiagnosed heart condition. Both *Mercy* and *Voices* are dedicated to the two children, though the earlier drafts of *Mercy* are dedicated only to Rica: Chan had yet not passed at their composition. *Mercy* mentions both by name, along with their dates, while the dedication page of *Voices* refers to them as "my little bird and my beamish boy." *Mercy* bears the epigraph underneath which gives the book its title, "the only mercy is memory,"—though its title can also be interpreted as a scream from an oppressed person for succor—while the dedication page of *Voices* bears the traditional Black lyric, "all goodbye ain't gone."

As clear-eyed as she was before, in these late poems Lucille Clifton opens herself up to spaces of deep and abiding grief, intense sorrow, pessimism, resentment, and the regrets of a lifetime. This is not the Clifton that is most often celebrated, but we have learned by now that precarity in the face of danger in the world has always been a part of her work. Indeed, though "won't you celebrate with me" is thought of as a highly jubilant poem, asking the reader to "celebrate" the poet's resilience, we must remember what has required this resilience: a world that is daily trying *to kill her*.

I identify two hinge moments in the poetry itself upon which this shifting emotional paradigm takes place. The first moment is quite subtle, one little shift at the end of a poem, while the second is more dramatic, announcing itself loudly and firmly.

Typical of the way Lucille Clifton makes rooms of meaning with a single syllable, the first moment happens in a single mark of punctuation at the end of the poem "dialysis," which appears among the new poems of *Blessing the Boats*. The poem describes Clifton's dialysis after kidney failure in the wake of the treatment for multiple cancers (the first of which is described in *The Terrible Stories*):

> We are not supposed to hate
> the dialysis unit.   we are not
> supposed to hate the universe.[323]

Clifton seems here willing to finally concede the unflagging optimism of "won't you celebrate with me," saying here, "this is not supposed to happen to me." When she finally comes to the end of the poem, she declares—with what might initially be taken to be courage:

after the cancer i was so grateful
to be alive.   i am alive and furious.

She echoes here both the "fury" of Thelma Sayles at burning her poems and also the fury with which Joanne C.'s mother
lifts her up by the scruff of her neck in *Next* and demands that she
"Live   Live   Live!"[324]

What follows is a line that a reader of Clifton would be
forgiven for thinking was along the lines of "won't you celebrate
me," but unlike in that poem, and many others of hers, here Clifton
does include a question mark at the end of the question:

Blessed be even this?

It is a devastating moment. Clifton will not make a declaration of survival or worth of struggle, or nobility in victory over the
degradation of flesh. In an interview following her (long overdue)
receipt of the National Book Award for this collection, she even
mentions this moment as atypical of her and unexpected for her
readers. "Some people would have expected me to just say 'Blessed
be even this' without that question mark." In her self-deprecating
way, Clifton comments, "But dialysis is not fun, you know? Kidney
failure is not fun."[325] Clifton makes light of the paradigm-shifting
question mark, but this is precisely what Judd was zeroing in on
when she said perhaps Clifton's "theology" was an "atheology."
After all, for a deeply physically afflicted person, what might it mean
to argue a philosophy that *everything* is part of 'God's plan?'

Atheology is a framework Crawley developed that Judd
explains is a spiritual outlook in which "God is not infallible, and
Lucifer ain't all bad." Certainly Lucille has uplifted the voice of
Lucifer, the fallen brother, throughout her poetry.[326]

If "dialysis" represents a turn in Clifton's writing about her
own body, the second moment I identify happens in a poem of hers
responding to external events in the world.

Clifton was a longtime member of the Community of Writers,
an organization founded by novelists Oakley Hall and Blair Fuller to
run writers' workshops in California, including a Poetry Program,

which to this day runs each summer in the mountains outside Tahoe for a week. She had been invited there by her friend Galway Kinnell, who had taken over direction of the Poetry Program and had given it a unique format. Halfway between a conference and a retreat, the Poetry Program participants do not bring previously published work, nor work with the same fixed workshop leader and classmates, as is typical in most writing workshops, but rather each day must write a new poem to share with a rotating workshop, run by a different poet. The workshop leaders—called by participants in egalitarian terms, "staff poets"—must also write a poem each day, and submit that poem for workshop feedback. Energized and inspired by the process, Clifton attended nearly every year from 1991 until her passing, joining regular staff poets—Kinnell, Sharon Olds, Brenda Hillman, and Robert Hass among them—as well as many other visiting writers, such as Li-Young Lee, Gerald Stern, Cornelius Eady, and C.D. Wright.

I was at the Community of Writers with Lucille Clifton in the summer of 1998 the morning she brought in the manuscript of the poem "jasper texas 1998." Though I myself heard Lucille say in a reading in 1995 that she revised all her poems heavily, with one single exception ("let there be new flowering"), I can attest that the version of "jasper texas 1998" published in *Blessing the Boats* is the same as the poem she brought into the workshop that day in the valley, with one single difference: her manuscript, produced on a typewriter, bore the slightly abbreviated title, "jasper tx 1998."

It was July. James Byrd, Jr., a Black man living in the Texas town named in the title of Clifton's poem, had just been murdered. The killing made national news, not solely because it was a hate crime—two of the three men who murdered Byrd were avowed white supremacists—but also because of the gruesome nature of the killing. The men, one of whom was acquainted with Byrd for many years, offered him a ride home from work in his pickup truck. Instead of taking him there, the men took him to an isolated area of forest, beat him senseless, then chained him up to the back of the pickup and drove off, dragging him down the road until his body was dismembered. The autopsy results confirmed Byrd was alive for some time before he died, and that he was struggling to hold his head up the entire time. While his head and one arm were intact, the rest of his remains were spread across eighty-one different forensic locations.[327]

Clifton takes the horrific nature of the crime and makes it—appropriately, perhaps, for the level of horror it involved—mythic. She begins, "i am a man's head hunched in the road./i was chosen to speak by the members/of my body." The bare facts of the case become a ghostly metaphor in Clifton's hands. Byrd's head—one of two intact parts of his body—must now speak for the whole. Rather than the earlier enjoinders to that generous union—"come into the black/and live"—the outlook here is far more bleak: Clifton's Byrd asks in desperation, "why and why and why/should i call a white man brother?" and later, "the townsfolk sing we shall overcome/ while hope bleeds slowly from my mouth":

> jasper texas 1998
> *for j. byrd*
>
> i am a man's head hunched in the road.
> i was chosen to speak by the members
> of my body.   the arm as it pulled away
> pointed toward me, the hand opened once
> and was gone.
>
> why and why and why
> should i call a white man brother?
> who is the human in this place,
> the thing that is dragged or the dragger?
> what does my daughter say?
>
> the sun is a blister overhead.
> if i were alive i could not bear it.
> the townsfolk sing we shall overcome
> while hope bleeds slowly from my mouth
> into the dirt that covers us all.
> i am done with this dust.   i am done.[328]

The speaker here turns from any sense of possibility of the future, any notion that there could be reconciliation, and even any concept of liberation following a sacrifice, as was present in the Christian mythos informing "some jesus," "tree of life," and "brothers." Byrd is perhaps closer to Clifton's regretful David, asking—in an inversion and echo of David's final question—"who is the human in this place,/the thing that is dragged or the dragger?"

Byrd ends in resigned acceptance of death, or with frustration and rage, depending on how you read "i am done." This ending utterance is also an echo of Jesus' final groan, "it is done." Clifton's last line reads sadder though, knowing that this is a poet who has spent a lifetime writing poems that affirm life and kinship through even the most challenging of moments. From "blessed be even this?" to "i am done with this dust.   i am done" we see a turn in Clifton, now profoundly alone, pessimistic in a way we have not seen before.

Two of the men involved in Byrd's killing received the death penalty, while the third received life in prison. Texas passed a hate crimes statute; and in 2007, the United States—nearly ten years after Byrd's murder, and Matthew Shepard's murder later that same autumn—followed suit. Byrd's son Ross, a conscientious objector to the death penalty, campaigned for years to have his father's killers spared, unsuccessfully. The first was executed in 2011, the second in 2018, the first white men ever sentenced to death for killing a black person in the history of Texas. Neither man ever repented of their crime.

As if to connect the violence done to Byrd's body with a historic lineage of the decimation of Black bodies, the poem on the facing page in the collection is one called "alabama 9/15/63." The poems are linked spatially, but also by the format of their titles— location and time of event. Their form links them as well: "alabama 9/15/1963" also appears in three stanzas—though not the same length—and includes questions in it, one more than in "jasper texas 1998." The title's location and date refers to the infamous bombing of a church in Alabama, in which four young Black girls were killed.

It's notable that in this poem, Clifton uses normative punctuation and capitalization. "Have you heard the one," she opens, establishing a conversational tone immediately, drawing the reader into a past, similar to the way the narrative voices in the novels *The Lucky Stone* and *The Times They Used to Be* and the poem "memory" frame the past as an active part of present life. In the case of the 1963 Alabama church bombing, it *was* and still is part of the present in which Clifton published the poem: by 2000, the year *Blessing the Boats* was published, only one of the four Ku Klux Klan members who had been found by the FBI to be responsible for the crime had ever been charged. Another of the four had long before died himself, without ever being charged, and the final two were just then being tried; the prosecutor in the case was Doug Jones, who decades later would serve a brief but notable term in the U.S. Senate.

Clifton mentions the four girls who were killed by name— "the one about Cynthia and Carole and Denise and Addie/Mae?"— asking again "Have you heard the one about/the four little birds/ shattered into skylarks in the white/light of Birmingham?"[329] The girls here become birds—facing Byrd in the book—shattered by the "white" light of the place Martin Luther King called the "most segregated city in America." If there is lightness in Dark Lucille, it is leavened—though only slightly—not within the poem "jasper Texas 1998," which is unrelenting, but in poems that follow. "[A]labama 9/15/63" ends with a more poetic evocation of the violence and grief: "Have you heard how the skylarks,/known for their music,/ swooped into heaven,/.../how the blast/is still too bright to hear them play?"[330] Despite the beauty of the image, Clifton is still mourning that the violence with which the young girls' lives ended has effaced their identities and destroyed any potential they might have had in their lives, personified here when she mentions their "never to be borne daughters and sons."

In the closing poems of the new poems section of *Blessing the Boats*, Clifton returns to figures from her earlier sequences, but with a more somber and less exuberant manner. Lazarus reappears, darker and more pensive about his experience of resurrection at the hands of Jesus, and one of the fawning angels from "tree of life" returns with a somewhat more sober outlook on the Fall.

Lazarus tells us his story in three "days," the same amount of time between the crucifixion and resurrection of Christ. In this way, he is likened as a mirror figure to Christ, a savior of a different kind, his bardo period being three days in new life, rather than three days after death and before rebirth. In the "first day," Lazarus describes rising from death, which he describes as a "stiffening" toward a voice calling him toward, not light, but "forever," and then another voice, that of Jesus, presumably, calling him back. Upon his return, he says to his sisters Mary and Martha that the voice calling him forth and the voice calling him back were "the same voice."[331] He seems to recognize the unity of the Divine, swimming in what he described as "a river of sound."

Lazarus, though, is mortal. The sameness of the divine, the union that Lazarus recognizes between Father and Son, seems to imply that death and life too are equal conditions, that it wouldn't have mattered if he had gone on rather than return. Such equanimity of the Divine does not seem fair to apply to the mortal. Lazarus says, "i am not the same man/borne into the crypt." His use of "borne" is hardly accidental: another kind of birth has happened there, if, indeed, he has been transformed by his ordeal. He clarifies, "what entered the light was one man./what walked out is another."[332]

In the earlier poem, "the raising of lazarus," the transformation from death to life is seen as liberation, especially in the political context that Clifton places figures like Daniel, Jonah, and Mary in other poems from "some jesus," and in the context of poems in the section, "heroes," about Angela Davis, Bobby Seale, Malcolm X, and other contemporary figures. Clifton continued this promise of resurrection, though in a darker fashion, in the poem, "atlantic is a sea of bones." Here in the later Lazarus poems, however, the return from death is seen as a burden, and is confusing to Lazarus. In "third day," he sits struggling with understanding "what i was moving from/what i was moving toward."[333] The others around him are equally hungry to know the secrets of eternity, asking him questions about his experience. Lazarus yearns for the one thing he is certain of, but also knows the price of such knowledge. The reader will have to wonder whether Lazarus intends entreaty or warning when he tells his sisters, "stand away/from the door to my grave/ the only truth i know."

Clifton presented a somewhat hopeful view of the expulsion from the garden in the sequence "tree of life." In those poems, it's true that the angels worry about the aftermath, but Eve herself walks proudly out of the garden and an unrepentant (pre-"brothers") Lucifer makes a pretty good case for himself having given carnal knowledge to humans for all the right reasons. The later poem, "report from the angel of eden," that closes out the new poems section in *Blessing the Boats* presents a somewhat different outlook. The angel knows the period of immortality is over and that death will follow, even for the angel themselves. The angel knows "they could do evil/...and i knew/they would."[334] As he watches the humans in their first sexual act outside the garden, he sees that "it was like dancing/creation flowered around them." Though he eventually comes to his senses and turns back to return to God in the garden, he is left with the lingering question (sans question mark): "what now becomes/what now//of Paradise."

Clifton doesn't only return and revisit past themes and subjects in the poems of the book alone. The title of the collection, *Blessing the Boats*, also bears a double meaning. Obviously, it is a reference to Clifton's poem of that same title, which in its original publication closed out the collection *Quilting*. Originally an occasional poem written to bless actual boats preparing to launch as part of an annual event held in St. Mary's City, Maryland, "blessing the boats" became a beloved and oft-quoted poem of Clifton's, an entreaty for an easy and peaceful journey through dangerous circumstances. It closes with one of Clifton's uncannily effective abstractions: "may you in your innocence/sail through this to that."[335] In the context of being the title of the entire book of new and selected poems, one is tempted to think that Clifton is using it as an expression of hope even through the difficulties she describes in "moonchild," "jasper Texas 1998," the lazarus poems, and others in the collection.

Yet, the painting that graces the cover of *Blessing the Boats* is "Siren's Song" by African American painter and collagist Romare Bearden. The painting depicts an episode from the Odyssey in which Odysseus and his ships are sailing close to the sirens, whose songs have been known to captivate sailors into jumping into the sea and drowning. In the epic, the witch Circe has taught Odysseus how he might hear the song: he is to have his men lash him to the mast of the ship and promise not to release him no matter how much he demands it. They are then to plug up their own ears with beeswax so they can steer the ship past the fatal musicians.

It is a curious story. On the one hand, Odysseus wants to hear the forbidden song. His story is analogous to Eve seeking knowledge, and notably it is the witch Circe—a goddess herself, an embodiment of feminine divinity, who, like Lucifer, knows the art of transformation and transmutation—who has the knowledge of how to access this experience. But it is also a story about hierarchy and power: Odysseus is given the tools with which to gain forbidden knowledge while his crew is not given the same opportunity. In Bearden's painting, the ship is in the background, the sailors and the captain are all black. Odysseus is tied halfway up the mast, hanging there, rather than at the base of the mast as described in Homer's epic. In the foreground of the painting are, presumably, the sirens. Undescribed visually in Homer's epic, here they are depicted in African dress and in an African landscape. They are pointing at the ship, reaching for it.

In other words, it is not Odysseus from the myths who is on the ship. It is a slave ship. With a prisoner lashed to the mast.

The "Siren's song" in this painting is the grieving wails of the Africans left behind, reaching for their stolen families. Perhaps the boats being blessed are those ships, sailing away into the unknown. In this case, the statement echoing in the air is not, "may you in your innocence/sail through this to that," but that haunting choral wail from the poem "slaveships," which also appears in *Blessing the Boats*, "can this tongue speak/can these bones walk/Grace Of God/can this sin live."

While *Mercy* contends with the deeply personal losses of Clifton's daughter Rica and her son Chan, it deals also with the crisis in the national psyche and consciousness engendered by the events of 9/11/2001. *Mercy* ends warily, even somewhat bleakly, with the inclusion of the sequence, "Message from the Ones," which Lucille said was drawn from the many transcripts of her experiences channeling in the 1970s, poems that she—with the exception of the short sequence, "the light that came to lucille clifton," included in *two-headed woman*—had elected not to include in any of her previous books.

It was very early in her work that Clifton began writing of the burden of being a poet, of having to bring work into the world. Some of the dramas Adam suffers around the naming of things could perhaps also be seen through this lens. In the poem "wild blessings" (whose title Holladay used for her book), published in 1991's *quilting*, Clifton confesses, "i am grateful for many blessings/ but the gift of understanding,/the wild one, maybe not."[336] It's a tentative statement here, but thirteen years later, after the deaths of two children, Clifton is less sanguine. In a poem called "children" which appears directly after "sonku," the haiku about Chan's death, she writes:

> children
>
> they are right, the poet mother
> carries her wolf in her heart,
> wailing at pain yet suckling it like
> romulus and remus.   this now.
> how will i forgive myself
> for trying to bear the weight of this
> and trying to bear the weight also
> of writing the poem
> about this?[337]

To be a poet means to suckle the pain, to allow it full expression and then to let it linger, to worry over it while one crafts language to better describe and share it. That Clifton feels there is something to be forgiven means the deed itself is somehow a transgression—against the memory of the deceased, perhaps against the purity of grief that ought to be personal and not shared. The poem "children" closes the first section of *Mercy*, and the untitled first poem of the following section seems to contend with what it means to be so governed by singular events, such as the death of children. Clifton *wants* to leave the pain behind, but it haunts every subject:

> surely i am able to write poems
> celebrating grass and how the blue
> in the sky can flow green or red
> and the waters lean against the
> chesapeake shore like a familiar,
> poems about nature and landscape
> surely   but whenever i begin
> "the trees wave their knotted branches
> and..." why
> is there under that poem always
> an other poem?[338]

This layering of fresh grief underneath all other experiences is reminiscent of the much earlier poem where Clifton points out that an ordinary landscape, "what white poets call the past" reads much differently to an African American person. There is always a fractured and multiple experience happening in life and in poetry, for example in a poem ostensibly about mulberry fields unable to produce fruit, Clifton describes the unacknowledged legacy of slavery on that same land, diffidently concluding, "bloom how you must i say."[339]

In a late poem, "man-kind: digging a trench to hell," that Clifton elected not to include in either of her last books, she contends with the problem of the poet's task even more bleakly:

> did i go deep enough?
>
> i've exhausted the earth,
> the plentiful garden,
> the woman,
> myself.

i've exhausted even the darkness now.

are you not done with me yet?[340]

    While the poems about Chan's death are full of grief, and end with his body cold, his heart stopped, the poems about Rica all take place after her death, with Rica present and active in some kind of afterlife. Unlike the poems of Thelma and Fred speaking to Clifton after their deaths, removed in various ways from mortal matters, Rica seems aware in the afterlife of Clifton's lived life, and concerned about it. She speaks across less of a distance and, like Lazarus, seems more aware that death and life are close experiences. She entreats Clifton, "try to feel me feel you/i am saying i still love you." In the end there is an odd interruption of voice, and it is unclear whether it is Lucille who is speaking to the spirit-Rica or if it is Rica speaking back, calling her own mother "baby," since the poem bears an odd parenthetical first line, "(mama)": "i am trying to say/from my mouth/but baby there is no/mouth."[341]

    Clifton somehow picks up and moves on from these unimaginable losses because, as she says in another later uncollected poem, "there were other children."[342] Among her papers is a list of New Year's resolutions Clifton wrote in a small notebook given to her by the Academy of American Poets. Beneath a heading "2005" surrounded by two capital L's in a looping cursive, Clifton wrote a poignant list of twelve resolutions, both practical and forward looking:

    1) lose weight (exercise, food, etc.)
    2) detach more from the past
    3) consistently try to look my best
    4) enjoy myself more (go out, etc.)
    5) try to be more emotionally stable
    6) do not procrastinate or put off stuff
    7) say yes less, don't worry about "shoulds"
    8) travel for fun
    9) seek medical care and advice consistently
    10) write better

11) try to feel less guilty
12) make a will[343]

Even before "the Message of the Ones," Clifton circles back in time by including the sequence "september song: a poem in 7 days," which she wrote in the week following September 11, 2001 before the loss of her children. The sequence has one poem for each of the days beginning with 9/11. She critiques American exceptionalism right away, recognizing amid the tragedy, as many did, that:

> they know this storm in otherwheres
> israel   ireland   palestine
> but God has blessed America
> we sing[344]

Once more Clifton's capitalizing of "God" and "America" here—while the names of Israel, Ireland, and Palestine (not quite such a random selection of exemplar countries, after all) are uncapitalized as standard in Clifton's work—is a pointed further critique. She further cites various examples of racist violence in America while honoring the actions and sacrifices of the first responders in New York City on that day.

Despite this, of course, Clifton is unwilling to accept the dominant narrative of victimhood. "Some of us know," she says, "we have never felt safe."[345] When many Americans, ordinarily inured from such a degree of violence both home and abroad, wondered what was the source of such violence and hate against the United States, Clifton answered with a pointed double-entendre:

> what have we done
> to deserve such villainy
>
> nothing we reassure ourselves
> nothing

That "nothing" of course means both the ignoring of the pain and violence America has caused around the world both in wars and in the impacts of its cold wars, secret wars, CIA-sponsored coups, and economic and political imperialisms, but also a *lack of action* in truly decolonizing and creating an environment of justice and equity around the world. The word also hearkens painfully back to "l. at nagasaki" where the speaker says:

> in their own order
> the things of my world
> glisten into ash. i
> have done nothing
> to deserve this,
> only been to the silver birds
> what they have made me.
> nothing.[346]

The sequence "message from The Ones" presents a starker and bleaker set of spiritual engagements than any of Clifton's earlier spiritual writing. Although the pieces were originally written/transcribed in automatic writing sessions in the 70s, their place in her work—as the concluding section of her penultimate book—feels appropriate. As far as her other spiritual writing goes, the growing pessimism that perhaps began with the very flawed speaker of "from the Book of David," and continued with the later "lazarus" poems, seem more in line with the tone and voice from these poems, a voice that is not always kind, often impatient, and at times feels unconcerned with whether or not Clifton is listening and what, if anything, she will do with the information she is receiving.

While Clifton may not have edited these texts—and the pages I saw in the archive seem to attest that she did indeed not—she still did select from the material and arranged it: the pages from which "messages from The Ones" was drawn comprises six folders, about two-thirds of one of the three boxes that hold Clifton's "spirit writing." There are numerous other sequences and notebooks included in the boxes, according to scholar Sumita Chakraborty, who studied them. "Most of Clifton's spirit writing, however," the archival note attached to the catalog for the item warns, "is inde-cipherable." In a fashion, this seems appropriate. The writing was personal and direct. It foregrounds its own source as external from Clifton as a poet herself by announcing before the first poem starts, "beginning of Message."

"Your mother sends you this," the voices begin by way of introducing themselves to Clifton through the familiar, though they are then quick to clarify their own status as strangers to her: "we are not she."[347] They are not friendly voices, and normally come across as brusque, even anticipating Clifton's doubts and questions and dismissing her, saying ,"why you/why not."[348] They do not aim to comfort her, but to strip her of her sense of her own impor-tance. At one point they dress her down, saying, "your tongue/is useful/not unique."[349] Of themselves and their own identity, they do not say much, but what they do say implies that they are both beyond knowing, and wholly ordinary. In one place they clarify, "we are ones/who have not rolled/selves into bone and flesh" and later simply "we are we," and "we are just here/where you are," implying, as in the Muslim view of life after death, described in the Quran, that the dead are wholly ordinary and present, just beyond the senses of the living.[350]

Though the Ones are physically present and aware of the quotidian and phenomenal world, they do possess an understand-ing and vision beyond the limits of the human—"what you have not noticed/we have noticed," they say, advising, "pay attention to/ what sits inside yourself/and watches you."[351] This last reference is a clear call-back to the *advaita Vedanta* studied and practiced by Fred Clifton, and which Lucille likely became familiar with during their relationship and marriage. In *advaita Vedanta* the nature of the world is not illusory but a manifestation of *Brahman*, the high-est Self, called *Atman*. The *jivatman*, or individual, is not separate from God, but a part of it, and the individual's path to liberation is in the realization that this separation is illusory. What "sits inside" the *jivatman* is *Atman*, God Itself, not the small lowercase indi-vidual "self," that a person normally identifies with, but a higher universal Self.

This moment is the first where the Ones really situate themselves in a spiritual system, but they do not return to the point. In fact, the Ones do not really get into the granular of any spiritual system; rather they speak in broader terms, often issuing warnings. As the Quran frequently says, the Ones reiterate, "we have no new thing/to tell," repeating:

only the same old
almanac
january
love one another
february
whatever you sow
you will reap[352]

By only giving two of the months of the year, the Ones imply there will be a whole calendar year of the most basic and essential rules from the Bible, and by implication other spiritual systems, which their listener (Clifton) may already be familiar with.

The Ones—unlike Thelma Sayles and Fred Clifton, and others who were alive and spoke to Lucille Clifton (like Aunt Margaret Brown, who through Clifton is able to have opinions of Martin Luther King and the lunar landing as well as a comparative analysis of the comedy of Murphy and Pryor)—are something other than human. "We/who have not been/human" is how they describe themselves later in the sequence.[353] Neither are they "angels" as they also describe how angels still appear to humans ("they have learned to love you/and will keep coming") though the angels are also not separate from humans and from human conceptions of them, as "they come to you wearing/their own clothes" and "have no wings."[354]

Throughout the "message," Clifton returns in ways to the concept of "nondualism" manifested in the ancient philosophy of advaita Vedanta. At one point, the "Ones" say "god/is/love" then correct themselves, amending it to "god/is love/is light/is god" and then further correcting themselves, advising instead, "place here/ the name/you give/to god....the name/you give/to//yes."[355] Rather than providing a description, no matter how expansive or generous, the Ones instead suggest that it is the individual who must define the relationship and that *any* effort to do so is part of the "god" they describe. This sense of inclusiveness returns to Lucifer's realization at the conclusion of "brothers" that "to ask you to explain/is to deny you."[356]

The lack of separation between human and divine is extended to the relationship between humans themselves. "You are not/ your brothers keeper," the Ones say, "you are/your brother."[357] They want to make sure their listener understands that this old familiar idea "is not/metaphor//you are not/your sisters keeper/ you are/your sister   yes." This lack of separation is, of course, also cause for concern as the Ones recognize the intimate connection between humans and their environment and ecosystem. They caution the listener that they are in "peril" and that "balance/ is the law."[358]

According to Marina Magloire, the poems "eerily forecast and corroborate the increasingly vocal chorus of scientists detailing the disastrous effects of anthropogenic climate change in the following decades."[359] Indeed, the "messages" were written—or "received," to use Clifton's term—in the early 70s right around the time that NASA scientist James Lovelock was formulating what would later be called "Gaia Theory," namely that the planet itself behaved like a self-regulating organism. In 1972 and 1974 Lovelock published the first scientific articles examining chemical compositions of the atmospheres of Mars, Earth, and Venus, and possible correlations between fluctuations in chemical atmospheres and the development of biological life. Lovelock later expanded his work into "Gaia Theory," a broad conceptual framework that allowed scientists from a range of disciplines to make connections between planetary processes and human behavior.

While Lovelock had already had significant and real impact in the accepted climate change science of the time—it was he who first posited the deleterious effect of chlorofluorocarbons (CFCs) on the ozone layer—his Gaia Theory was not widely accepted in scientific circles; it was thought of mainly as a critical or philosophical lens through which to approach scientific problems. It was not until 2000, at a *third* international conference (the early two happened in the 1980s) on climate change, that the theories Gaia Theory proposed became more broadly accepted as scientifically proven fact.

It was atmospheric chemist Paul Crutzen who coined the term "Anthropocene" at the beginning of the new millennium to define an age in the planet where ecosystems were impacted primarily by human endeavor. In 2016, philosopher Donna Haraway started using the term "Chthulucene" to imply that whatever humans had wrought had now traveled quite beyond them. While she was definitely referencing the monstrous or demonic of Lovecraft's Cthulhu, her spelling hearkened, rather, back to the "chthonic": that things were beyond mere control of the human. The "Anthropocene" was over. That human and non-human, including the planet itself, were now bound together inextricably. Years before all of this, Lucille Clifton, in the early 1970s, seemed to be tapping into the same gut feeling that had been driving James Lovelock to realize that the planet behaved like a single organism, when "the Ones" confessed to her:

> whether in spirit
> or out of spirit
> we don't know
>
> only that balance
> is the law
>
> balance
> or be balanced
>
> whether in body
> or out of body
> we don't know[360]

The closing pages of the "message" make clear the "grave danger" impending. The ones caution, "the patience/of the universe/is not without/an end,"[361] and that "what has been made/

can be unmade."[362] The close of the sequence echoes the Christian iconography of Clifton's sequences "some jesus" and the "mary" poems, which she would have been writing around the same time as these channelings:

> there is a star
> more distant
> than eden
> something there
> is even now
> preparing[363]

In discussing their place within the volume *two-headed woman*, Marina Magloire points out the "mary" poems serve as a "bridge between the embodied poems of the beginning of the collection and Clifton's narration of her own spirit visitation [in "the light that came to lucille clifton"]."[364] Furthering the belief that Clifton's unpublished "spirit writing" is essential to understanding all of her writing about spiritual figures, Bettina Judd argues that "to analyze Clifton's work is to take seriously her spiritual subjectivity."[365] Even the supposed "illegibility" of Clifton's spirit writing is, to Judd, part of the deeply embedded tradition of mediumship and speaking in "tongues" present in early Black American religious and spiritual cultural traditions.

In this sense, Clifton's spiritual approaches have always been less Western, and more closely allied with African shamanistic and pantheistic traditions. Indeed, the last poem of "Message from the Ones" (before the phrase "end of message" appears at the bottom of the following page, announced like a telegraph signal), does seem to imply that there have been many iterations of the world and that there will be another after. This sense of reincarnation or repeated worlds may stem from *advaita Vedanta*, but also has an analog in Quranic descriptions of the afterlife being a repeated or second version of life as it is lived in the present moment. Judd explains, "This pantheist spirituality and her creative practice allows Clifton to grapple with the theodical question with a more robust set of tools than biblical text alone."[366]

Even if Lucille Clifton did not share these poems at the time of their writing, she did write of the feeling of being "summoned," or spoken to, both in the sequence "the light that came to lucille clifton," but in other poems as well, including ones treating the goddess Kali. It wasn't until *an ordinary woman*, after the early familial and community-based poems of *good times* and the broader and more historical and social poems of *good news about the earth*, that Lucille Clifton began getting individually personal in her work. Published in 1974, just a few years before *generations*, and in the midst of her most productive period of writing children's books, *an ordinary woman* includes poems that are both intensely private and poems that are mythical in nature. The Kali poems fall into the overlap of both of these categories.

Kali is one of the most important goddesses in the Indian pantheon. She is a goddess of destruction, similar to Shiva, but unlike the calm Shiva who sits in repose, Kali is a manifestation of *shakti*, the divine and feminine energy active in the world. There are various myths about her origin and nature, but most commonly she is a counterpart of Shiva, born out of, and as, another version of his canonical consort/wife Parvati. Unlike Parvati, who in the somewhat caste-ist and colorist context of Indian mythology, is fair-skinned and delicately featured, Kali is dark—often depicted as black or blue—and has a fierce and ferocious countenance. Clifton, lover of fierce warrior women, tapped into the blackness—and the Blackness—of Kali, as a figure.

Like the "buffalo war" poems and the "mary" poems, the Kali poems in *ordinary woman* appear to be a sequence, but are embedded in the book without demarcating them as a sequence per se. There is one Kali poem (untitled, but with the single word "Kali" as its first line) late in the first section of the book, and then early in the second section appear six more Kali poems. Because there is no transition into or out of them as a cycle or sequence, it is possible to read the poems preceding and following as potentially part of the series (as I did with the poems preceding and following the four poems named for Tyrone and Willie B.).

The poem "Kali," in the first section of the book, begins with a list of her attributes and mythological qualities—"queen of fatality," "nemesis," "the permanent guest/within ourselves," "bitch/of blood sacrifice and death."[367] In addition to the typical aspects of the dread mother goddess, Clifton also digs under the myth to reveal the metaphorical meaning of any god of death, "the mystery/ever present in us and/outside us." Death also, as Clifton well knows, is a metaphor for transformation and includes in it the notion of rebirth. Clifton claims Kali, depicted in traditional iconography with (literally) black skin, as a Black ancestress, even though she is of Hindu and Desi origin: "Kali./who is black."

The full sequence of Kali poems does not appear until the second section of the book. Six of them appear back-to-back, after two of Clifton's most famous poems about transformations, "the lesson of the falling leaves," and "i am running into a new year." Both of these poems deal with the ending of one stage of life and the beginning of another, which always involves letting go of what one has held dear and important. In other words, it is only after Clifton has said, "i beg what i love and/i leave to forgive me," [368] that Kali—already invoked by the earlier poem—arrives "terrible/with her skulls and breasts."[369]

As Kali was drawn from Parvati, Clifton feels that Kali is a part of her, but a part that worries her. Kali sings to her, "you know you know me well," while the poet grouses, "running Kali off is hard./she is persistent with her/black terrible self."[370] Even though Clifton would rather not be the subject of Kali's attention, she does concede, "she/knows places in my bones/i never sing about." This ambiguity continues in the following poems where Kali insists on the poet accepting her and the poet does finally accept that Kali understands her as no one else does. There grows actual love between the two, but it is tempered with fear on the human's part about what the divine goddess wants with her. In one poem she contends that even though she is empowered by the goddess' presence, "she is always emptying and it is all/the same wound the same blood the same breaking."[371] She also wonders, regarding the psychic wound the goddess' presence represents, "will it scar or/

keep bleeding."[372] Despite these worries, she finally accepts in the final poem here, "awful woman,/i know i am your sister."[373]

Clifton takes in the aspect of Kali that is clear-eyed about the role destruction and death plays in creating the possibility of new growth and rebirth, but there is a very late appearance of a Kali-like figure who is more frightening, less generous in her capabilities. In an uncollected poem, "she leans out from the mirror," which Glaser and Young date to 2006—meaning it could have been included in *Voices* had Clifton chosen to include it—a woman appears, perhaps a manifestation of the self-empowered woman from "if i stand in my window." This woman "leans out from the mirror,/big-breasted woman/with skinny legs," calling also to mind earlier, more empowering poems like "what the mirror said."[374] This woman is ruder and more forthright, lifting her gown up over her head, saying "put this/into your poems":

> and there is nothing there, not
> the shadow of paradise even,
> only the empty glass and the   echo
> of bitch   bitch bitch.

It's a startling ending, denying any sense of empowerment or even a darker illuminating realization of any kind ("not/the shadow of paradise even"). The only thing left to the woman in the mirror—Clifton after all, or whoever is looking out at her, which is some literal reflection of her—after a life of loss and pain is resentful anger and accusations.

Kali was only one of the warrior figures who captivated Clifton's attention. She also had a lifelong interest in the Indigenous leader Tasunka Witko, commonly known as "Crazy Horse." While Clifton believed there may have been Indigenous ancestry somewhere in her southern family's line—she remembers her Aunt Timmie chanting poetry both Cherokee and Masai while ironing—her fascination with Witko was more related to his reputation as a warrior and general. In a late interview, when asked which three historical figures she would want to host at a dinner party, along with the Virgin Mary and King David, she included Witko.[375] She was equally fascinated by the name of Witko's lover, Black Buffalo Woman. "How much more obvious can you get?" Lucille joked, masking in humor her likely very serious thought of relationality between the historical Black Buffalo Woman and herself, a Black woman born in Buffalo, NY. In four poems from *Next* she writes about Witko, calling him Crazy Horse, and then later, in her final book, she writes of him, but using his Indigenous name, one last time.

In the early poems about Witko, she uses his voice—as the Ones spoke in their "message"—to warn of environmental destruction. The first poem featuring him, "the death of crazy horse," shows him leaving the mortal world, which he calls "shadow" and entering the afterlife, called by him "the actual world."[376] While this inversion agrees with Muslim conception of the afterlife as merely another life, it also hearkens to the later poem in which Fred Clifton also realizes that the afterlife is *realer* in some way: once dead, he no longer sees "the shapes of things," but "oh, at last, the things/themselves."[377]

From this vantage point, Clifton's Witko is unable to effectively guide and warn his people after his somewhat mysterious death, though he promises a resurrection. Throughout Clifton's political poetry—though without much specificity—she creates mythical alliances between Black people and Indigenous people. Perhaps due to her commitment to simplicity of expression and economy of words, she often falls back on abstractions ("the red road," "red dust and black clay," etc.), and in the case of the Crazy Horse poems, upon mythic figures rather than the individuals, like Miss Rosie or Tyrone and Willlie B, who populate her poems about Black life. I cannot but believe that Clifton's explorations of Indigenous life and of Black-Indigenous solidarity would have deepened as our own national consciousness around Indigenous politics and social issues evolved in the new millennium.

The final poem about Witko that Clifton would publish for some decades was called "the message of crazy horse." It immediately precedes the poems about the deaths of Thelma Sayles, Joanne C., and Fred Clifton, with the poems beginning "message of" that accompany each of those other deaths. In doing this she makes Witko personal to her, as personal as these other intimate family members, and at the same time she elevates Thelma, Joanne, and Fred to mythical status. The poem is a hinge moment in that Witko begins by describing his own world and his love for the historical Black Buffalo Woman, but then—having failed to include the young men of his community in the previous poem—pivots to saying, "i am dreaming now/across the worlds.../i come through this/Black Buffalo Woman," meaning Clifton herself. He warns of the destruction of the world, warning also that from his vantage point in the afterlife, it is all past tense: "i have seen it. i am crazy horse."[378]

I was standing in a line once—it was in October of 2000—waiting to get my copy of Next signed. The man in front of me was talking to Clifton. He said to her, "I love your poems about Crazy Horse, but I have to tell you that that is not his Lakota name." She looked up with interest, and asked the Lakota name. He told her, and when she finished signing his book on the title page, she opened it to the page where "the message of crazy horse" was and she drew a slash through the last sentence and wrote underneath it, "i have seen it. i am tasunka witko."

Nearly twenty years later, in Voices, Clifton returns again to the old spirit, calling him this time "Witko" in a poem of that name. This time, unlike his earlier appearances, "the man/who wore a blue stone/behind his ear/did not dance."[379] This later appearance of Tasunka Witko is restrained, quieter, the lines are less exuberant. He is ready to "rebone" and return and fight whatever battle may be left to fight. His horse, who in previous poems "danced under him," in this poem rises only to prepare, "whispering/Hoka Hay brother/it is a good day/to die." These final words are supposedly those said by Witko as he called the warriors to battle, though they have entered American popular culture as the battle cry of Clifton's favorite science fiction aliens, the Klingons. An avid fan, she would have been aware of the overlap.

Throughout her published work Clifton, explored mythologies and belief systems from the Books of Moses, from the

Gospels, from Indian mythology, and even imagining the spiritual systems of animals. In each of these endeavors she was speculative, plumbing the depths of the received stories for additional layers and nuances of meaning. As I mentioned earlier, she intentionally included previously unpublished sections in both her last two volumes. In the case of *Voices*, the presence in her archives of large amounts of unpublished material from the same time period as she was writing the poems that appear in *Voices* shows that she made an intentional craft decision to include the earlier sequence, "ten oxherding pictures," originally published in a limited edition letterpress chapbook in 1988, rather than what seems to me to be a complete—and stunning—later sequence called "Book of Days," found later in her papers and included in *Collected Poems*.

The "ten oxherding pictures," as I mentioned before, were based on paintings (with accompanying poems) used as teaching tools in Zen Buddhism. The original images and poems first appeared in the early 12th century, but the paintings and poems as we know them, with canonical titles, date from the mid-fifteenth century. Although there are numerous contemporary depictions— including those that accompanied Clifton's poem when it appeared in its original chapbook form—the 15th century canonical images were painted by Zen monk Tensho Shubun in the mid-fifteenth century. The poems, which exist in multiple translations, were written by Kuoan Shiyuan. Clifton claimed only to have seen the traditional names of the ten paintings upon which she wrote her poems; she had not seen the canonical images, nor read the traditional verses that accompany each painting.[380] In that sense, electing not to include the images from the chapbook in the *Collected Poems* makes good sense: the reader, like Clifton, has only the traditional title with which to understand Clifton's accompanying text.

Before she begins the ten poems, there is an invocation of sorts, "a meditation on ten oxherding pictures." In this prefatory poem, Clifton raises her own hands, the polydactyl ones, to prepare for the journey. Throughout the poems that follow, her hands will guide her in the search for the ox, feeling her way forward with only the titles of the paintings as a guide. It is remarkable how often Clifton's intuitions lead her in the same areas of inquiry as the classical poems. It is even more interesting where her poems diverge, and in such divergence provide a different view from the canonical received wisdom. Such divergence is appropriate since a large part of traditional Zen practice is rigorous critical inquiry and interrogation, including of koans.

In the first poem, "1st picture: searching for ox," Clifton declares herself ready for this journey into the practice of transformation of the mind that Zen Buddhism attempts:

> they have waited my lifetime for this
> something has entered the hands
> they stir
> the fingers come together[381]

While the original poem cautions, "the way to proceed is unclear," Clifton has intuited that the process of seeking knowledge is not merely intellectual or abstract, but immediate and physical, and will require physical engagement, particularly if such knowledge is represented in the poems by an animal as fearsome—the very metaphor for strength, after all—as the ox. While the classical meaning of the first poem is frustration at feeling lost, Clifton is feeling more practical; she does not view the search as a "hunt" of any kind, but rather as a "summons" from the ox itself. Thus summoned, as she has proven over and over again, she will follow.

In the second poem, the seeker finds the footprints of the ox. Clifton invokes the cities of her life—Buffalo with its snow, and Baltimore where she became a poet. The traces of her own life lead her on, and she, like the classical poet, wonders how she will be able to tame whatever it is that she finds. The ox is not spotted by the seeker until the third poem, "seeing the ox." Interestingly, Clifton has intuited what both the painting and poem depict: only part of the ox is seen and the seeker must chase after it still. In this way the object of knowledge never reveals itself completely. "[N]ot the flesh/not the image of the flesh" is seen, according to Clifton's poem. Clifton's seeker has not seen the ox either, rather they say, "we are coming to the ox."[382]

The fourth poem, "catching the ox," is really where Clifton diverges from the classical depictions. While the fifteenth-century poem and painting depict a great and violent struggle by the seeker to control the wild ox, Clifton's poem is small and brief, and the apprehension of the ox is easy: "i whisper come/and something comes," though her hands do "caution" her, as if in recognition that the struggle cannot be so simple.[383] This divergence of method and intention continues in the fifth and sixth poems, "herding the ox," and "coming home on the ox's back." While in the classical poems, both the whip and harness are required to tame and ride the ox, Clifton's seeker has a more reciprocal relationship with the animal. In the first of these poems, she tames the ox with only a word—her own name—though once again her hands caution her, "what can be herded/is not ox."[384]

The ease with which the ox has allowed itself to be mastered ought to make the seeker aware of the difference between the "shape of things," to quote "the message of fred clifton" one more time, and "the things themselves." In the second of these two poems, Lucille and the ox return to the city "together"—they have a companionable relationship that is not combative, nor the relationship of beast and master:

> our name is inflated
> as we move   lucille
> who has captured ox
> ox who supports lucille[385]

Clifton injects a new character here who does not appear in the original poems. She meets a man on the road who assumes he knows what the relationship between beast and rider is. The man in the road may be a guard at the gate as he "wears authority," and "describes" and "defines" the ox. She denies both his claim on the ox, and his attempted definition of the relationship.

In the next two classical poems, first the seeker forgets the ox, and then the seeker and ox are both forgotten. It takes the monk in the classical poems until the seventh poem to finally abandon his whip and rope; meanwhile Clifton has not, in fact, forgotten the ox.

She describes a life lived over fifty more years, including children and family, but in the end none of these have actually distracted her from the journey she once took—at the close of the poem she wonders, "where is ox."[386]

You will by now recognize the power of Clifton's signature eschewing of punctuation, but it should be taken as even more particularly pointed here: in the original chapbook publication, the poem, though still all lowercase, was normatively, though minimally, punctuated with commas, periods, and question marks. When the poem was reprinted in *Voices,* she removed every piece of punctuation. The absence of the question mark here is most powerful because it highlights the endlessness of the question: it will be a perpetual asking.

In the eighth poem, where both the man and the ox are "forgotten," the classical painting is blank except for an "ensō," a simple circle drawn with a calligraphy brush. This drawing, common in Zen Buddhism, is a meditative practice meant to symbolize the paradox of everything and nothing being present at once. The classical poem points out that the whip, the rope, the ox, and the man have all merged into nothing or more properly—and Clifton would approve—"no thing." Clifton seems to have apprehended the same concept in her version of the same poem: "man is not ox/i am not ox/no thing is ox/all things are ox."[387]

In the classical ninth poem, the seeker returns back to his origin, wishing—or realizing—he never left. There was nothing to be found in the outside world, after all, that could not be discovered at home. Clifton agrees, knowing the ox is only found in one's own personal experience and life:

9th picture:
    returning to the origin
    back to the source

what comes
when you whisper ox
is not
the ox

ox
begins in silence
and ends
in the folding
of hands[388]

The cycle ends with the seeker re-entering the city they had left. As the old and weary traveler enters and passes by a dead tree, the branches break into blossom. In Clifton's poem, it is the hands that tremble and rise. Life has returned to weary limbs. In contemplating the pointlessness of the long journey and the purposelessness of conquering the ox, life and energy has returned to the aged wanderer.

Dark Lucille, like Kali, like Witko, knows the dangerous parts of life. She does not look away. The "oxherding pictures" end not with any easy answers, but with another endless question, this one in three terse lines:

end of meditation

what is ox
ox is
what[389]

This particular short poem has affinities—not solely because it follows Clifton's meditation on Zen teaching texts, both verbal and visual—with the tradition in Zen study of the "koan." The koan is a short poem or story or question meant to provoke thought and questioning on behalf of the student. They are not riddles intended to be "answered," but rather texts meant to open inquiry. They are dense with meaning, often using wordplay or allusion to call a reader's attention to previous texts and teachings, and they sometimes use indirection or a seeming disconnect or disjunction of meaning to introduce additional potential meanings. Frequently, the actual koan is accompanied by a series of illuminating notes or commentary, and paired with a teaching story. Despite a tantalizing tendency to think of their questions as "unanswerable," a student is meant to engage with them, and rigorously.

It makes sense to me that Lucille Clifton would choose to end *Mercy*—a deeply mournful book—with the distant and sometimes chilling voice of the "Ones." Somehow, it feels equally appropriate that *Voices*, a volume focused on mortality and abiding loss, would end, rather than with the concurrently written "Book of Days," which returns to her earlier engagement with Edenic and Biblical texts and contexts, but with "ten oxherding pictures." This series of poems departs from her normal spiritual framework, and it is by its nature speculative, since Clifton only looked at the titles of the paintings themselves. In a way, these became *her* koans to consider, and "scour for meanings," to return to Morrison's term. The sequence allows the reader also to take a breath, and take a step back from the precipice of death and loss that had suffused the earlier parts of the book.

Clifton did not intend, of course, for the "end of meditation" to be her last published poem while alive, but the words are appropriate as a valediction nonetheless. The questions of this final poem do leave the reader in the dark, but it is in the darkness one is able—from the very beginning of discerning shapes in the complete absence of light—to learn to see. Clifton was able to incorporate what others might think of as "darkness" into her vision, the same way Lucifer becomes included as an equal of God. As Judd concludes, "Lucille Clifton's atheology of joy demonstrates how felt knowledge is multi-dimensional and resists binary modes of categorizing lived experience."[390]

Neither the poet nor the oxherder has any choice but to continue trying "to bear the weight of this/and trying to bear the weight also/of writing the poem/about this."

It is the asking always that is the answer.

Chapter 10: Last, First, and Yet Unseen

Throughout her last years, in addition to writing the poems that would become a part of *Voices*, Lucille Clifton was working on a nearly book length sequence called "The Book of Days," as well as numerous other poems which remain so far unpublished. Running twenty-two pages in a clean unedited manuscript, "The Book of Days" was found in her papers after her passing by Kevin Young and Michael Glaser, the editors of her *Collected Poems*. Of the sequence, Young writes, "the sequence is a wonder, a manuscript that seems quite complete, mournful yet mindful, concerned with birth, death, and that 'what we will become/waits in us like an ache.'"[391]

"The Book of Days" is a polyvocal epic in the tradition of Louise Glück's *The Wild Iris*, a poem in which God, the flowers of the garden, and humans all speak. In Clifton's epic, rather than flowers, the angels of paradise speak, as well as two other speakers, who seem to each be aspects of Lucille Clifton herself: one a mother who speaks in a series of poems called "mother-tongue," and the other, that crafty old brother himself, Lucifer, who speaks twice in poems called "lucifer morning star."

There are a handful of other poems, some lyric utterances in a collective "we," and others spoken from scriptural stories about places, including Babylon, Armageddon (Megido), the doomed cities of Sodom and Gomorrah, and Nineveh, the city to which Jonah had been sent by God. The sequence is a breathtakingly well-cadenced crescendo of numerous of Clifton's lifelong concerns—motherhood, mortality, the difficulty of incarnation of the spirit into flesh, and a painful revisiting of Lucifer's final questions to God at the end of "brothers":

> tell me, tell us why
> You neither raised Your hand
> nor turned away, tell us why
> You watched the excommunication of
> that world and You said nothing.[392]

The series opens with a poem called "birth-day" that hearkens back to the poem "spring song," which closed the earlier series "some jesus" in *good news about the earth*. In that poem, "the green of Jesus/is breaking the ground," like a seed, though of course, "breaking" implies this transformative process is not without pain. Once that physical duress is borne, however, "the future is possible."[393] In "birth-day" the poet has arrived at the knowledge first: "today we are possible" because "the morning, green and laundry-sweet,/opens itself and we enter/blind and mewling."[394] The speaker once again invokes the color "green" to represent fertile new life, and like seeds, the speaker and her comrades are as newborn in the world. Along with the more abstract "green" we get the very specific adjective "laundry-sweet," which summons up Clifton's busy home, with six young children, four of them in diapers, before the days of disposable diapers. Indeed, in such a home, each morning would have begun with the domestic chore of laundry.

As was the pain in his body described by Adam ("I would rather have been born"), the "birth-day" ends with the realization Young quoted, "what we will become/waits in us like an ache."[395] By this we know Clifton always knows knowledge and experience come at a price, often painful, but also that—as with the stars that choose and the narrative style of *generations*—the future is present, as is the past.

God and Lucifer each speak to humans first. God, impatient as Glück's irritated divinity, scolds as a parent might: "what more could you ask than this/good earth, good sky?/you are like mad children/set in a good safe bed/who by morning/will have torn the crib apart."[396] Lest one think Clifton is adopting Glück's critical distance, one must remember Clifton's own childhood bed was neither safe nor good.

In a poem taking place "after the fall," Lucifer says that "bright things/winged and unwinged/fall still/through the dark closets of night." By this reference one may imagine Clifton has greater trust in the fallen angel to speak the truth to her about her own experiences. Lucifer is quick to remind humans that they were made by the "same perfect reckless hand." If God is "reckless," and the devil and angels and humans are all siblings, jointly made, why, Lucifer wonders:

> will you still insist
> you cannot understand
> how it is possible to stumble,
>
> one eye filling with darkness,
> the other bright with heaven-light,
> with its unreachable unbearable glory?[397]

The divided nature of Lucifer is another manifestation of Lucille's identification with him. Throughout her work, she has used the image of physical bifurcation or duality (including in a poem from ordinary woman called "lucy one-eye") as a metaphor for physical division, her own ability to see the past and the future, or, as in the case of the "two-headed woman," the ability to see the inside and the outside. This Lucifer also recognizes Heaven as "unreachable," and perhaps because of this unreachability, or because of its own nature, or perhaps hers, also "unbearable."

The distance of this heaven, the very political and social troubles of the end of the last century and the beginning of the new one, as well as Clifton's own personal tragedies, have all created much higher stakes for the conflict between humans and their divinity. In a poem called "man-kind: in the image of," humans who were created in the image of God supposedly, call Him an "enemy": "we learn what it is to live/inside the enemy's skin."[398] In this poem, too, the image of the stone carried as reminder returns as a metaphor for the spirit. This greater distance is commented upon by the angels in their first poem, "angelspeak." They recognize that God has increased His distance between Himself and mortals, saying, "in order for us to abandon him again/we'd have to hurl ourselves/from such a height that/to survive another fall would be impossible."[399]

If the closing of *Voices* felt valedictory, then "The Book of Days" feels very much like what was supposed to come next. Throughout the poems, as in "birth-day," Clifton returns to images (and even phrases) from earlier poems. Even the "stone" image of the previous poem calls to mind Tee's precious talisman in Clifton's book *The Lucky Stone*.

In a poem called "mother-tongue: the land of nod," Clifton returns to one of her most famous and oft-quoted poems. While Clifton has written of Cain and his exile in the land of Nod twice before, she had never identified herself as strongly with the residents of Nod as she does in this poem, which imitates the form and structure of her earlier poem, "won't you celebrate with me." Clifton she made this poem practically an anthem, often reciting it from memory at the conclusion of her readings, sometimes inviting the audience, who often also knew it from memory, to recite along with her.

According to Kevin Young, she even intended to use the phrase as the opening of her acceptance speech for the Poetry Society of America Frost Medal ceremony, a speech which was the last text written in her diary before her death.[400] Though "mother-tongue: the land of nod" mirrors the structure and even language patterns of "won't you celebrate with me", it is more sorrowfully introspective, less defiant in the face of danger. "True, this isn't paradise," she confesses in its opening lines, "but at last we come to love it." It is a different kind of acceptance than that which appeared in the earlier poem where she is both wary of danger, since she had been "born in babylon/both nonwhite and woman," and also defiant, adopting a tone that celebrates survival when she declares, "everyday/something has tried to kill me/and has failed."[401]

Twenty years later, Clifton has come to a new relationship with the barren world around her, the "rocky/land of nod," as she referred to in an earlier poem.[402] She notices the "sweet hay" and the "mourning doves who/open the darkness with song," and, in a softer echo of the phrasing of the conclusion of the earlier poem, she is grateful "for how, each day,/something that loves us//tries to save us."[403]

It's an even more daring statement to be this vulnerable, realizing it comes after the losses of her children, and the decline in her physical condition. The poem is followed by four more poems in the "mother-tongue" that mourn both the losses of a child, an extremely personal loss, and the communal losses after the Biblical flood, which returns to a broader and more abstract loss, less intensely personal. Speaking of the "martyrdom of love," the mother warns the child that love "can cost you everything," but loneliness can "do you in." There is no escape from the pain of experience, she now knows, and god will not answer her desperate question, "in which room of the heart/is the fortress,/is the inside wall that saves you?"[404]

If Clifton echoes the earlier "won't you celebrate with me" in "mother-tongue: the land of nod," she once more gestures to her earlier poem "Jonah," in "nineveh: waiting," which revisits the story of biblical Jonah from the other side: not that of the prophet fleeing his work, but of the people in the city, waiting to be saved. In Clifton's earlier poem on Jonah, she focuses on the ordeal inside the belly of the beast—a Leviathan in the scripture, but a slaveship in Clifton's conception.

Those left behind, those waiting for Jonah's arrival, are the subject of this later poem. The people in Nineveh know his journey to their city would be "terrible," they know that they are "unloved," but even still they predict, "he will find that even its memory//will cling, like salt,/to every thing."[405]

These kinds of bittersweet realizations are quite different from the bold pronouncements of Clifton's other books, even the late books. Something shifted in her irrevocably after the death of her children, as anyone would reasonably expect. "[D]eath is a small stone," the mother says later, trying to make sense of things, "from the mountain we were born to."[406] Again the stone appears to remind a human that they are fated to die, but the stone also—as it has from the beginning—functions as a talisman, a lucky stone to remind them they are part of something much larger: "we put it in a pocket/and carry it with us/to help us find our way home."

The mother's voice disappears long before the end of the sequence, which is dominated by poems from "man-kind," god, and the angels, and she does not speak in the final poem that bears her name: in "mother-tongue: in a dream before she died," the mother figure—perhaps Mary, perhaps Lucille, perhaps just any generic mother— is spoken about in the third person, perhaps the only real way one can imagine one's own death. Jesus appears in the most unlikely of places—the living room—and in the most unlikely of raiments—her blue housecoat. He completes three tasks there, apparently in preparation for assumption: he raises the blinds, he frees the bird from its cage, and then, startlingly, he transforms "all her fresh-baked bread/back to stones."[407] This moment of transformation is jarring, but like the other two actions, is a motion against continuance, a denial of the will to live that the freshly baked bread may symbolize.

Clifton's relationship to God revealed itself in "brothers"—a cheerful mistrust—but shifted toward more overt wariness in this later sequence. First, in a poem named "sodom and gomorrah," the poet bemoans the fate of people "too frail in sin/to be any good at it" who must now drown "in the weight of commandments/that broke at the ends of their fingers."[408] In the following poem "prodi- gal," perhaps conflating God with her own problematic father, she challenges the divinity outright:

prodigal

illusion is
your prettiest trick.

free will, you said.

but all the roads
that seemed to lead away
have circled back again to you,
old father, old necessity.[409]

The picture Clifton paints of God as a manipulative parent is not a pretty one. If I compared this sequence to *The Wild Iris* earlier, it was only in shape and scope. In Glück's sequence, the humans are either petulant or oblivious, and the God wise, but removed; the flowers are the only ones who really know what's going on. But here in Clifton's "Book of Days," Clifton has lots of bones to pick with God, the humans who speak in the "man-kind" poems are aware of the danger they are in, and God—who speaks rarely, but unlike in "brothers," *does* speak—seems human himself: somewhat annoyed, and growing more and more so. Humans he finally calls "small and treacherous," asking them, "why would you believe that *I* punish you/who punish each other relentlessly/and with such enthusiasm?"[410]

No one finds hope at the end of this sequence—neither humans nor angels. Even old Lucifer knows that he has no further part in salvation, neither in a sacrifice nor rebirth. In the last poem bearing his name, Lucifer finds himself on a road "that does not go/ all the way in any direction." Far from finally wising up, he is still "always falling/far from the glory gallows/and the resurrection."[411]

Whether he means it or not, God taunts humans throughout the sequence—and Lucille too, one imagines—with a potential truth that has perhaps occurred to none of them—humans, god, angels, or poet—to be the case:

godspeak: kingdom come

you, with your point-blank fury,
what if i told you
this is all there ever was:

this earth, this garden, this woman,
this one precious, perishable kingdom.[412]

It's a breathtaking conclusion to a sequence that has continued the spiritual drama of "some jesus," the mary poems, "tree of life," and "brothers" in remarkable and unsettling ways.

In her last poems and drafts, Clifton was returning to the beginning, to some of her earliest concerns. Young recounts in his afterword that Alexia Clifton recalled her mother talking about a book she was planning to call "God Bless America." With such a title, it is unlikely that the "Book of Days" was intended to be included in this book either, but Young and Glaser did discover a brief three-line poem bearing that title which may remind a reader of the pithy and epigrammatic nuggets of wisdom propounded by Margaret Brown:

God Bless America

You don't know the half of it, like the old folks used to say
but the half of it is what I do know
What I don't know is the other[413]

It calls to mind one of the criticisms that had been leveled at Clifton early in her writing career: that her so-called "simple" language betrayed a simplicity of ideas. Clifton addresses it in a short essay called "A Simple Language." "Sometimes people have asked me," wrote Clifton, "when I was going to try something hard or difficult, as if my work sprang from my ignorance. I like to think I write from my knowledge not my lack, from my strength not my weakness."[414] And what that strength was, as she went on to explain, "I am a Black woman and I write from that experience...other people's craziness has not managed to make me crazy."[415] Plus she knew exactly why her so-called simple language was singled out for comment: "there is a bit of snobbishness, even a little racism" in the critique, she pointed out.[416]

In the end, she knew that her own knowledges, knowledges that non-Black people and non-women would not have access to, were the things to be privileged and prized, which the short riddle-like paradoxical text of "God Bless America" clearly states. As for what Clifton planned to follow it up with, that is anyone's guess.

Perhaps surprisingly, considering how spontaneous the poems sometimes sound, how "simple" their language may be, Lucille Clifton was a perfectionist. There are many poems she worked on for years, even decades, finally including them in books, and countless others that she wrote and revised but never included in books. Among her papers at her passing, Young and Glaser found twenty-eight poems from her early career that she did not include in her first book, seventeen more throughout the following decade she did not include in any book, and—along with "The Book of Days"—eleven more poems from the period after she published her last book. In working on the posthumous selected poems volume, *How to Carry Water*, Aracelis Girmay and Kamillah Aisha Moon found ten more paper drafts of unpublished poems.

In August of 2023, I went to visit the archives myself, and I was one of the first scholars who examined the files downloaded from her computer and files preserved from diskettes from the word processor she used in the late 1980s and early 1990s. In these electronic files I found a voluminous number of poems, some one hundred of them, from the period between 1987 and her passing in 2010 that she did not include in the books published in those years. These are not half-finished drafts, but fully realized poems, often themselves existing in multiple drafts and worked on over a number of years.

Of her own writing practice, Clifton said, "by the time I get to where I'm sitting down to print out on a word processor I've edited in my head. I work in my head a lot." And despite the harried mother in her poem from "somewhere," who at the end of a long day after putting the children to bed fumbles between the couch cushions for a pen to start writing poetry, Clifton claims, "I can't work with a pen and paper either. I need to see the look of the thing as close to print as I can."[417] That was one thing she did share in common with the woman from her poem (besides the fact that each writes a poem with the title "Good Times")—Clifton says, "I learned to work in my head a lot because I had the kids."

The presence of this large number of uncollected poems teaches us two things: first of all, that Lucille Clifton was exacting, both in the construction of an individual poem, but also in the construction of the books themselves. She had specific intentions for them. Clifton herself said, about the construction of a collection, "a manuscript is not only word following word, line following line, space after space, but poem following poem."[418]

The very first early uncollected poem printed in *Collected Poems*, "BLACK WOMEN," offers the opportunity to look at the generative way Clifton revised, often borrowing language and creating whole new poems.[419] She wrote "BLACK WOMEN" as a free verse poem first, but then revised and re-wrote it as a dialogue between Harriet Tubman and Sojourner Truth, calling it "Conversation Overheard in a Graveyard."[420] These two drafts are from the 1960s and are included in *The Collected Poems*, but I found another version of this same poem in her papers from the mid 1970s, using only the first half of the text included in *Collected Poems*, and not the second half. This version is again called "Black Women" (without the all caps).

She didn't discard the ending of the poem: she used the last two lines in a different poem from the late 1980s that she included in the earliest drafts of *quilting*, but eventually excluded from the book, a poem called "Recalling":

Recalling

Of the babies I could not bear to bear
I start a cake
I carefully close my opinion
to other sweets
stir tenderly the ingredients
ignore the soft
insistent baby cry not occurring
around my martyred rooms.

What mirror will remember us as truly
suckling strangers and sons?
oh history.[421]

One of the other early unpublished poems included in
Collected Poems, "OLD HUNDRED," (Clifton seems to have been
fond of all-caps titles in her earlier work) refers to a tune often
accompanying the one hundredth psalm; the capitalized words
are an adaptation of the most common lyrics for the hymn. Clifton
intersperses private thoughts between the lines of the hymn. It is an
uncharacteristically formally innovative poem for her:

OLD HUNDRED

NOW LET US MAKE
     nobody knows
A JOYFUL NOISE
     under the cry
LET US SHOUT
     under the glistening
HALLELUJAH
     sleeps goodbye
AND LET US MAKE
     God is a friend
A JOYFUL NOISE
     standing between
UNTO THE LORD
     what I've been told
AMEN   and the trouble I've seen. [422]

In this formally complex and interwoven poem, Clifton juxtaposes the very public language of a homily and the private worries
of an individual supplicant. Of course, as I mentioned previously,
it also takes the shape of the call-and-response common to both
Black church services and Muslim prayers. The columns interleaved
with each other make for some surprising phrasing, for example,
"nobody knows/A JOYFUL NOISE" and "under the cry/LET US

SHOUT." But when one reads only the small lowercase text, one hears the whisper of a very significant theological belief that would continue to haunt Clifton throughout her body of work: "God is a friend/standing between/what I've been told/and the trouble I've seen." This last extrapolated passage is one which Clifton would refine herself toward writing without the armature of the external.

Thelma Sayles' frustrated ambitions as a poet, expressed singly and powerfully in Clifton's poem "fury," in fact recur through Clifton's unpublished work. It is in "the message of thelma sayles," from *Next* (1987) that the mother urges her daughter to allow the frustrations and setbacks of her own life to become poetry. One finds this sentiment explored again in an unpublished poem from the same time period called "your life," that Clifton worked on since at least the late 1970s. In that poem, the speaker is fashioning sons with an absent father: when the sons ask "their father's right name/ make poems, i will tell them,/make poems."[423] The entreaty to write poetry becomes more and more important to Clifton.

In her unpublished prose memoir "Curiosities," she mentions that Thelma would find it extraordinary that Lucille has raised a family—Lucille calls it "her"—meaning Thelma's—family—and also written books, more than either woman could have imagined. In an early unpublished poem called "Dear Mama," one of a series that bore that title, Clifton writes, "here are the poems/you never wrote."[424] Nearly a third of the unpublished poems from that period mention Thelma or are addressed to her, but Clifton didn't include any of them in *good times* save one, and that poem, "now my first wife never did come out of her room," is from her father Sam's perspective. Lucille Clifton wouldn't publish poems about Thelma until her fourth book, *two-headed woman*, and then, of course, she couldn't stop.

Though she was poet laureate of the state of Maryland for many years, one thing she barely did was write incidental poems. There are some few among those she did not publish herself. One such poem was "Phillis Wheatley Poetry Festival," composed on the occasion of the inaugural festival convened by Margaret Walker at Jackson State University, to which Walker had invited thirty Black women writers including Clifton, June Jordan, Nikki Giovanni, Sonia Sanchez, Mari Evans, Audre Lorde, Alice Walker, and many others. In a three-part poem, Clifton creates a litany of the various writers' names. "Hey Nikki/wasn't it good, wasn't it good June," she begins and ends with an invocation to both Margaret Walker and Gwendolyn Brooks as maternal figures to the younger Black women writers, saying, "you such a good mama we/got to be good girls."[425]

Many years later, during the US military inventions in Iraq and subsequent nationwide (and international) protests against the invasion, Clifton composed a poem called "Make the Pie Higher," comprised of found text, namely the various malapropisms of President George W. Bush. Even though the poem is humorous, it still has its moments of poignancy, such as the opening, "I think we all agree, the past is over. /This is still a dangerous world." No doubt.

Clifton became Maryland's poet laureate in 1979, and served in that role until 1985, when she departed for California. She succeeded the one-time segregationist Vincent Godfrey Burns, who served in the role for seventeen years and spent the whole time writing incidental poems, something Clifton refused to do. "You don't go around asking poets to write verse on request," she declared, saying that poetry was "beyond assignment."[426] Of the previous laureate, she was asked to give an opinion on whether his verse was truly poetry or not and though she did try to avoid the question, when pressed she confessed, tersely, "I don't think so."

Not only her forms of poetry but also her language was her own. While in the beginning her verse was thought of and regarded by its own practitioners, such as Haki Madhubuthi, as part of the Black Arts Movement, Clifton soon began shifting into other dictions, and registers, as William Fogarty shows in his scholarly work. Even by the mid-seventies, when Clifton was still writing and publishing both poetry and childrens' books written in Black English, she was not fully embraced by the community of Black Arts Movement writers. For example, the book *A Capsule Course in Black Poetry Writing*, written collectively by Gwendolyn Brooks,

Keorapetse Kgositsile, Haki Madhubuti, and Dudley Randall, and published by the legendary Black Arts Movement-affiliated Broadside Press in 1975—just two years after Frederick Turner and others had praised the blend of registers in good news about the earth—does not mention Clifton.

What I find particularly interesting is that Clifton was very aware of the various boxes reviewers and audiences tried to fit her into, trying to define her as a Black poet, or a not-Black-enough poet, or a Christian poet—particularly bemusing because of her avowed interest in alternative practices sometimes termed "occult" as well as non-Abrahamic African, South Asian, Buddhist, and Indigenous American spiritual systems. "One set of my godchildren is Jewish-Catholic and the other set is Hindu," she said. "I've been to all those places of worship. In my house I have a Bible, a Bhagavad-Gita, a Torah, and the Bahai book. My husband was a Yogi. I do believe in spirit and the world of spirits but I don't think of myself as a Christian because that word is so laden with baggage."[427]

She even resisted the geographical association some critics made of her as a Southern poet—though she conceded that she had a "Southern upbringing" since her father was from Virginia and her mother from Georgia—or even a Maryland poet. In an interview with Roland Flint, who succeeded her as poet laureate of Maryland, given upon Clifton's return to the state in 1989, she commented, "People say 'oh, she's coming home,' but I'm not 'coming home.' Buffalo, New York is my home."[428]

In one particular unpublished poem she commented on a quote from a review of The Book of Light:

"always calm"
a good review

what do they know of the calm eye
where you are still as it all
whips around you, toward you
and you hold as you were born to hold
the sharp edge of it? what
do they know of the cold fist

your hand makes as it enters
under your heart and leaves there
what no lone heart can carry?
and the knife of sight
and the children bleeding from your
bony thighs and ears? what
do they know the one who look at
only what they see what do they know
of here where the storms and the wars
live here at the center inside you?[429]

It is a serious plaint and indictment from a woman who never in her life stopped struggling with the burden of what she had committed with her life to do—to be a poet, to write poems. It opens with the image of the "calm eye," which can be understood both as Lucille's "one off eye," the one that allowed her visions, and by extension poetry, but also of course more literally here, the eye of a storm passing over, the "calm" center, which is of course nothing but the origin point around which all the tempests turn in their gyre.

The propulsive line breaks make the reader go along with the growing rage of a misunderstood woman who challenges her readers to see deeper. Clifton, capable of raising her voice indeed, sometimes preferred to read with a quieter voice. Anyone who heard Clifton read in person might be able to tell you that occasionally someone from the audience would call out to her to "speak up!" at which point Clifton would pause and cast a stern look across the crowd and say, respectfully, "I'm going to ask you instead to listen harder." As kind and generous of spirit as she was—and she was—she was not above challenging her audiences and readers, requesting them to move out of their own comfort zones.

The poem was in a folder on Clifton's computer marked "Memphis," meaning it was probably written during a semester that Clifton taught in that city. There is a section of poems called "A Term in Memphis" that appeared in The Terrible Stories, but it did not include this poem "always calm." The poems from the Memphis period were written during one of Clifton's bouts with breast cancer; one recognizes the image of the "cold fist/your hand makes as it enters/under your heart" as it later appears in the poem "1994," written at the same time: "a thumb of ice stamped itself/ heard near your heart."[430]

Another unpublished poem from the Memphis period, called in the manuscript "la lorena," bears similarities to both the poem "lorena," about Lorena Bobbitt, and the published poems from "A Term in Memphis" like "slaveships" and "auction street," both of which discuss Middle Passage, the crossing of African people into slavery across the Atlantic. It is unclear to me whether the title "la lorena" is an unintentional misspelling of the Mexican folk figure La Lloronad, or if Clifton meant to make some link to Lorena Bobbitt as a Kali-like destructive goddess figure.

La Llorona, in the myth, drowns her own children as revenge against their transgressing father. Filled with regret, she then haunts waterways, mourning for her lost children. Though Clifton gave the poem the title of "la lorena," the larger metaphorical reference in the poem is not to Bobbitt but to children lost during Middle Passage, some indeed—as Clifton referenced in "lost baby poem"— cast into the seas by their own mothers as a last desperate act of maternal agency:

> la lorena
> (a mythical woman who cries up and down water
> sources looking for her lost children)
>
> i exist and no anchor can still me
> i will search out the mouth of the ocean
> and steal any tongue that fails
> to remember my story the story
> of the cursed ships that stole away
> my waterlost children   oh the years
> on their fading faces   oh the terrible sea
> of their names[431]

Finally, these yet unpublished poems continue to teach us about Clifton's trajectory and cast new light on the extant published poems. One way we might think now of the stone imagery that kept recurring throughout "The Book of Days," and is that this recurring image of a stone represents some kind of an elemental shift in Clifton. A water sign, Cancer, Clifton wrote often of the ocean— the Atlantic of Middle Passage, but also the Mississippi River, the seas beneath the city in "lost baby poem," the waters of Niagara. However, we begin to see in the later poems an elemental shift from water to earth. In an unpublished poem written after Rica's passing, Clifton writes of this shift:

elements

i was a water sign
when my little bird died
and i sank
down into the roots of grass
and trees all the while
flooded with rage
at the lying gods

what remained above was air
bodiless and still
as eden was before
the serpent spoke
naming the actual names
of things

now i attempt
to ground myself
in earth   though
fire is always raging
water always bitter
as styx is sorrow
as ganges is regret[432]

Not only does this poem chart her shift from water to earth (though fire and air are still present), but there is another shift: she once more reassigns the role of the naming of things—this time from eve to lucifer. It is also a resigned poem, mournful. She had previously written that "the only hell is regret," but regret is where she leaves herself at the end of this poem.

Back in Buffalo one winter, I found myself thinking of Lucille Clifton. I knew the two street addresses of her childhood homes, the Sayles' houses, named in the poem "lot's wife 1988," but I knew Lucille and Fred Clifton had also lived in Buffalo for a time. I called Sidney Clifton and asked her what houses the family had lived in when they were there. I copied down the addresses she gave me. Barbara Cole, then the artistic director of the Just Buffalo Literary Center, but who has now become the executive director, was going to meet me. I'd long had this fantasy of getting the city of Buffalo or Erie County or New York State to put up historical markers in the city in front of the houses important to Lucille Clifton.

I pulled up in front of the empty lot in front of what used to be 254 Purdy Street. Barbara was waiting. We both knew from the poem that the house wouldn't be there, but I still felt unprepared for how I would feel looking at the empty lot. I'd seen the pictures— of Sam in his Sunday suit, of Lucille in a white pinafore—standing in the alley between the house that no longer exists and the house just to the east of it which is still there. There is still something haunting about looking at the empty space. I walked into it, through it, as if it were still there. The house to the east is now a church, called the Refuge Temple. To the west, the house seemed lived-in. We knocked on the door. An older woman answered. We asked her if she knew that there had been a house next to hers. She did. The lot was appended to her property now—she leases it to the Refuge Temple to use as a parking lot.

We asked her if she knew the family that lived there. *Sayles, their name was Sayles.* She didn't know them. There was another neighbor, a much older woman, who had lived on the street her whole life. She would know.

We went to 11 Harwood Place after that, but it was Purdy Street that haunted me, that day and all the days after. Lucille felt like a spiritual mother to me. She always had, I guess. I was looking at my houses, or the empty spaces they used to be. I was looking at the ghosts of my own family. I went haunted, not only by memory, but by the emptiness of the lot, the music that must roll over it the congregation in the church sings. I wrote:

Refuge Temple

*254 Purdy Street, Buffalo, NY, childhood home of
Lucille Clifton*

There will be another storm always on the air
Or in the air or are you the air
Cold unrecognizable following
The inside road
This vessel bears one through
Snow or time to find the house
Paint peeling and maybe unfamiliar but the address
Is to a place that doesn't exist anymore
An empty lot
Now owned by the woman
Next door who leases it to a
Storefront church that needs the space for parking
I take a selfie with the snowbank
254 Purdy Street
Sunday morning they will plow and cars will fill the place
Worshippers filing next door
Names of the family who lived here forgotten
Sayles their name was Sayles
Well there's Miss Bowden says the neighbor
Who lives over there
Ninety years old
Lived here her whole life
If anyone'd remember she would
Though if the house don't hold against the world

And the body don't hold against the world
Snow falling down
What can hold
The church house the neighbor next door
The snow Old Miss Bowden
This empty lot
We empty now
Everybody drive home
Song done over
Snow river hover
House is gone
Storm-sent era
That Miss Bowden may remember
The twelve-fingered girl who lived here
We tell the neighbor: her name was Lucille
Playing in the street
No longer afraid of the dark
Now with fiery words bringing the light

Conclusion: Refuge Temple

Seven years later. Another winter. This time south, in Baltimore. I'd been in DC giving a reading at the Lannan Center for Poetry and Social Practice, housed at Georgetown University. I asked to stay an additional day. I woke up early the next morning and got on a train from Union Station. I had a copy of Clifton's book *Mercy* with me. I read it on the train.

Upon arriving in Baltimore, I called a ride-share. I admired my driver's box braids and fuchsia streaks, her incredible nails curling around the wheel as she steered. I debated talking to her about the purpose of my visit. "I am visiting the house of a poet," I would say. "Who?" she would say. "Lucille Clifton," I would say. "Oh, I love her!" she would exclaim. We would launch into a spontaneous recitation of "won't you come celebrate with me" that Lucille often recited collectively with her audiences at the end of her readings.

I am quiet. I don't say anything. Shonta pulls onto Clifton Street. Clifton Street? It was so named before Fred and Lucille Clifton moved onto nearby Talbot Street in 1967. They raised their six children in a beautiful three-story house built in 1908. They lost the house to foreclosure in 1980. It was years later that Sidney Clifton awoke from a dream. She had been dreaming of the house. It was February 13, 2019; February 13 being the date on which both Lucille Clifton and Thelma Sayles had each—51 years apart—passed away. Conscious that it was the nine-year anniversary of her mother's passing, Sidney felt moved to reach out and get in touch with the present owner of the house. Both women were astonished by the coincidence: the house had gone on the market that very morning. It did not stay on the market very long.

Sidney Clifton bought the property and created The Clifton House, a literary center devoted to promoting Clifton's work. The house had always been a sanctuary, Sidney remembers, back in the days her parents had owned it. It had been "a righteous womb nurturing artists and activists, truthtellers and revolutionaries. No one was turned away if they stepped to us right. No one who stepped off incorrectly did so twice."[433] Fred and Lue, as they were known to the community, had a synergy, Sidney explains: "Mom and Dad's metaphysical combination healed the sick and straightened out the crooked. There was historical, hysterical, freedom-inducing magic in that house." Under Sidney's guidance and vision, the Clifton House currently offers classes and workshops and aims to support creative workers in the city of Baltimore. Her vision is to convert it to a live-work space complete with residencies and housing programs for both established and emerging writers. "Mom's magic is still alive within those walls," wrote Sidney. "In reclaiming our home, I reclaim our legacy of place."

When I approach the front the door, it swings open. I am expected. Graham Clifton, Lucille's second youngest, lets me in. He is rail-thin, like a yogi or long-distance runner. He moves with deliberateness and thought. His smile is soft and kind. He has the same features as his younger sister Alexia, whom I have also met. Looking at the two of them it does seem that Clifton had, as she had always imagined, some Indigenous heritage in her Southern family's background.

Graham shows me the house, the living room where they used to play, the place Lucille sat to write her poems, the window where they all climbed out onto the roof to watch fireworks. Later he leaves me at the dining room table with a stack of Lucille's childrens' books and the deck of divination cards that Tracy K. Smith created using quotes of Lucille's poems. I don't know how I feel about the deck, but I pull a card. "Your tongue is useful, not unique," the card cheerfully announces. Lucille—or someone—is putting me on notice! I like it. I sit down at the table in the same place I had seen Lucille sitting in a photograph. I turn the pages of The Black BC's. I write. Graham brings cookies and sweet tea.

Later, I lie down on the carpet in the living room in corpse pose. I wonder if spirits are real and if they are real if they have the same sense of location we do. I think about calling out to Lucille, but I remember what she herself once said about her mother in the afterlife—that she seemed busy, she seemed to have a life separate from worldly concerns. I decide Lucille probably knows I'm here, that it would be rude to call out.

I spend the whole day in the house, reading, writing, wandering from room to room, imagining the family that lived here. Graham shows me the place the elevator used to be, shows me pictures of the family, the newspaper article announcing Fred Clifton's death. I think of the children here. I do not try to imagine Fred or Lucille. I do not want to inadvertently summon anybody out of rest. It is enough to be here.

Later, as I am waiting for the car that is going to take me back to the train station, Graham and I talk about ghosts. He says he often feels like he has company in the house, that he is being kept and watched over. He wants to give me a gift and though I already have a copy of *Voices*—Lucille signed it for me the last time I saw her—it is home in California, so I ask for one.

This time as the ride-share driver, Martin, drives me back to the train station, I tell him whose house he has just picked me up from. He tells me about spoken word artists he likes listening to. I recite "the lesson of the falling leaves." He asks me if poetry is the same thing as spoken word. I tell him that it probably is.

When I climb the stairs to the tracks, a wind blows in. I lean over the railing, looking down the tracks toward the house. That's when I feel her. Lucille. Just a sense of her, an awareness. A feeling. It grows. My skin feels warm. I look up at the sky, tears in my eyes. "Lucille," I whisper. I feel her presence, immediate and sure, more than in the house.

Here, at the end of the book, is what I believe: Lucille Clifton was one of the greatest poets of the twentieth and twenty-first centuries and one of the greatest in the English language.

She is equal to Dickinson or Auden or Whitman or Brooks. Her body of work is timeless, an essential part of American literature.

Who is going to tell now how it is? Lucille is.

Acknowledgments

Always: to Rukia Ali, whose name means: One Who Ascends. Would that I could put this book in your hands.

Its seed was a four-lecture series on Clifton I gave in the spring of 2022 for the Community of Writers. Aishvarya Arora helped me by transcribing the four lectures I had delivered for the course. Thank you to Brett Hall Jones for the original invitation to lecture on Clifton, and to Hunter Jones who did so much advance and on-the-spot work making that course work.

There are my sibling poets to thank who have done important editorial and archival work on Lucille Clifton: Kevin Young and Michael Glaser co-edited *The Collected Poems of Lucille Clifton*. Aracelis Girmay edited *How to Carry Water: Selected Poems*, and along with Kamilah Aisha Moon, worked in the Clifton archives and discovered manuscripts for ten yet unpublished poems; Tracy K. Smith wrote the introduction to the new edition of *generations* and curated a deck of divining cards using quotes from Clifton's work; Remica Bingham-Risher wrote about Clifton in her book *Soul Culture;* and finally, there is friend and sisterpoet Honorée Fannone Jeffers, with whom I share a love and devotion for Lucille Clifton; to all of you, my thanks and affection.

Thank you to all the staff at the Rose Library at Emory University, which holds Lucille Clifton's archives. In particular, thank you Kathy Shoemaker for making the process so smooth and helping me get extra hours with the documents. The Black Studies Project at the University of California, San Diego, gave me a research grant that enabled me to spend time in Atlanta. Thank you to the Black Studies Project and to Dr. Sara Johnson, its director.

Thank you to Lucille Clifton's children Sidney, Gillian, Graham, and Alexia; they have been generous and supportive of this project and are passionate advocates and caretakers of their mother's legacy.

Hilary Holladay and Mary Jane Lupton both wrote previous books on Clifton. Holladay's is a scholarly monograph that examines the breadth of Clifton's work to date of publication (2004) and includes a comprehensive bibliography; Lupton's book (2006) focuses on a biographical interpretation, and includes previously hard-to-find information on Fred Clifton, an important influence on Lucille Clifton both personally and artistically.

Some chapters from this book previously appeared in the *Barn Owl Review*, poetryfoundation.org, *Jewish Currents*, *Mississippi Review*, *Georgia Review*, *American Poetry Review*, *Hopkins Review*, and *Mentor and Muse*. Thank you to Mary Biddinger, Michael Slosek, Claire Schwartz, Adam Clay, Gerald Maa, Elizabeth Scanlon, Dora Malech, Blas Falconer, Beth Martinelli, and Helena Mesa for giving these essays homes.

Thank you Beacon Press: "Personal Letter No.2" from *Home Coming* by Sonia Sanchez. Copyright © 2021 by Sonia Sanchez. Reprinted with permission from Beacon Press, Boston, Massachusetts.

And finally, great and everlasting gratitude to Dr. Barbara McCaskill, who first showed me Lucille Clifton's poetry and taught me about the profundities within.

Notes

1. Introduction
    Collected Poems, 173.
    Collected Poems, 183.
2. *Collected Poems*, xxx-xxxi.
3. *Collected Poems*, xxxiii.
4. https://familyguy.fandom.com/wiki/Ms._Clifton
5. *Collected Poems*, 370.
6. *Collected Poems*, 371.
7. DiFranco.

Chapter One: Buffalo War

8. *Collected Poems*, 173.
9. *Collected Poems*, 57.
10. *Collected Poems*, 58.
11. Fogarty, 162-163.
12. *Collected Poems*, 59.
13. *Collected Poems*, 60.
14. *Collected Poems*, 61.
15. *Collected Poems*, 62.
16. *Collected Poems*, 63.
17. Ali spoke to reporters in his hometown Louisville, KY, about his decision to refuse the draft in March of 1967; qtd. in Barbash.
18. *Collected Poems*, 174.
19. Bartsch, 323.
20. *Collected Poems*, 64.
21. *Collected Poems*, 331.
22. *Collected Poems*, 333.
23. *Collected Poems*, 172.
24. *Collected Poems*, 65.
25. *Collected Poems*, 66.
26. *Collected Poems*, 67.

Chapter 2: All Clay is Kin

27. *Collected Poems*, 9.
28. *How to Carry Water*, xvii.
29. *Collected Poems*, 77.
30. *Collected Poems*, 82.
31. Asante and Miike, 4.
32. *Collected Poems*, 338.
33. *Collected Poems*, 268.
34. *Collected Poems*, 431.
35. *Collected Poems*, 515.
36. *generations*, vii.
37. Sharpe, 13.
38. Sharpe, 14.
39. *generations*, 5.
40. Sharpe, 21.
41. *Collected Poems*, 264.
42. *Collected Poems*, 267.
43. *Collected Poems*, 266.
44. *Collected Poems*, 265.
45. Hayden.
46. *Collected Poems*, 503.
47. Thyreen-Mizingou, 88-89.
48. ibid.
49. Jeffers, 176.
50. *Collected Poems*, 262.
51. *Collected Poems*, 516.
52. *Collected Poems*, 508.
53. *Collected Poems*, 378.

Chapter 3: The Blacker She Do Be

54. Somers-Willett, 74-75.
55. Ibid.
56. *Collected Poems*, 45.
57. Hennenberg, 62.
58. Brooks.

59. *Collected Poems*, 80.
60. *Collected Poems*, 549.
61. Kekatos.
62. *Collected Poems*, 103
63. Clark.
64. *Collected Poems*, 446.
65. Walker, 629.
66. *Collected Poems*, 18.
67. Cunningham, 31.
68. Hennenberg. 62.
69. *Collected Poems*, 197.
70. Cunningham, 32.
71. *Collected Poems*, 198.
72. *Collected Poems*, 199.
73. *Collected Poems*, 380.
74. *Collected Poems*, 200.
75. Cunningham, 31.
76. *Collected Poems*, 481.
77. *Collected Poems*, 482.
78. *Collected Poems*, 483.
79. *Collected Poems*, 484.
80. *Collected Poems*, 426.
81. *Collected Poems*, 485.
82. Kinnell, 208.
83. Kinnell, 204.
84. *Collected Poems*, 486

Chapter 4: Trouble is Coming Round

85. *Collected Poems*, *157*.
86. *Collected Poems*, 183.
87. Rowell, 68.
88. Rowell, 66.
89. *Collected Poems*, 39.
90. *Collected Poems*, 206.
91. Holladay, 151-152.
92. *Collected Poems*, 413.

93. Rowell, 59.
94. Holladay, 41.
95. *Collected Poems*, 253.
96. *Collected Poems*, 297.
97. *Collected Poems*, 298.
98. *Collected Poems*, 299.
99. *Collected Poems*, 303.
100. *Collected Poems*, 305.
101. *Collected Poems*, 296.
102. *Collected Poems*, 306.
103. Lupton, 23.
104. *Collected Poems*, 307.
105. *Collected Poems*, 308.
106. *Collected Poems*, 309.
107. *Collected Poems*, 310.
108. *Collected Poems*, 490.
109. *Collected Poems*, 491.
110. *Collected Poems*, 492.
111. *Collected Poems*, 427.
112. *Collected Poems*, 493.
113. Rowell, 63.
114. Jordan, 49.
115. *Collected Poems*, 104.
116. *Collected Poems*, 373.

Chapter 5: Things Don't Fall Apart

117. Holladay, 163.
118. Clifton, *Ms.*, 45.
119. Wall, 553.
120. Holladay, page 168.
121. Rowell, 56.
122. Wall, 554, quoting bell hooks, 48.
123. Wall, 556-557.
124. Whitley, 48.
125. Wall, 557-558.
126. *generations*, 12.

127. ibid.
128. Brand, 3-5.
129. Wall, 561.
130. *Collected Poems*, 53.
131. *Collected Poems*, 86.
132. *Collected Poems*, 28.
133. *Collected Poems*, 347.
134. *generations*, 37.
135. *generations*, 12.
136. *generations*, 32.
137. *generations*, 36.
138. *generations*, 38.
139. *generations*, 39.
140. *generations*, 38.
141. *generations*, 39.
142. Clifton Archives, Born Digital Materials.
143. *generations*, 43.
144. *Collected Poems*, 78.
145. *Collected Poems*, 378.
146. *generations*, 45.
147. *generations*, 82.
148. *generations*, 45.
149. *generations*, 46.
150. *Collected Poems*, 76.
151. *generations*, 50.
152. *generations*, 54.
153. *generations*, 84.
154. *generations*, 82.
155. *Collected Poems*, 172.
156. Rowell, 57.
157. Lucille Clifton Papers, Box 1, Folder 4.
158. *generations*, 83.
159. *generations*, 84.
160. Kallett, 83.
161. *Collected Poems*, 594.
162. *Collected Poems*, 205.
163. *Collected Poems*, 207.

164. *Collected Poems*, 208.
165. *Collected Poems*, 272.
166. Box 29, Folders 1-4, Lucille Clifton Archives.
167. Box 29, Folder 5, Lucille Clifton Archives.
168. Kallett, 80.
169. Somers-Willett, 74.
170. *Collected Poems*, 446.
171. Somers-Willett, 83.
172. *Collected Poems*, 445.
173. *Collected Poems*, 316.
174. *Collected Poems*, 317.
175. *Collected Poems*, 416.
176. Lucille Clifton Papers, Box 1, Folder 2.
177. *Collected Poems*, 447.
178. *Collected Poems*, 520.
179. *Collected Poems*, 37.
180. *Collected Poems*, 377.
181. *Collected Poems*, 414.
182. *Collected Poems*, 520.
183. *Collected Poems*, 547.
184. *Collected Poems*, 554.
185. *Collected Poems*, 583.
186. *Collected Poems*, 587.
187. *Collected Poems*, 657.
188. *Collected Poems*, 587.
189. *Collected Poems*, 588.
190. *Collected Poems*, 658.
191. Ostriker, 42.
192. *Collected Poems*, 659.
193. *generations*, 28 and 63.
194. *generations*, 86.
195. *Collected Poems*, 660.
196. *generations*, 87.

197. Young, in *Collected Poems*, 741.

198. Hull, 273.

199. Hull, 274.

200. Magloire, 318.

201. Magloire, 317.

202. Werbanowska, 91.

203. Clifton Archives, Boxes 29, Folders 5-9.

204. Lupton, 11.

205. *Collected Poems*, 557.

206. *Collected Poems*, 116.

207. *Collected Poems*, 117.

208. Jonah 2:10, *King James Bible*.

209. Jonah 4:10-11, *King James Bible*

210. *Collected Poems*, 118.

211. *Collected Poems*, 119-120.

212. *Collected Poems*, 122.

213. Richard Foerster, Email to Kazim Ali, February 17, 2023.

214. Zapf, 37.

215. *Collected Poems*, 123.

216. *Collected Poems*, 124.

217. *Collected Poems*, 125.

218. *Collected Poems*, 88.

219. Magloire, 325.

220. *Collected Poems*, 227.

221. *Collected Poems*, 228-229.

222. *Collected Poems*, 231.

223. *Collected Poems*, 232.

224. *Collected Poems*, 233.

225. *Collected Poems*, 239.

226. *Collected Poems*, 245.

227. *Collected Poems*, 248.

228. *Collected Poems*, 249.

229. *Collected Poems*, 250.

230. *Collected Poems*, 264.

231. *Collected Poems*, 216.
232. *Collected Poems*, 348.
233. *Collected Poems*, 393.
234. ibid.
235. ibid.
236. *Collected Poems*, 394.
237. *Collected Poems*, 395.
238. *Collected Poems*, 239.
239. *Collected Poems*, 396.
240. *Collected Poems*, 397.
241. *Collected Poems*, 398.
242. *Collected Poems*, 399.
243. *Collected Poems*, 111.
244. *Collected Poems*, 348.
245. *Collected Poems*, 400.
246. *Collected Poems*, 401.
247. *Collected Poems*, 402.
248. *Collected Poems*, 515.
249. *Collected Poems*, 466.
250. *Collected Poems*, 466-467.
251. *Collected Poems*, 467.
252. *Collected Poems*, 468.
253. ibid.
254. ibid.
255. *Collected Poems*, 469.
256. ibid.
257. ibid.
258. qtd. in Holladay, 188.
259. *Collected Poems*, 470.
260. *Collected Poems*, 527.
261. *Collected Poems*, 528.
262. *Collected Poems*, 530.
263. *Collected Poems*, 532.
264. *Collected Poems*, 535.
265. *Collected Poems*, 537.
266. *Collected Poems*, 538.
267. *Collected Poems*, 539.

268. *Collected Poems*, 424.
269. *Collected Poems*, 442.
270. ibid.
271. *Collected Poems*, 443.
272. *Collected Poems*, 444.
273. *Collected Poems*, 448.
274. Lucille Clifton Papers, Born Digital Materials.
275. *Collected Poems*, 449.
276. *Collected Poems*, 460.
277. ibid.
278. *Collected Poems*, 461.
279. ibid.
280. *Collected Poems*, 459.
281. *Collected Poems*, 523.
282. *Collected Poems*, 640.
283. *Collected Poems*, 641.
284. ibid.
285. *Collected Poems*, 175.
286. *Collected Poems*, 93.
287. *Collected Poems*, 122.
288. *Collected Poems*, 642.
289. *Black BC's*, 29.
290. *Black BC's*, 32.
291. *Everett Anderson's Goodbye*, unnumbered.
292. Lucille Clifton Papers, Box 1, Folder 4.
293. Fogarty, 174.
294. Fogarty, 175.
295. Lucille Clifton Papers, Box 1, Folder 5.
296. *All Us Come Cross the Water*, unnumbered.
297. ibid.
298. Fred Clifton, *Darl*, 23.
299. *The Times They Used to Be*, 1.
300. *The Times They Used to Be*, 10.
301. *The Times They Used to Be*, 41.
302. Lucille Clifton Papers, Box 2, Folder 2.

303. *Collected Poems*, 590.

Chapter 8: Adam and His Mother

304. *"A Simple Language,"* 137.
305. *Collected Poems*, 113.
306. Longenbach, 53
307. Sanchez.
308. *Collected Poems*, 150.
309. *Collected Poems*, 576.
310. Molinaro, 48.
311. Molinaro, 49.
312. Wilson, *Odyssey*, #159.
313. *Collected Poems*, 456.
314. Finch, 12.
315. DiFranco, "32 Flavors."
316. *Collected Poems*, 427.
317. Miranda, 128.

Chapter 9: Dark Lucille

318. Kunitz, qtd. in Glück, 111.
319. *Collected Poems*, 90
320. Crawley, qtd. in Judd, *Feelin*, 70.
321. Judd, *Feelin*, 73.
322. *Collected Poems*, 515.
323. *Collected Poems*, 548.
324. *Collected Poems*, 298.
325. Interview with Hilary Holladay, *Poets and Writers*.
326. Judd, *Feelin'*, 71.
327. Wikipedia, "Murder of James Byrd Jr."
328. *Collected Poems*, 552.
329. *Collected Poems*, 553.
330. ibid.
331. *Collected Poems*, 558.
332. *Collected Poems*, 559.
333. *Collected Poems*, 560.

334. *Collected Poems*, 564.
335. *Collected Poems*, 405.
336. *Collected Poems*, 369.
337. *Collected Poems*, 577.
338. *Collected Poems*, 581.
339. *Collected Poems*, 582.
340. *Collected Poems*, 710.
341. *Collected Poems*, 570.
342. *Collected Poems*, 723.
343. Lucille Clifton Papers, Box 59, Folder 16.
344. *Collected Poems*, 601.
345. *Collected Poems*, 604.
346. *Collected Poems*, 266.
347. *Collected Poems*, 611.
348. *Collected Poems*, 612.
349. *Collected Poems*, 613.
350. *Collected Poems*, 614-616.
351. *Collected Poems*, 619.
352. *Collected Poems*, 620.
353. *Collected Poems*, 621.
354. *Collected Poems*, 623.
355. *Collected Poems*, 622.
356. *Collected Poems*, 470.
357. *Collected Poems*, 626.
358. *Collected Poems*, 629.
359. Magloire, 326.
360. ibid.
361. *Collected Poems*, 631.
362. *Collected Poems*, 632.
363. *Collected Poems*, 633.
364. Magloire, 324.
365. Judd, "Glossolalia," 113.
366. Judd, *Feelin'*, 77.
367. *Collected Poems*, 152.
368. *Collected Poems*, 158.
369. *Collected Poems*, 159.
370. ibid.

371. *Collected Poems*, 161.
372. *Collected Poems*, 162.
373. *Collected Poems*, 164.
374. *Collected Poems*, 720.
375. Holladay, Interview.
376. *Collected Poems*, 290.
377. *Collected Poems*, 307.
378. *Collected Poems*, 293.
379. *Collected Poems*, 648.
380. Rowell, 67.
381. *Collected Poems*, 672.
382. *Collected Poems*, 674.
383. *Collected Poems*, 675.
384. *Collected Poems*, 676.
385. *Collected Poems*, 677.
386. *Collected Poems*, 678.
387. *Collected Poems*, 679.
388. *Collected Poems*, 680.
389. *Collected Poems*, 682.
390. Judd, *Feelin'*, 90.

Chapter 10: Last, First, and Yet Unseen

391. Young, in "Afterword," *Collected Poems*, 747.
392. *Collected Poems*, 469.
393. *Collected Poems*, 126.
394. *Collected Poems*, 689.
395. *Collected Poems*, 689.
396. *Collected Poems*, 690.
397. *Collected Poems*, 691.
398. *Collected Poems*, 692.
399. *Collected Poems*, 693.
400. Young, "Afterword," in *Collected Poems*, 749.
401. *Collected Poems*, 427.
402. *Collected Poems*, 458.
403. *Collected Poems*, 694.
404. *Collected Poems*, 696.

405. *Collected Poems*, 699.
406. *Collected Poems*, 703.
407. *Collected Poems*, 704.
408. *Collected Poems*, 705.
409. *Collected Poems*, 706.
410. *Collected Poems*, 702.
411. *Collected Poems*, 708.
412. *Collected Poems*, 711.
413. *Collected Poems*, 726.
414. Clifton, "A Simple Language," in Evans, 137.
415. Clifton, in Evans, 138.
416. Somers-Willett, 85.
417. Somers-Willett, 81.
418. Somers-Willett, 79.
419. *Collected Poems*, 3.
420. *Collected Poems*, 12.
421. Lucille Clifton Papers, Born Digital Materials, Rose Library.
422. *Collected Poems*, 4.
423. Clifton, Born Digital Materials.
424. *Collected Poems*, 18.
425. *Collected Poems*, 129.
426. Neale.
427. Somers-Willett, 75.
428. Howard Country Poetry and Literature Society.
429. Clifton, Born Digital Materials.
430. Clifton, Born Digital Materials.
431. ibid.
432. ibid.

Conclusion: Refuge Temple

433. Sidney Clifton, Mentor and Muse.

Works Cited

Asante, Molefi Kete, and Yoshitaka Miike. "Paradigmatic Issues in Intercultural Communication Studies: An Afrocentric-Asiacentric Dialogue." *China Media Research*, Vol. 9, Number 3, July 2013.

Barbash, Fred. "50 years Ago today Muhammad Ali was told to 'step forward.' He refused," in *Washington Post*, 4/28/2017. Archived at: https://www.washingtonpost.com/news/morning-mix/wp/2017/04/28/muhammad-ali-50-years-ago-today-was-told-to-step-forward-he-refused/

Bartsch, Shadi (translator). *The Aeneid* by Vergil, Modern Library, New York, NY, 2021.

Brand, Dionne. *A Map to the Door of No Return: Notes on Belonging*, Vintage Books Canada, Toronto, ON, CA, 2002.

Brooks, Gwendolyn. "The Mother," *Selected Poems*, Harper Perennial, New York, New York., 2006. Reproduced at https://www.poetryfoundation.org/poems/43309/the-mother-56d2220767a02.

Chakraborty, Sumita. "Poetic Networks Begin After Death," College Literature, Volume 47, Number 1, Winter 2020, pp. 230-239.

Clark, Sonya. "The Hair Craft Project." Artist's Statement, http://sonyaclark.com/project/the-hair-craft-project/.

Clifton, Fred J. *Darl*. Third Press, New York, NY, 1973.

Clifton, Lucille. *All Us Come Cross the Water*, Henry Holt, 1973.

Clifton, Lucille. *The Black BC's*, illustrated by Don Miller, Dutton, New York, NY, 1970.

Clifton, Lucille. *The Collected Poems of Lucille Clifton,* edited Kevin Young and Michael Glaser, BOA Editions, Rochester, NY, 2012. Introduction by Toni Morrison. Afterword by Kevin Young.

Clifton, Lucille. *Everett Anderson's Goodbye*, illustrated by Ann Grifalconi, Henry Holt, 1983.

Clifton, Lucille. *generations*, New York Review Classics, New York, NY, 2021. Introduction by Tracy K. Smith.

Clifton, Lucille. *How to Carry Water: Selected Poems*, edited by Aracelis Girmay, BOA Editions, Rochester, NY, 2020. Introduction by Aracelis Girmay

Clifton, Lucille. "If I Don't Know My Last Name, What is the Meaning of My First?: Alex Haley's *Roots: The Saga of an American Family,*" *Ms.*, Volume V, No. 8, February 1977, pp. 45.

Clifton, Lucille. "A Simple Language," in *Black Women Writers 1950-1980: A Critical Evaluation*, edited by Mari Evans, Anchor Press/Doubleday, Garden City, NY, 1983.

Clifton, Lucille. *The Times They Used to Be*, Henry Holt, 1974.

Clifton, Sidney. "Reclaiming Her Voice," in *Mentor and Muse: Essays from Poets to Poets*, Lucille Clifton Tribute, edited by Blas Falconer, Helena Mesa, and Beth Martinelli. https://mentorand-muse.net/sidney-clifton/.

Crawley, Ashon T. *Blackpentecostal Breath: The Aesthetics of Possibility*, Fordham University Press, 2016.

Cunningham, Scarlett. "The Limits of Celebration in Lucille Clifton's Poetry: Writing the Aging Woman's Body," in *Frontiers: A Journal of Women's Studies*, Vol. 35, No. 2 (2014), pp 30-58, stable URL: www.jstor.org/stable/10.5250/fronjwome-stud.35.2.0030.

DiFranco, Ani. "Lost Woman Song," on *Ani DiFranco*, Righteous Babe Records, Buffalo, NY, 1990.

Finch, Annie. "Gwendolyn Brooks' 'the mother,'" Poetry Foundation, https://www.poetryfoundation.org/articles/159670/gwendolyn-brookss-the-mother.

Finch, Annie. *The Ghost of Meter: Culture and Prosody in American Free Verse.*

Fogarty, William. "Mortal Tongues: Lucille Clifton's Local Speech Admonitions," in *The Politics of Speech in Later Twentieth Century Poetry: Local Tongues in Heaney, Brooks, Harrison, and Clifton,* Palgrave McMillan, New York, NY, 2022.

Glück, Louise. *Proofs and Theories: Essays on Poetry*, Ecco Press, New York, NY, 1995.

Hayden, Robert. "Middle Passage," from *Collected Poems*, Liveright, New York, NY, 1985. Reproduced at https://www.poetryfoundation.org/poems/43076/middle-passage.

Hennenberg, Sylvia. "Fat Liberation in the First World: Lucille Clifton and the New Body," *Women's Studies*, 47:1, pp. 60-79, https://doi.org/10.1080/00497878.2017.1406354.

Holladay, Hilary. *Wild Blessings: The Poetry of Lucille Clifton*, Louisiana State University Press, Baton Rouge, LA, 2004.

hooks, bell. "In Our Glory: Photography and Black Life." *Picturing Us: African American Identity in Photography*. Ed. Deborah Willis. New York: NY, 1994, pp. 43-54.

Howard County Poetry and Literature Society. *The Writing Life*, Lucille Clifton, in conversation with Roland Flint, September 1991: https://www.youtube.com/watch?v=PPr6EOggzm0.

Hull, Akasha (Gloria). "In Her Own Image: Lucille Clifton and the Bible," in *Dwelling in Possibility*, edited by Yopie Prins and Maeera Shreiber, Cornell University Press, 1997, pp. 273-295, https://doi.org/10.7591/9781501718175.

Jeffers, Honorée Fanonne. *The Age of Phillis*, Wesleyan University Press, Middletown, CT, 2021.

Jordan, Shirley. *Broken Silences: Interviews with Black and White Women Writers*, Rutgers University Press, New Brunswick, NY, 1993.

Judd, Bettina. *Feelin: Creative Practice, Pleasure, and Black Feminist Thought*, Northwestern University Press, Evanston, IL, 2023.

Judd, Bettina. "Glossolalia: Lucille Clifton's Creative Technologies of Becoming," in *Black Bodies and Transhuman Realities: Scientifically Modifying the Black Body in Posthuman Literature and Culture*, edited by Melvin G. Hill, Lexington Books/Rowan and Littlefield, Lanham, MD, 2019, pp. 133-150.

Kekatos, Mary and Katie Kindelan. "What would have been 50th anniversary of Roe v. Wade sees protests, celebration," January 22, 2023, 6:13 am, EST. https://abcnews.go.com/US/50th-anniversary-roe-wade-sees-protests-celebration/story?id=96533967.

Kinnell, Galway. "The Bear," in *Collected Poems*, Mariner Books, New York, NY, 2017.

Longenbach, James. *The Art of the Poetic Line*, Graywolf Press, Minneapolis, MN, 2007.

Lucille Clifton Papers, Stuart A. Rose Manuscript, Archives, and Rare Book Library, Robert W. Woodruff Library, Emory University, Atlanta, GA.

Lupton, Mary Jane. *Lucille Clifton: Her Life and Letters*, Praeger/ Greenwood Publishing, Wesport, CT, 2006.

Magloire, Marina. "Some Damn Body: Black Feminist Embodiment in the Spirit Writing of Lucille Clifton," *African American Review*, Volume 55, Number 4, Winter 2022, pp. 317-330.

Miranda, Omar. "On Phoenix Wings: Lucille Clifton's Romantic Renewals," in *Studies in Romanticism*, Volume 61, Number 1, Spring 2022, pp. 125-135.

Molinaro, Ursule. *The Autobiography of Cassandra: Princess & Prophetess of Troy*, McPherson and Company, Kingston, NY, 1979.

Neale, Dennis. "Poetry Not Greeting Cards," Washington Post, 8/9/1979.

Ostriker, Alicia. "Kin and Kin: The Poetry of Lucille Clifton," in *Literary Influence and African American Writers: Collected Essays*, edited by Tracy Mishkin, Garland Publishing, New York, NY, 1996.

Rowell, Charles. "Interview with Lucille Clifton," *Callaloo*, Vol. 22, No. 1, Winter 1999, pp 56-72. Stable URL: https://www.jstor.org/ stable/3299938.

Sanchez, Sonia. "Personal Letter No. 2" in *Shake Loose My Skin: New and Selected Poems*, Beacon Press, Boston, MA, 2000.

Sharpe, Christina. *In the Wake: On Blackness and Being*, Duke University Press, Durham, BC, 2016.

Somers-Willett, Susan B. A. "Music in Language: A Conversation with Lucille Clifton," *American Voice* 49 (Summer 1999), pp 73-92.

Thyreen-Mizingou, Jeannine. "Grace and Ethics in Contemporary

American Poetry: Resituating the Other, the World, and the Self," in *Religion and Literature*, Spring 2000, Volume 32, No. 1, University of Notre Dame, pp. 67-97.

Walker, Barbara G. *The Woman's Encyclopedia of Myths and Secrets*, HarperOne, New York, NY, 1983.

Wall, Cheryl. "Sifting Legacies in Lucille Clifton's *generations*," in *Contemporary Literature*, Volume 4, No. 4, Winter 1999, pp. 552-574, University of Wisconsin, stable URL: www.jstorg.org/stable/1208794. Accessed 08/06/23.

Werbanowska, Marta. "There is Hope in Connecting: Black Ecotheology and the Poetry of Lucille Clifton," ISLE: Interdisciplinary Studies in Literature and Environment, 26.1, Winter 2019, pp. 83-96.

Wilson, Emily. *The Odyssey*, W.W. Norton, New York NY, 2018.

Zapf, Hermann. *About Alphabets: Some Marginal Notes on Type Design*, MIT Press, Cambridge, MA, 1970.

BOA Editions, Ltd.
American Reader Series

No. 1 *Christmas at the Four Corners
of the Earth*
Prose by Blaise Cendrars
Translated by Bertrand
Mathieu

No. 2 *Pig Notes & Dumb Music:
Prose on Poetry*
By William Heyen

No. 3 *After-Images: Autobiographical
Sketches*
By W. D. Snodgrass

No. 4 *Walking Light: Memoirs and
Essays on Poetry*
By Stephen Dunn

No. 5 *To Sound Like Yourself: Essays
on Poetry*
By W. D. Snodgrass

No. 6 *You Alone Are Real to Me:
Remembering Rainer
Maria Rilke*
By Lou Andreas-Salomé

No. 7 *Breaking the Alabaster Jar:
Conversations with
Li-Young Lee*
Edited by Earl G. Ingersoll

No. 8 *I Carry A Hammer In My
Pocket For Occasions Such
As These*
By Anthony Tognazzini

No. 9 *Unlucky Lucky Days*
By Daniel Grandbois

No. 10 *Glass Grapes and Other
Stories*
By Martha Ronk

No. 11 *Meat Eaters & Plant Eaters*
By Jessica Treat

No. 12 *On the Winding Stair*
By Joanna Howard

No. 13 *Cradle Book*
By Craig Morgan Teicher

No. 14 *In the Time of the Girls*
By Anne Germanacos

No. 15 *This New and Poisonous Air*
By Adam McOmber

No. 16 *To Assume a Pleasing Shape*
By Joseph Salvatore

No. 17 *The Innocent Party*
By Aimee Parkison

No. 18 *Passwords Primeval: 20 American
Poets in Their Own Words*
Interviews by Tony Leuzzi

No. 19 *The Era of Not Quite*
By Douglas Watson

No. 20 *The Winged Seed: A Remembrance*
By Li-Young Lee

No. 21 *Jewelry Box: A Collection
of Histories*
By Aurelie Sheehan

No. 22 *The Tao of Humiliation*
By Lee Upton

No. 23 *Bridge*
By Robert Thomas

No. 24 *Reptile House*
By Robin McLean

No. 25 *The Education of a Poker Player*
James McManus

No. 26 *Remarkable*
By Dinah Cox

No. 27 *Gravity Changes*
By Zach Powers

No. 28 *My House Gathers Desires*
By Adam McOmber

No. 29 *An Orchard in the Street*
By Reginald Gibbons

No. 30 *The Science of Lost Futures*
By Ryan Habermeyer

No. 31 *Permanent Exhibit*
By Matthew Vollmer

No. 32 *The Rapture Index: A Suburban
Bestiary*
By Molly Reid

No. 33 *Joytime Killbox*
By Brian Wood

No. 34 *The OK End of Funny Town*
By Mark Polanzak

No. 35 *The Complete Writings of Art Smith,
The Bird Boy of Fort Wayne, Edited
by Michael Martone*
By Michael Martone

Colophon

BOA Editions, Ltd., a not-for-profit publisher of
poetry and other literary works, fosters readership and
appreciation of contemporary literature. By identifying, cultivating,
and publishing both new and established poets and selecting
authors of unique literary talent, BOA brings
high-quality literature to the public.

Support for this effort comes from the sale of its publications,
grant funding, and private donations.

■

*The publication of this book is made possible, in part,
by the special support of the following individuals:*

Anonymous

Angela Bonazinga &
Catherine Lewis

Mr. & Mrs. P. David
Caccamise, *in memory of
Dr. Gary H. Conners*

Bernadette Catalana

Daniel R. Cawley

Jonathan Everitt

Bonnie Garner

Robert L. Giron

Margaret B. Heminway

Charlotte & Raul Herrera

Kathleen C. Holcombe

Nora A. Jones

Christopher Kennedy

Paul LaFerriere & Dorrie
Parini, *in honor of Bill Waddell*

Jack & Gail Langerak

Tony Leuzzi

Barbara Lovenheim

Joe McElveney

Daniel M. Meyers, *in honor of
J. Shepard Skiff*

Boo Poulin

John H. Schultz

William Waddell & Linda
Rubel